THE

THE WITCHES' GOD

Lord of the Dance

by
Janet and Stewart Farrar

With line illustrations by Stewart Farrar

PHOENIX PUBLISHING INC.

This edition printed 2008

PHOENIX PUBLISHING, INC.
1160 Yew Avenue
PO Box 3829
Blaine, WA 98231

ISBN 978-0-919345-47-8

Printed in the U.S.A.

Contents

Part III: Gods of the World 149

Illustrations

PHOTOGRAPHIC CREDITS

Stewart Farrar: 1, 3-6, 8, 12-13, 16-19, 21. Museum of Mankind: 1, 9, 13. National Gallery, London: 2, 11. British Museum: 3-6, 8, 12, 16-19. Rick Welch: 7. Ian Rorke (photographer): 9-10, 14. D. Hooley: 20.

Figures

In loving memory of
DON PLEASANCE,
our very first initiate,
who passed to the Summerlands
while this book was in preparation.

Introduction

This book is intended as a companion volume to our earlier one, *The Witches' Goddess*. In the pagan cosmic view, the supreme creative polarity is that of the Goddess and God principles, for without polarity, from divinity downwards, there can be no manifestation. 'As above, so below.'

In our introduction to *The Witches' Goddess*, we said that the re-emergence of the Goddess 'may well prove to be one of the most significant spiritual, psychic and psychological developments of our lifetime', and added that, under the patriarchal domination of Western society and religion in the past two millennia, 'Even the God has suffered, for without his complement he is emasculated, his image distorted and impoverished.'

This being so, once we have readmitted the Goddess, we must reassess the God; otherwise the imbalance, though changed, remains. And since the readmission lays the foundations for the reassessment, we wrote *The Witches' Goddess* first.

For our own reassessment, we have followed the same pattern as we did in the first book. Part I exports the history of mankind's

1

god-concepts, and the various aspects in which the masculine principle of divinity has appeared. Part II consists of a selection of individual god-forms in history, with their mythology and symbolism, and suggests a ritual for each by which we can attune ourselves to that particular aspect. Part III is a directory of gods of the world, past and present, with a brief definition of each.

What do we mean by 'the masculine principle'?

Briefly, we would say that it represents the linear-logical, analysing, fertilizing aspect, with its emphasis on Ego-consciousness and individuality, while the feminine principle represents the cyclical-intuitive, synthesizing, formative, nourishing aspect, with its emphasis on the riches of the Unconscious, both Personal and Collective, and on relatedness. In human terms, these two principles can be said to correspond to the left-brain and right-brain functions respectively.

These are the two complementary terminals of the cosmic battery at all levels; without their creative difference, no current flows.

The denial of this has been the main flaw in patriarchal thinking. For Polarity it has substituted Dualism; for the creative complementarity of God and Goddess it has substituted the confrontation of God and Devil, of Good and Evil.

We must emphasize that the masculine and feminine principles are not mutually exclusive; each contains the seed of the other, just as in the Chinese Yin-Yang symbol (the perfect expression of the polarity concept) the dark Yin contains a bright Yang spot, and the bright Yang a dark Yin spot. Otherwise they could not relate to each other.

At the human level, in Jungian terms – the Goddess whispers to a man's anima, his buried feminine aspect, and the God speaks out loud to his male emphasis; while the God whispers to a woman's buried male animus, and the Goddess speaks out loud to her female emphasis.

Both whisper and the clear voice must be listened to. Otherwise, like patriarchy itself, we are incomplete and inviting trouble.

Both the readmission of the Goddess and the reassessment of the God are essential to health on all the levels; and this book concerns itself with the latter task.

In pursuing that task, why do we rely so much on ancient mythology? For two reasons.

First, because the god-concepts of pagan times were still undistorted by the banishing of their consorts – or, at most, were only beginning to be so distorted, as in the case of Zeus (see Chapter XXV). So they are still conceived in terms of polarity with their corresponding goddess-concepts, and therefore have much to teach us while we are trying to rediscover that polarity during the death-throes of patriarchy.

Second, because mythology, like poetry, expresses truths which cannot effectively be expressed in cold technicalities. From it, we can learn with our souls, while the Ego-consciousness is still struggling to define the lessons in its own limited language.

As John Gray puts it (*Near Eastern Mythology*, p. 135): 'Modern "demythologizing" brings its own perplexities and may well result in the great truths it seeks to elucidate becoming intelligible only to a limited circle inducted into the jargon of its own exponents and only to a certain age and theological tradition.' He adds that to 'seek rather to understand the traditional idiom and imagery of the mythology' (of the Near East, in his case) seems 'a safer way to objective truth'. Mr Gray is talking, in this passage, of the 'demythologizing' of Christ, but we believe his approach is sound in a wider field as well.

It also points to another principle which must always be remembered. This book is largely concerned with the analysis and intellectual understanding of the various god-forms which man has developed, and with tracing the course of that development. This, we believe, is a worthwhile exercise. The intellect is a tool which should always be kept sharp and clean – but there are times when it must be left on the bench.

Such advances as herd-raising, agriculture and the development of human society inspired mankind's god-form concepts. Time-measuring, wisdom, vegetation, war and craftsman gods and goddesses evolved in step with human evolution. Which does not, we must emphasize, mean that these deities were man-made or unreal; they were and are channels and tuning-signals to cosmic reality, filled with life and responsiveness by that reality.

The particular deities we invoke depend on our own individual tuning, which in turn is determined by historical, cultural and environmental factors. What matters is that our choice should be individual, and not dictated to us from outside. Otherwise we shall not be tuning in effectively to the cosmic source.

We, for example, are writers. If we feel at ease calling upon Thoth, Egyptian god of scribes, or upon Brid, Celtic goddess of inspiration – while other writers are at ease invoking Apollo and his Muses, or Benten, the Japanese goddess of eloquence, or Christ of the golden words – that is as it should be, for them and for us. In the end we are all tuning in to the same source.

Magical or religious practice is a communion with the reality which lies behind such god-forms, which are tuning-signals to aspects of that reality. When one is in the Magic Circle – or in church, synagogue, mosque or temple – one must relate to it directly, resonating with the chosen god-form or goddess-form, not analysing it intellectually.

Understanding the nature of the deity-form one is using, defining precisely the aspect one wishes to commune with – all this is useful preparation; it helps to perfect the tuning. But one must not fall into the trap of thinking: 'These are useful psychological devices, merely representing archetypes of the human Collective Unconscious. They have no reality outside that.'

They are indeed more than that. The gods and goddesses exist, and ensoul the archetypes. They are living, active faces of the ultimate Unknowable. And unless we lay intellect aside at the right moment and surrender ourselves to the mystery of communion with them – unless we give free rein to an innocent sense of wonder – the tuning will be in vain.

'Whosoever shall not receive the Kingdom of God as a little child shall in no wise enter therein.'

A point on the rituals at the end of each chapter in Part II. Some of them contain substantial dialogue. It is of course entirely up to you whether you learn this by heart, read it out or grasp the gist of it and express it in your own words. These rituals are meant to stimulate ideas, not to lay down chapter and verse.

We have called this book *The Witches' God*, as we did the earlier one *The Witches' Goddess*, because we ourselves are practising witches and because Wicca is probably the most widespread and fast-growing of the many paths of the current pagan revival. But we fully acknowledge the validity of those other paths, and hope that their followers will find that these books express, and contribute to, the thinking of that revival as a whole.

Our earlier books have provoked a great deal of correspondence, and we apologize to those to whom we have not been able to reply adequately because of pressure of work and the sheer volume of letters. We have always given our address before, but we may move again, so we suggest that any readers who wish to write to us should use the publisher's address as given below. (And, if we may say so, a stamped addressed envelope from Ireland, or an International Reply Coupon from abroad, does help!)

JANET FARRAR
STEWART FARRAR

c/o Robert Hale Ltd,
Clerkenwell House,
45-7 Clerkenwell Green,
London EC1R OHT

Part I
Faces of the God

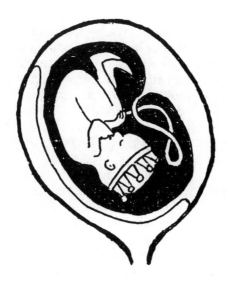

I The Son-Lover God

Sons, I have borne many sons, but my dugs are not dry.
Rudyard Kipling

'It was Neith, the mighty mother,' the Egyptian priest told the King of Persia, 'who gave birth to Ra; she was the first to give birth to anything; she did so when nothing else had been born, and she herself had not been born.'

Or, according to the witches of Tuscany: 'Diana was the first created before creation; in her were all things; out of herself, the first darkness, she divided herself; into darkness and light she was divided. Lucifer, her brother and son, herself and her other half, was the light. And when Diana saw that the light was so beautiful, she yearned for it with exceeding great desire.' (Leland, *Aradia: The Gospel of the Witches*, p. 18).

One Gnostic school said of Sophia, the Ancient Wisdom: 'She is an old woman because she was first, and the world was made by her.' She birthed the universe in a vast self-induced orgasm, because she wished 'to generate out of herself without spouse'.

In Genesis 1:2 in the beginning, 'The earth was without form, and void; and darkness was upon the face of the deep. And the Spirit of God moved upon the face of the waters.' The word for 'deep' here is *tehom*, and for 'waters' *tohu*, Hebrew forms of Tiamat, the goddess who personified the primordial waters from which all things sprang. (The Hebrew word for 'spirit', incidentally, is also feminine in gender; and it is interesting, in view of the translations to which the Bible was subject in the patriarchal centuries, that the corresponding Greek noun is neuter and the Latin one masculine.)

And on the other side of the world, the Australian Aborigine Sun goddess Yhi, the Great Spirit, pre-existed all manifestation; she created her consort, the All-Father Baiame, and together they made all living creatures.

It is this pattern – of the primordial, uncreated Mother giving birth to all things, including her own male counterpart – which is the earliest foundation of all mythology and all religion.

In palaeolithic days, a girl would normally mate, and start to conceive offspring, at puberty, so the fact that the one caused the other would not be obvious. Many 'primitive' tribes in recorded history believed that pregnancy was bestowed by moonlight or by ancestral spirits – and even some of those who knew otherwise maintained that it used to happen that way.

With man's impregnating role unrealized, or only half-realized, Woman naturally personified the archetypal Creator. And when mankind, as is its nature, began to conceive of transcendental deities and to worship and propitiate them, the obvious (almost the only possible) symbol of such a concept would be the Earth Mother – or, in some environments, the Primordial-Waters Mother.

To begin a book on the God with such an explanation may seem strange. But to explain the God, we have to start with his birth. And to human understanding, his Mother preceded his birth. All pre-patriarchal mythology points in this direction; and the more ancient and undistorted our sources, the more strongly it does so.

In pre-agricultural times, when mankind lived by hunting or fishing, woman was the home base, even if the home was nomadic. She was in charge of the young, and doubtless of the preparation of the food which the men brought in. There is little doubt that she invented agriculture, by finding, safeguarding and eventually learning to multiply by planting the vegetable supplement to the hunters' meat.

But as agriculture expanded, till it was no longer a supplement but had become the economic basis of human society, that society changed. Man, too, was now part of the home base, and the division of labour became more complex. The new system was economically more efficient, in that it provided not merely the means of survival but (at least locally or in phases) a surplus. This is proved by the fact that tribes which were still hunting-based came to be dependent satellites of the agricultural peoples, trading for their surpluses or, when opportunity offered, raiding for them.

This in turn added another aspect to man's growing importance in the agricultural economy. He was its warrior, the defender of its all-too vulnerable crop-raising territory.

This increasing complexity of society naturally gave rise to new deity-concepts. The Earth Mother, on whom everything (and certainly the crops) depended, was still the primal factor. At the human level, her daughters continued her function – procreativity being, if anything, more important to the tribe's success than ever. But her sons' functions were becoming more clearly defined and differentiated, too. They were field-workers, especially useful for their physical strength, and when necessary warriors. And with increasing sophistication and observation, their impregnating function would have become conscious. So these developments were projected onto the divine level.

What, then, would be the first male god-form to emerge?

He would be the son of the Earth Mother, his only possible origin. He would be young and strong, both as a warrior and as a virile impregnator.

To define him further, though, we must come back to the human level for a moment. Royalty (which evolved with more complex and settled societies) was certainly matrilinear; how often it was also matriarchal is still a matter of debate. It was the queen (whether as focus of a major community or as chieftainess of a small tribe) who personified the continuity of rule, and her daughter who inherited it; the male consort who impregnated her, even the commander of her warriors, was secondary to that continuity and could fulfil his role only as long as his virility and his warrior-qualities could meet the demands on him.

This situation was formalized into the custom of selecting the consort by mutual challenging between the likeliest candidates; the man finally selected would become the queen's consort for a fixed term – say, three or seven years – at the end of which he would be ritually sacrificed or slain in combat by his successor. (The major breakthrough in recognizing this system was J.G. Frazer's *The Golden Bough* – see Bibliography.) The queen, on the other hand, was continuous, merely handing over to a daughter when the time was ripe.

At divine level, of course, the Mother was truly continuous; no daughter would succeed her or be there for the young god to relate to.

So the young god was both her son and her lover. Often the periodic nature of human kingship would be reflected in the god; this overlaps with the vegetation-god and sacrificed-god themes, which we shall consider in Chapters V and X. But he often appears as being constantly reborn, the son-and-lover cycle being endless.

Vestiges of this concept are to be found in much later mythologies; for example, one of the titles of the Child Horus was 'Bull of his Mother', and he was regarded in many ways as his father Osiris's reborn self.

Erotic desire was one of the observable characteristics of the human woman; so the divine Woman must possess it too. Having given birth to her complementary other half, she desired union with it, as Etruscan Diana did with *her* other half, Lucifer, pursuing him across the sky till she caught him and lured him into bed.

The incestuous nature of the Earth Mother/Young God relationship is shocking only to the modern mind. To the ancients, where magical power or the numinosity of royalty was involved, in some circumstances incest could merely reinforce it. Political interest, too: in matrilinear Egypt, Pharaohs secured the legitimacy of their kingship by marrying their sisters, or even their daughters, as Rameses II did with Nefertari. (The late Omm Seti, whom we had the privilege of meeting at Abydos before her death, thought it was a good idea: 'It does away with the mother-in-law'!)

Perhaps the latest example of this attitude, in the sphere of magical power, was Merlin and his sister Gwendydd. She was said to have been the only person who could approach her brother when he retired to the woods, and finally to have joined him there, where he taught her the gift of prophecy, and in the original version doubtless became his mistress. Subsequent versions, such as that of Geoffrey of Monmouth, replaced her with Vivienne or Nimue; but Gwendydd's story 'bears the traces of a time when fraternal incest was not forbidden, at least not in the case of exceptional people who thereby re-created the perfect couple' (Markale, *Women of the Celts*, pp. 56, 134).

'Exceptional people' obviously included gods and goddesses; throughout pagan mythology, it was almost the norm for a god's wife also to be his sister; and many Earth goddesses, such as the Greek/Phoenician Gaia, had offspring by their sons.

This, then, was the earliest of all gods: a virile young warrior, born of the self-created Earth Mother, mating with her and constantly reappearing as his own reborn self. As yet, he represented only in embryo the linear-logical, left-brain aspect of masculine polarity which we defined on p.2; his emphasis was still on the fertilizing and warrior aspects of that polarity. But, from him, all later god-forms evolved.

II   The Time-Measuring God

A time, and times, and half a time.

Revelations

Man the hunter needed no more than the rising and setting of the Sun, and experience of the rhythm of the seasons, to know when to seek his quarry. Women the child-rearer needed no more than a baby's cry to know when to put it to her breast, the waning of the campfire to know when to throw wood on it, and the ripening of berries to know when to gather them.

Life called for little forward planning beyond co-ordinating migration with the movement of game, and being wherever one could best survive the winter before it actually set in.

But once men and women had become farmers, they began to need to measure time more exactly. Not only was much more forward planning called for; with more complex social organization, mutual arrangements for future actions, events and meetings required a mutually agreed time-measuring standard.

The only precise time-definer available was the Moon. Its phases, to careful observation, could be pinpointed within, say, five or six hours. The solar cycle, on the other hand, was much less easy to pinpoint. The exact day when the Sun reversed its decrease in elevation at the winter solstice, for example, did not define itself as the new or full moon did; it might take a week or two to be recognized. Also, for mankind's first time-measuring methods, a monthly, accurate indication was more useful than a yearly, vague one.

'We will meet at the next full Moon' was a practical arrangement. 'We will meet when the Sun is one-sixth of the way from its maximum elevation to its minimum' obviously was not.

Mankind's first time-measurer, then, was the Moon; and the first calendars were lunar – a fact which survives in the awkward division of our present solar calendar into months ('Moonths'). The incompatibility of solar and lunar calendars did not create real problems until later.

It may be said that the deliberate use of the Moon for accurate time-measuring is essentially an intellectual process. The human intellect, the left-brain, linear-logical function, had been in successful use for a very long time. But conquering fire, making tools, building huts, planting seeds – these all involved its application to material problems, to things which could be handled. Lunar time-measuring, on the other hand, was the application of intellect to an abstract problem. Mankind observed a phenomenon that could not be touched, observed its laws and then used them for practical purposes.

And time-measuring was perhaps the first linear-logical aspect to be added to the son/lover, virile warrior god whom we considered in the last chapter. The more fully rounded God of later times was beginning to emerge.

It was understandable, in view of all this, that many of the first lunar deities should be masculine.

Typical of these Moon gods was the Egyptian Thoth, whom we shall consider in detail in Chapter XX. He later, as god of wisdom, became primarily involved in Earthly affairs, but he remained Egypt's titular Moon god.

Another example was the Chaldaean, Sumerian and Assyro-Babylonian Moon god Sin, after whom Mount Sinai was named. One of his attributes was that he was the enemy of evildoers (because they tend to operate at night, whose darkness the Moon illuminates). He like Thoth, was a wisdom god. The Babylonian calendar was one of the first major lunar ones.

And, as we have seen, the Moon often also stood for the God-function of fertilization; the belief that women were impregnated by the moonlight was widespread.

The evolution of Moon deities was a complex one, because the

Moon does not only symbolize time-measuring. It also vividly symbolizes goddess-aspects, in that it is the light of the Unconscious, the illuminator of intuition – and is also cyclical, its cycle corresponding to that of women.

So from earliest times there were Moon goddesses as well as Moon gods. And the emphasis tended to move in the direction of the goddesses as the solar time-measuring function gained in importance.

Pinpointing the nodal points of the solar year is also an intellectual achievement.

The simplest method is to stick two poles, or place two stones, in the ground before midwinter, and to align them with the point where the Sun rises from the eastern horizon, correcting the alignment day by day. As midwinter approaches, the sunrise-point continues (in the northern hemisphere) to move further to the right. On the day of the solstice, it halts, and thereafter it moves to the left. It will appear to be static for a few days, but the solstice can still be pretty accurately determined as the mid-point of that static period. The poles or stones could be left in place, as indicators for succeeding solstices.

Stone Age brains managed this measurement, and from then on the solar year was definable. This would have encouraged a swing towards the importance of the Sun gods, helped by the fact that, to farmers, the Sun was the obvious fertilizer of the crops.

Although there remained exceptions (such as the Japanese Sun goddess Amaterasu and Moon god Tsukiyomi, and the Australian Aborigine Sun goddess Yhi and Moon god Bahloo), the mainstream tradition of later paganism became that of a fertilizing, time-measuring Sun god and a menstruating Moon goddess, illuminator of the Unconscious.

The impressive megalithic structures of the neolithic peoples gave us, if not exact answers, at least food for speculation about their ritual practices.

One of the most remarkable of these is Newgrange, the great megalithic mound which overlooks the River Boyne. It is the focal point of the Boyne Complex, a rich aggregate of structures within a mile or two of each other, built by the thriving agricultural community which lived there around 3000 BC.

Newgrange is usually described as a passage grave. It consists of a stone-built passage, 62 feet (18.9 metres) long, leading to a central chamber with three recesses, in a cruciform layout. This chamber has a corbel roof, still as sound and dry as ever after 5,000 years. Over the passage and chamber was built a huge mound of stones, now covered by grass, and the mound was surrounded at its foot by great kerb-stones. The whole structure covers an acre (0.4 hectares) of ground, is estimated to contain about 200,000 tons (203,200 tonnes) of stone and was made without metal tools or the use of mortar.

Newgrange was always known; and as Brugh na Bóinne ('Palace on the Boyne') it played a significant part in Celtic mythology (see p.110). It was not until the 1960s and 1970s that Professor Michael J. O'Kelly and his team brilliantly excavated and restored it, and in the process they discovered an astonishing feature. Over the entrance was a stone-framed slit which they called the Roof Box; on the morning of the winter solstice, the rising sun throws a pencil of light the whole length of the passage and chamber, to illuminate the central of the three recesses for about seventeen minutes. The same effect is seen, though less strongly, from three mornings before the solstice to three mornings after.

Prompted by this discovery, research at other Irish megalithic mounds revealed that many of them were also solar-oriented, though some to different nodes on the solar cycle.

Newgrange is often, all too glibly, thought of as a group tomb and as a structure for determining the winter solstice for the advantage of an agricultural community. If it is merely a tomb, because the cremated remains of a few people have been found there – then so is a cathedral a tomb, because some people have been buried there. And if its builders were knowledgeable and skilful enough to incorporate the winter solstice feature, they must have known how to determine the solstice long before that, with two sticks or two stones, and without the need for 200,000 tons of building-stone, much of it brought from miles away.

One can envisage the annual rebirth of the Sun god being celebrated there, with the dramatic enhancement of the reborn Sun actually announcing his arrival by lighting up the heart of the tribe's most sacred shrine.

And perhaps, on that solemn morning, a High Priestess would sit in the central recess, awaiting spiritual impregnation by the God himself, so that she could prophesy for the tribe. Perhaps, as elsewhere, there would also be a *hieros gamos* (sacred marriage) with a High Priest personifying the God; but even if there was, the true moment of conception must have been in the seventeen minutes of the God's own light.

Perhaps, perhaps ...

But whatever the facts, one thing is certain. The Sun God, fertilizer and time-measurer, still vividly manifests at Newgrange at the dark turn of the year.

III   The Sun God

Nor dim nor red, like God's own head,
The glorious Sun uprist.

S.T. Coleridge

We have spoken of the early development of the Sun god in the last chapter, and we shall consider one of the most important Sun gods, the Egyptian Ra, in Chapter XXVII. But there are one or two points which should be looked at separately, to fill in the gaps.

Quite apart from his fertilizing and time-measuring aspects, it is easy to see why the Sun has always been such a compulsive god-symbol. He rules the sky during our hours of activity, to the bulk of which his rising and setting mark the limits, because we need his light to see what we are working at. The Moon-light of intuition can, with an effort, be ignored (at our peril, it should be emphasized); the Sun-light of Ego-consciousness cannot.

We said in the Introduction that the masculine aspect is analytical, the feminine aspect synthesizing. The analytical function takes things to pieces to see what they are made of; the synthesizing function puts them together to see how they relate. Sunlight is relentless, discriminatory; it starkly emphasizes the differences between things. Moonlight is soft and harmonizing; it seems to blend all things into a whole.

The Sun is also seen to rule impartially the activities of the various, and often mutually hostile, phenomena which emerge from his existence. The Egyptian Ra, for instance, kept scorched the arid desert of his terrible great-grandson Set – but he also kept fruitful the rich Nile valley of his other great-grandson, Osiris.

As his rising and setting govern our daily activity, so does his annual rhythm govern our long-term activity and the Earthly fruitfulness on which we depend.

A vivid god-symbol, indeed. And he remained so, it may be noted, for rising Christianity. The Gospels give no date for Jesus's birth; but as the early Church raised him to god-status, the deep-rooted human instinct to celebrate the Sun's annual rebirth demanded that the Christ-god, too, should be born at the midwinter solstice. And it was so decreed, in AD 273, and has been so accepted, both officially and popularly, ever since.

The emphasis on the masculinity of the Sun, and the Sun deity, is most marked in the tropical and sub-tropical regions. Around the Mediterranean (and, remember, Christianity in its formative centuries was a Mediterranean religion) both Sun and Sun-god are almost universally masculine. (The only Sun-goddesses of the region we have been able to find are comparitively minor – the Phoenicians' Nahar and Samas, mentioned in the Ugarit scripts, the Sumerian Shapash and the Hittite Wurusumu.) The Egyptian Ra, the Greek Helios and the Roman Sol are all words meaning 'Sun' as well as being the names of gods; and all are masculine nouns. This is understandable, because in those regions the masculine aspects of brilliant light and great heat are inescapable.

But further north, where the Sun is gentler, its light more often misted or clouded, and its heat less predictable, the reverse often applies. The Germans' *Sonne*, and the Gaels' *Grian*, their names for the Sun, are both feminine nouns.

The Gaelic Celts, in particular – or at least their warrior aristocracy who formed the Celtic mythology which has come down to us – were cattle-raisers, not farmers; so the male fertilizing aspect of the Sun, which was so important to agricultural communities (and, in Ireland, to the neolithic peoples who preceded them), would be comparatively irrelevant to their ways of thought. It is interesting that both the Eskimos and the Australian Aborigines were among the minority who had Sun goddesses; and neither of those peoples was even marginally agricultural.

Whatever the light or heat of the Sun, up north it is lower in the sky, and its lateral movement is therefore much more obvious. So the idea that a Sunwise, *deosil* (Gaelic *deiseal*) movement, particularly in ritual, was propitious, and a counter-Sunwise or *widdershins* (Middle High German *widersinnes*) movement unlucky was strongly held in northern latitudes and survives in folklore as well as in occult and Wiccan ritual tradition.

Around the Mediterranean and farther south, where the vertical and not the lateral movement of the Sun is what strikes you, this deosil convention seems non-existent. Watching traditional Greek dancing, much of it dramatizing mythological themes, we have been struck by the fact that movements are just as likely to be widdershins as deosil and that, as far as we can see, the direction has no symbolic significance.

In the neo-pagan movement today, including Wicca, not many of its followers are farmers or cattle-raisers but all are striving to achieve a more living attunement to Nature; so it is not surprising that the Sun tends to be often used as a god-form, especially in the seasonal rituals. And for this, a greater understanding of what the Sun has meant to our forebears helps us to envisage our own concepts more clearly.

QUOD SUPERIUS
EST SICUT QUOD
INFERIUS ET
QUOD INFERIUS
EST SICUT QUOD
SUPERIUS AD
PERPETRANDA
MIRACULA
REI UNIUS

IV   The Wisdom God

But lo, thou requirest truth in the inward parts: and shall make me
to understand wisdom secretly.

Psalms

What is wisdom, whose value we are told is above rubies? It is not
simply intelligence, or knowledge, or intuition, or even understanding, though all these faculties enter into it.

Wisdom is the successful blending of all these abilities. It tells us
when and how to act on the sum of their contributions – or,
sometimes, when to refrain from acting until the time is ripe, and
what attitude to take while we are waiting.

Now, if we examine these abilities in terms of our definition of
masculine or feminine emphasis – of Gifts of the God and Gifts of the
Goddess – we find that overall they are a blend of the two. Intelligence
and knowledge certainly belong to both, while understanding
(intellectual grasp of truth) and intuition (direct grasp of truth) are the
God and Goddess faces of the one function. Which is why neither a
god-form nor a goddess-form alone would be adequate to personify

wisdom. And, in fact, in pantheon after pantheon we find both wisdom gods and wisdom goddesses. Neither is redundant, because wisdom itself arises from the polarity of the two.

Significantly, in the few cases where a pantheon has one major wisdom deity, the gender often seems ambiguous. The Japanese Buddhist wisdom deity Dainichi, for example, is sometimes referred to as a goddess and sometimes as a god.

To the Greeks, the major wisdom deity was Hermes, adopted by the Romans as Mercury. So perhaps it is not strange that the symbol of Hermes/Mercury (see Figure 1) is a combination of the male and female symbols; or that one of Hermes' offspring, by Aphrodite, was the strange Hermaphrodite, who was of neither sex but included the qualities of both.

Fig. 1 – The Mercury (Hermes) symbol is a combination of the male (circle and arrow) and female (circle and cross) symbols.

Usually, though, wisdom was represented by a god and a goddess acting in polarity.

The Egyptian Thoth, whom we touched on in Chapter II and will consider more fully in Chapter XX, is perhaps the classic example. He appears time and again as the working partner of the supreme goddess Isis; their polarity achieved magic which neither could have effected alone. And his wife was Ma'at, the goddess of truth, justice and the natural order of the universe, with which aspects wisdom must always be in harmony.

In the Brahmanic Hindu pantheon, Sarasvati was the goddess of wisdom, knowledge and speech, and inventor of the Sanskrit alphabet. She was born of Brahma himself, from his own immaculate substance, and when he saw her, he fell in love with her and married her. Together they 'begat all kinds of living things'.

A closeknit Assyro-Babylonian team was Nabu (the biblical Nebo), god of wisdom and teaching, and his wife Tashmit ('Hearer'), goddess of letters and opener of the eyes and ears of those receiving instruction. Together they invented writing. They also found their way into Egyptian mythology as Nabu and Tashmetu.

Invention of writing, understandably, is almost universally ascribed to wisdom deities. Thoth, too, is credited with inventing hieroglyphics.

Oghma Grianaineach ('of the Sunlike Countenance'), the Irish Gaelic god of wisdom and learning, one of the Tuatha Dé Danann and son of the Dagda, was said to have invented the Ogham script. This script appeared about the fourth century AD but 'almost certainly continues an older system of magical symbols' (Proinsias MacCana, *Celtic Mythology*, p. 40). Typically of a warrior society, to which shrewdness and quick thinking in warfare are of major importance, Oghma was no cloistered scholar; he was also a champion in battle, as was his Gaulish equivalent, Ogmios.

But, in this, Oghma/Ogmios is an exception. The mainstream concept, in many pantheons round the world, is that of the complementary partnership of god and goddess.

And there is food for thought here, both in the selection of deity-forms for matters of wisdom and in our whole approach to it in everyday life. The use of intelligence, the marshalling of available knowledge – these are obviously necessary. But the moment of truth comes when we have learned to harmonize logical understanding and the intuition which stirs below the surface, and to be able to integrate and rely on both. It is the moment of magic, when the Gift of the God and the Gift of the Goddess, together, give birth to that bright flash of confident awareness which tells us that wisdom has spoken.

V The Vegetation God

For out of olde feldes, as men seith,
Cometh al this newe corn from yeer to yere.

Geoffrey Chaucer

The vegetation god is the full flowering of the son/lover god, once the great agricultural communities had become firmly established. As the lover of Mother Earth, he is the Sun and the rain which fertilize her; and as her son, he is the crops to which she gives birth as a result. The cycle is endless.

Supreme examples of this concept were the Middle Eastern Tammuz, whom we shall consider in Chapter XIX, and the Egyptian Osiris (Chapter XVIII), who carried the concept one stage further by introducing the child Horus, who was both his own son and his reborn self.

The actual form of the vegetation god varied according to the environment of the people who conceived him. Let us look, for example, at the Canaanite Baal, whose story is vividly told in the verses of the Ras Shamra tablets.

He was the son of the supreme god El. His sister, and firm ally, was the fertility goddess Anat, who seems originally herself to have been an Earth Mother. She was also a battle goddess, which can be said to reflect the fact that in Canaanite territory agricultural success did not come easily but had to be fought for.

Baal's fertilizing function was primarily that of rain and thunderstorms, because it was those highly seasonal phenomena which caused the crops to spring up.

During the fertile season, Baal could enjoy the company of his three maidens, a happy young Triple Goddess of fertility – Plump Damsel the Daughter of Mist, Dewy the Daughter of Showers and Earth Maiden the Daughter of the Wide World.

But, however organized the fields, however safeguarded the wells, one enemy could never be permanently overcome – the aridity of the parched summer, when Baal's life-giving thunderstorms were absent. This dry period was personified by the terrible god of sterility and death, Mot.

His city, Ruin;
Dilapidation is the throne on which he sits,
Loathsomeness is the land of his inheritance.

Mot confronted Baal and slew him. But before his death, Baal did one apparently strange thing; he mated with a heifer. Now the bull was his cult-animal – and the Canaanites would depend on cattle as well as crops. So Baal's act would doubtless represent the careful provision, at the onset of the arid season, for the survival of adequate breeding-stock till that period was over.

With Baal banished 'as the dead' to the Underworld, it was time for his sister Anat (warrior goddess and indestructable fertility goddess) to take a hand. She set out to recover Baal's body, calling for help on the Sun goddess Shapash, who sees everything, including the Underworld, through which she travels at night.

When at length she was sated with weeping,
Drinking tears like wine,
Aloud she shouts to Shapash, the Light of the Gods:
Lift upon me, I pray thee, Baal the Mighty!

She herself travelled (like Ishtar for Tammuz) to the Underworld and pleaded with Mot. But Mot was adamant, so Anat's battle goddess aspect took charge.

She seizes the god Mot;
With a blade she cleaves him;

With a shovel she winnows him;
With fire she parches him;
With a millstone she grinds him;
In a field she scatters him;
His remains the birds eat,
The wild creatures consume his fragments,
Remains from remains are sundered.

The agricultural language is significant; at the end of the fertile
period, the products of the harvest are reaped, winnowed and ground.
But in Canaan it was also the custom to offer the firstfruits of the crop,
milled and fire-dried, to the gods.

As we shall see later (p.48), the Israelites assimilated much of the
Canaanites' agricultural seasonal ritual, and even its language; and
Anat's action is echoed in Leviticus 2:14: 'Thou shalt offer for the
meat offering of thy firstfruits green ears of corn dried by the fire, even
corn beaten out of full ears.'

So Baal was reborn, and the time had come for rejoicing:

For Baal the Mighty is alive,
For the Prince, Lord of the Earth, exists! ...
The skies rain oil, the wadis run with honey.

Year after year, the gods of fertilization and sterility are alternately
victorious – with the fertility goddess, who never dies even seasonally,
playing her part.

The corresponding human cycle of rituals – the seasons of
mourning, sacrifice and rejoicing – has an inevitable family likeness,
however much local conditions may vary. There is no doubt that, in
earlier days, the sacrifice was human. The Corn King would be
selected for his physical perfection, treated with honour as the
personification of the seasonal fertility god, mated at the harvest with a
priestess representing the goddess, and then immediately put to
death, either by her or on her behalf. Enacting the roles of the
appropriate deities in ritual drama was seen (as it still instinctively is
seen) as a way of attuning humanity to those deities' purposes, thus
ensuring their success.

There is a hint of this in a passage of the Ras Shamra text, where
Anat

... prepares seats for the warriors,
Dressing-tables for the soldiers,
Footstools for the heroes ...

after which hospitable welcome, she proceeds to slaughter them. This done, she purifies herself (as the sacrificing priestesses also doubtless did) with Baal's own water:

She scoops up water and washes,
Even dew of heaven, the fatness of the earth,
The rain of Him who Mounts the Clouds.

This washing follows the pattern by which many goddesses, after their ritual mating, washed or bathed to restore their virginity – in the old sense, not of celibacy but of independent status, property of no male, whether man or god.

The mating-and-sacrifice of the corn king/god would have been seen as a sad but loving necessity, not as a sadistic orgy. Robert Graves (*The White Goddess*, p. 316) says: 'There can be no doubt that, in the original legend of Osiris, Isis was a willing accomplice in his yearly murder by Set.'

The harsh tragedy of the primitive ritual, with priestess-goddess Isis's inescapable role of lover/sacrificer, was forgotten in the classic legend, by which kindlier period the human-victim custom had been long abandoned. But we can be sure that Graves is right.

(Christians who see the Corn King's sacrifice as evidence of pagan barbarity should consider this: Christ's own sacrifice – which was accompanied by mockery, not honour – is also seen as a sad but inescapable part of the divine purpose, for the well-being of mankind; and Christendom's most sacred symbol is an instrument of execution by torture. Spiritual truths are not always comfortable.)

Anat's slaughter of the 'heroes' may, of course, have been merely a memory of the much earlier human practice; mention of the firstfruits offering in the passage we quoted on p.23 above and in the verse from Leviticus suggests that these offerings had already replaced the human sacrifice.

And such offerings still survive today, in the hundred-and-one varied but similar folk-customs by which the first sheaf of the harvest is specially treated.

We shall return to another aspect of the cyclical fertility god theme in Chapter IX, Oak King and Holly King, and the Sacrificed God theme in Chapter X.

VI   The War God

He saith among the trumpets, Ha, ha; and he smelleth the battle afar off, the thunder of the captains, and the shouting.

Job

Homo sapiens, we are always being told (with the phrase 'survival of the fittest' usually thrown in), is an agressive species. In truth, though, mankind's strongest survival attribute lies in the fact that (like wolves, bees and baboons) we are social animals; from the very earliest times, we have achieved results by teamwork which we could never have achieved alone.

Nevertheless, it must be admitted that the ability to be aggressive, for the defence of the team (whether family, tribe or nation), has been a necessary element in our survival capacity.

The size of the typical 'team' has increased steadily since the Stone Age; and in this century, common sense and efficiency alone would suggest that the human race as a whole should become the team if our species is to survive and flourish, especially as warfare can now mean total mutual destruction. Fortunately, more and more people are realizing this.

These thoughts about our present situation may seem irrelevant to our historical study of god-forms, except perhaps to observe that the days when Army church parades could sing 'Onward Christian soldiers, marching as to war' (or its equivalent in other languages) without any sense of incongruity must be rapidly fading.

So let us look at the war gods of history.

They seemed to personify two aspects. On the one hand, the death and destruction which war entailed; such war gods (and goddesses, of whom there were plenty) were frightening. On the other, the conviction that 'our' cause was *ipso facto* just and that our god would support it; such war deities were encouraging and reassuring.

To take some examples. It would be over-simplifying things, of course, to say that the Romans on the whole regarded military conquest as a normal State function, while the Greeks tended to think in terms of independent city-states and to fight when that independence was endangered; but there is a considerable element of truth in it, and it is reflected in their war gods.

The Roman one, Mars, was integral with his people's history and was also called Marspiter (Father Mars). He was originally an agricultural deity, as Mars Gradivus (from *grandiri*, to grow). He was the son of Juno, not by Jupiter but by her union with a flower. By his wife, the vestal virgin Rhea Silvia, he became the father of Romulus and Remus, twin founders of the city of Rome.

He was in many ways more important to early Rome than the more remote figure of Jupiter; as farming Rome became conquering Rome, he retained that importance, changing his nature as that of his worshippers changed. He became a god of battle – at first in defence of the fields over whose produce he had presided, and later in the conquest of other people's fields. Even his title of Gradivus became reinterpreted as coming from *gradi* (to march).

Rhea Silvia faded into the background. His goddess companions were now themselves warriors – Bellona and Vacuna, and his general staff included Honos (Honour) and Virtus (Virtue) to inspire his troops, and Pavor (Quaking) and Pallor (as in English) to terrify the enemy.

He had a major temple on the Palatine Hill, and Bellona – regarded as his wife, sister or daughter – had hers near the Carmenta gate. Her priests, appropriately enough, were recruited from gladiators.

The Greeks' conception of their war god, Ares, was very different. It was best summed up in Homer's *Iliad*, which has his father Zeus telling him: 'Of all the gods who live on Olympus, thou art the most odious to me; for thou enjoyest nothing but strife, war and battles. Thou hast the obstinate and unmanageable disposition of thy mother, Hera, whom I can scarcely control with my words.'

Even his battle companions were purely destructive: his reputed sons Deimos (Fear) and Phobos (Fright), with Eris (Strife), 'insatiable in her fury', Enyo, 'destroyer of cities', and the blood-drinking Keres, Bitches of Hades. No honour, virtue or noble warrior goddesses here.

The Greeks knew that battle was sometimes justified, and it is significant that the championship of such battles was never attributed to Ares but normally to the patron deity of the city-state concerned. For example, Pallas Athene, goddess of Athens, was seen as a noble and intelligent warrior, taking up arms only when they were needed and not out of lust for destruction. She loathed Ares and all he stood for. Often, as in the Trojan War, they fought on opposite sides. Outside Troy, he attacked her, and she defeated him soundly. Standing over his prostrate body, she told him: 'Vain fool! Hast thou not yet learned how superior my strength is to thine?'

It must be admitted that the Hebrew god of the Old Testament, Yahweh, was a supreme example of the concept 'Our cause is just and justifies any atrocity.' Time and again conquered cities were wiped out, together with every man, woman and child in them, and their riches looted, all in the Name of the Lord. Unhappily, in his later Christian form his name has been all too often abused in the same way. One feels that Jesus and Pallas Athene would have been equally furious over such blasphemy. But more about Yahweh, both negative and positive, in Chapter XII.

Modern pagans use many ancient god- and goddess-forms to attune themselves to the ultimate divine essence, and their flexibility in this is one of the strengths of the movement. But war gods, today, we can do without.

And if ever battle is regrettably unavoidable, we would do well to reject firmly Mars, Ares and the primitive form of Yahweh and brace ourselves for it in the spirit of Athene. For, as she rightly said, her strength is in the end superior to theirs.

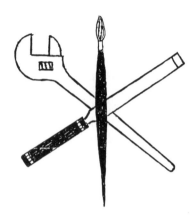

VII   The Craftsman God

Be no longer a chaos, but a world, or even worldkin. Produce!
Produce! Were it but the pitifullest infinitesimal fraction of a
product, produce it in God's name! 'Tis the utmost thou hast in
thee: out with it, then.

Thomas Carlyle

Greece has many lovely temples. Athene's own Parthenon, crowning
the heights of her sunlit city. Poseidon's lonely shrine at Cape
Sounion, surrounded on three sides by his great sea far below. The
stark columns of Apollo's temple in the heart of timeless Delphi. And
countless others, small and great.

But one in particular has a special place in our affection. It has stood
on a hillock overlooking Athens' Agora for more than twenty-four
centuries, and it is dedicated to Hephaestus, smith and craftsman of
the gods.

The spell of good craftsmanship must have blessed it, for it is
virtually complete; less elegant than some of the others, perhaps, but
with a workmanlike dignity of proportion. It is the oldest temple to be
built entirely of marble. The flanks of its hillock have in recent years

been lovingly replanted with myrtle and pomegranate, to restore the greenery as it is known once to have been.

But the truly magical circumstance is that, flanking the Agora and also immediately overlooked by the Hephaestion, are two streets called Hephaistou and Adreinou – which are occupied by craftsmen's workshops and sales counters, as their sector of the city always was.

Hephaestus looks down from his hillock to see the glow of smiths' furnaces and the flashing violet lights of the arc-welders, and to hear the banging of hammers and the buzz of power-driven saws – a strange blend of the ancient and the modern.

Does this puzzle him? We doubt it. True craftsmen take new discoveries in their stride, adopting them when they are useful. Over the centuries, he must have seen many such changes, as he watched over his protégés in their Athenian workshops.

Which he still does today.

Craftsmen – metalworkers in particular – were always regarded as people of magical power. This would have stemmed originally from the awe-inspiring effect of bronze weapons on the Stone Age peoples they overran, and the later corresponding superiority first of iron over bronze and in due course of tempered steel over plain iron. The possessors of the superior weapons and tools obviously had powerful gods on their side; and the craftsmen who made the weapons, and used the tools, were clearly in direct communion with these gods.

This is still reflected in the tradition, universally observed, that ordinary people nailing up horseshoes as good-luck talismans must do so points-upwards, or the luck will run out; while blacksmiths display them points-downwards, to pour power onto their anvils. Only for the magical blacksmith is that particular source of power permanently on tap; lesser mortals must carefully hoard such of it as comes their way.

This is of family interest to us, because Farrar, a Yorkshire name,

Fig. 2 – The Farrar (=farrier) coat of arms shows the points-down horseshoe display permitted only to smiths and farriers.

means 'farrier'. Stewart's own family is not entitled to a coat of arms (so far as we know), but every shield of Farrars or Farrers who are so entitled is a variant of that shown in Figure 2 with its points-down horseshoes.

A very old Irish hymn, known as 'The Deer's Cry' or 'St Patrick's Breastplate', has St Patrick calling on the powers of God to protect him 'against spells of women and smiths and wizards'

And of course there has always been, and still is, the sense of wonder inspired in all of us by some people's gift of taking metal, stone, wood or rough gems and transforming them into objects of beauty with a magical life of their own.

It is not surprising, then, that pantheon after pantheon had important deities of craftsmanship. Let us look at some of them.

Hephaetus himself, like most of the Olympians, had earlier origins. He was a fire god of Lycia, on the southern coast of Asia Minor (the Greeks learned metal-working from the East).

In Classical legend, he was the son either of Zeus and Hera or of Hera spontaneously. He was born lame and ugly, and his mother, out of shame, threw him from Heaven into the sea. There he was adopted by the sea goddesses Thetis and Euronyme, who brought him up for nine years. Gifted from childhood, he 'forged a thousand ingenious objects' for his foster-mothers. Finally, he persuaded Zeus to give him Aphrodite, loveliest of all the goddesses, as his wife, and he became craftsman of the gods.

His talents seemed limitless. He built bronze palaces for the gods. He made Zeus's throne, sceptre and thunderbolts; fabulous jewellery for many goddesses; the arrows of Apollo and Artemis; the armour of Herakles, Peleus and Achilles; and so on.

He could create robots – for example, the bronze giant Talos who was a formidable sentry; and for himself, two girls of gold who took his arms to help him walk when his stunted legs had difficulty supporting his massive body.

He even created, on Zeus's orders, a living woman – Pandora, whom Zeus sent to punish mankind with her fateful box of disasters.

Hephaestus's Roman counterpart, Vulcan, in his Classical form merely took over Hephaestus's attributes and legends – even marrying Venus, who from being a very minor Latin goddess had done the same with the attributes and legends of Aphrodite.

But this Hellenization obscured Vulcan's much older image, which unlike that of Venus had been far from minor. He was older even than Jupiter, and as Volcanus was in fact an earlier version of him. he had been a solar, thunderbolt god and above all a fire god, as his name suggests. As with the Asian Hephaestus, it was natural for ancient Stone Age gods of volcanic fire to become gods of the forge-fire with the dawn of the age of metal.

The Egyptians' craftsman god, Ptah, was of great importance throughout their long history. He was one of several deities, such as Ra and Thoth, who were regarded by their own priesthoods as creator gods; he even shared in one of the others, by collaborating in Thoth's creation myth. Ptah's principal cult-centre was Memphis, but his patronage of skilled artisans was country-wide. His high priest had the title Wer Kherep Hemut, 'Supreme Leader of Craftsmanship'. Imhotep, the great architect who built Egypt's first pyramid and major stone temple at Saqqara and who was one of the few known historical Egyptian figures to be later deified, was said to be Ptah's son.

Ptah created the cosmic egg from the mud of the Nile and formed man upon his potter's wheel. He was seen as the fashioner of Pharaohs' bodies – making that of Rameses II, for example, out of electrum, with limbs of copper and iron.

At Elephantine, the attributes of Ptah were attributed to Khnum.

The Hindu craftsman god, Tvashtri or Tvashtar, was also a solar-type god, known as 'the universal exciter'. He, too, was very ancient, probably coming to India with the first Vedic invaders. He forged the thunderbolt of Indra, and the Moon-cup which held ambrosia, nourishment of the gods. He was the father of Saranyu, the cloud goddess who married the Sun god Surya or Vivasvat, and father-in-law to the architect god Visvakarma. He trained the Ribhus, three artificer brothers who became so skilled that they were rewarded with immortality.

In northern mythology, craftmanship was the province not of a single deity (except for Volund/Wayland – see Chapter XXVIII) but of a large number of dwarfs employed by the gods. These dwarfs made everything from the spear of Odin and the hammer of Thor to the necklace of Freya and the golden hair of Sif.

These craftsmen-dwarfs, described as short and round-headed, are almost certainly a memory of a Central European tribe with a high reputation for metalworking and with access to the necessary raw materials; more on this on p.142.

In the last chapter, we said that war gods were better dispensed with. The opposite is true of craftsman gods such as Hephaestus, Ptah, Tvashtri or Wayland the Smith, or craft-inspiring goddesses such as Athene or Brid. They are immortal, and well worth invoking whenever we set chisel to wood, brush to canvas, drill to metal, wire to circuit, or pen to paper, for in all these activities there is, or should be, a touch of the fingers of the gods.

And a final thought for our Christian friends: Jesus himself was a carpenter.

VIII   The Horned God

The horn, the horn, the lusty horn,
Is not a thing to laugh to scorn.

Shakespeare

Of the male god-forms of history, one predates agriculture by
countless thousands of years; he has survived indestructibly in
harmony with it, and in spite of monotheist attempts to banish him.

That is the Horned God of Nature.

Originally he was a hunting god. The hunter identified with, and
respected, his prey; he imitated it in rituals of sympathetic magic, as
many prehistoric cave paintings tell us.

The American Indians' attitude to the buffalo, the myths they
attached to it, and the respect with which they treated that which they
hunted, is typical of this. Unfortunately their attitude was not shared
by the white immigrants.

Siberian hunters round Lake Baikal used to give formal burial to
the bones of the reindeer whose flesh they had eaten.

When the Stone Age hunter personified the vigour, strength,
beauty and procreative force of Nature in a god-form, what more

obvious model than the magnificent horned stag or bull or mountain goat which challenged his skill and on which his survival depended?

The Horned God was a vivid expression of the son/lover of Mother Earth – swift-moving, wide-roaming, concupiscent, respectfully killed to feed her other creatures and yet eternally reappearing as strong and splendid as ever.

Agriculture and social complexity did not push him aside, because mankind knew instinctively that, without the raw force of Nature underlying them, crops and community alike would wither and die.

This instinctive attitude to horns as a symbol survived, for example, among the ancient Hebrews. Few people realize, till it is pointed out to them, that throughout the Old Testament horns are a symbol of God-given power.

The equipping of Satan with horns, and the identification of horns (contrary to all Biblical tradition) with evil power only, was a medieval Church invention, a propaganda trick against the Horned God of the witches; the persecutors could then say, 'They worship the Devil, and he has the horns to prove it.'

The Horned God has survived all this, very thinly disguised, in such folk-customs as the Abbots Bromley Horn Dance. And he certainly flourishes again today as a God of the Witches.

He is probably the modern witches' favourite god-form; and the horned crown is the favourite ritual headgear of the High Priest, as the lunar crown is of the High Priestess.

His popularity in the Craft is understandable and appropriate. Wicca is a Nature-based religion. Its primal goddesses are the fertile Earth Mother and the cyclical Moon Lady of intuitive wisdom. And its primal god is, literally 'naturally', the mighty Nature-force which is ignored at our peril.

He is that which impregnates Mother Earth, and shepherds and defends her creatures. He is the true wisdom of cosmic and terrestrial law, from which mankind has tended to become estranged.

He is indeed the Lord of the Dance, for the rhythms of life, growth, death and rebirth are his, in creative counterpoint to the Earthly seasons and monthly phases of the Lady.

We shall examine two outstanding forms of the Horned God in detail in Chapters XVII, Pan, and XXI, Herne/Cernunnos.

Never was the Horned God of Nature more needed than today. Mankind's technological revolution is a gift of the God of Wisdom, which can be used or abused like any other – and it has been both. We are exploiting Mother Earth to a perilous extent, and have the power to destroy her and ourselves. We are in imminent danger of overpopulating her disastrously, though the means are at hand (in spite of Vatican prohibitions) to control the trend without frustrating our normal instincts. We are chopping down the rain forests which are our global lungs, and aerosoling great holes in the ozone layer which is our protective shield. We are polluting our oceans and imperilling whole species.

And so on and so on.

On the other hand, all these dangers have become the subject of lively public debate and positive counter-activity to a far greater extent than ever before. Exploiters and polluters of the environment, slaughterers of whales, believers in nuclear weapons – all these have to defend themselves against, or manoeuvre to divert, a rising tide of criticism not merely from ordinary citizens but from conscientious scientists and specialized experts.

One of the positive aspects of the technological revolution is that we have learned more about the Earth, its metabolism and its biosphere in the past thirty years than we did in the previous 3,000. We know the score – and with increasing certainty we know what to do about it, and how.

In the battle to see that it is done, our greatest allies are Mother Earth herself and the Horned God who is her wise and vigorous consort and champion.

IX Oak King and Holly King

Tall oaks, branch-charmed by the earnest stars,
Dream, and so dream all night without a stir.

John Keats

Of all the trees that are in the wood,
The holly bears the crown.

The Holly and the Ivy

The cycle of fertility has been expressed in many god-forms. One of these – or, rather, one pair – which has persisted from pagan times to contemporary folklore is that of the Oak King and Holly King, gods respectively of the Waxing Year and the Waning Year.

The Oak King rules from midwinter to midsummer, the period of expansion and growth; the Holly King from midsummer to midwinter, the period of withdrawal and rest. They are the light and dark twins, each being the other's alternate self. They are not 'good' and 'evil'; each represents a necessary phase in the natural rhythm, so, in this sense, both are good.

At the two change-over points, they meet in combat. The incoming

twin – Oak King at midwinter, Holly King at midsummer – 'slays' the
outgoing one. But the defeated twin is not truly dead; he has merely
withdrawn, during the six months of his brother's rule, into Caer
Arianrhod, the Castle of the ever-turning Silver Wheel (see *The Witches'
Goddess*, pp. 156-7).

We wonder how many of today's Yuletide Mummers realize just how
ancient a theme they are enacting. In the mummers' drama, which
varies little (for example) throughout the British Isles, St George
defeats the Turkish Knight in a sword fight – and then immediately
cries out that he has slain his brother. On comes the Doctor with his
black bag and restores the Turkish Knight to life.

The Yuletide St George is the Oak King, and the Turkish Knight is
the Holly King. The present pattern of mummers' plays dates back to
the fifteenth century, but its foundations are obviously very much older
than that.

Another folk-custom survival of the theme is that of Hunting the
Wren at the winter solstice. The wren is the Holly King's bird, and the
robin – his red breast doubtless proclaiming the reborn Sun – the Oak
King's. (On this widespread attribution, see the many wren and robin
references in Robert Graves' *The White Goddess*.) Hunting the wren
used to be done in actuality, the killing of the unfortunate birds being
sympathetic magic to ensure the end of their master's reign. Today, it is
merely symbolic. In scattered places in Ireland, for instance, adult
'Wren Boys', wearing conical straw hats completely covering their
heads and faces, still dance and sing around their villages on St
Stephen's Day, 26 December. And more universally, on the same day,
in the West of Ireland at least, children (usually in fancy dress and with
their faces made up) go from door to door carrying bunches of holly and
reciting their rhyme:

The wren, the wren, the king of the birds,
On Stephen's Day was caught in the furze;
Up with the kettle and down with the pan,
And give us some money to bury the wren.

Inevitably, the two brothers are also rivals for the favours of the
Goddess; and this theme crops up frequently in legend – for example,
in that of the Welsh maiden Creiddylad, for whom the Oak Knight
and the Holly Knight must fight, by King Arthur's ruling, 'every first
of May, until the Day of Doom'. Graves (*The White Goddess*, p. 180)
identified her with the lady in the ballad of *Sir Gawain's Marriage*:

... as I came over a moor,
I see a lady where she sate
Between an oak and a green hollèn,
She was clad in red scarlèt.

Creiddylad was the daughter of Llud, Nudd or Llyr (Lir), the original of Shakespeare's King Lear, and equatable to Cordelia – the only one of Lear's daughters who defied her father's orders and picked her own man.

Sir Gawain in *The Romance of Gawain and the Green Knight*, incidentally, is a type of the Oak King, and his rival the Green Knight, with his holly-bush club, represents the Holly King. They agree to behead each other alternately, each year.

Let us look at the significance of these two trees.

'The worship of the oak tree or of the oak god appears to have been shared by all the branches of the Aryan stock in Europe,' says Sir James Frazer in *The Golden Bough* (p. 209).

The oak obviously symbolizes strength and longevity; its acorn is expressively phallic; and its roots are said to extend as far below ground as its branches do into the air – the oak god thus having dominion over Heaven, Earth and the Underworld.

The oak was central to Celtic religious symbology. It was the tree of the Dagda, the supreme Irish father god. The Druids' very name probably derives from a root meaning 'oak-men'. They did not worship in buildings but in oak groves.

The wood of the ritual midsummer fire was always oak, as was the Yule log. It was on this fire that the Oak King's human representative was at one time ritually burned alive. And the Yule log often recalled its sacrificial significance by having a man's figure drawn on it.

In Christian times, the summer solstice has been taken over by St John. When we lived in County Mayo in the far West of Ireland, every St John's Eve, 24 June, bonfires jewelled the landscape from horizon to horizon when the Sun set. All the associations of this custom, which is not an official Church one, were transparently pagan – which is why we, as witches, also lit our midsummer fire on 24 June, instead of on 21 June as is the usual Craft practice. When all our neighbours were honouring such an ancient tradition, why leave ourselves out?

So to the holly. Although the Holly King's reign is one of withdrawal culminating in apparent lifelessness, his symbology reminds us all the time that he is his brother's other self and holds life in trust while it rests. The holly's leaves are evergreen, and its bright berries glow red when all else is bare of fruit. And, of course, in these islands at least, the harvest comes early in his reign; it is he who oversees the product of his brother's fertility.

It used to be considered unlucky to keep any holly, with its waning-year symbolism, in the house after Twelfth Night.

If the Holly King's reign begins with the harvest, it ends with the Saturnalia, with the revels of Yuletide. And its god, Saturn to the oak's Jupiter, tends to appear as a lovable buffoon, red-cheeked, jolly and bearing gifts. The Holly King is the true origin of Santa Claus, rather than the fourth-century bishop of Myra who is his official prototype and whose factual history is virtually non-existent, in contrast to his body of kindly legend.

In some Wiccan traditions, the Goddess is seen as ruling the summer, and the God the winter. For ourselves, we find this a restricting concept. After all, Mother Earth and her mysterious lunar sister are powerfully there all the time; and so is the Horned God of Nature, whether he roams the cornfields or the snowfields.

So to represent the god-aspect of the cycle of the seasons, both conceptually and ritually, who better than 'the lily-white boys, clothèd all in green O' – the twin Gods of the Waxing and Waning Year? For they are the two faces of the One who is One – but, unlike the One in the song, never alone.

X   The Sacrificed God

Uneasy lies the head that wears a crown.

Shakespeare

The concept of the Sacrificed God is linked directly to the ancient concept of kingship. This was that the king was the human representative and incarnation of the god, and that the welfare of his people, and the fertility of their lands and their herds, depended directly on his capable functioning in that role.

It implied that the king must be at the height of his powers – physical, mental and sexual – to fulfil his role, and that, before those powers were in danger of waning, he must be sacrificed, the elements of his body and spirit returning at their maximum power to the soil and atmosphere of his realm, for the benefit of its people.

This was, in fact, his accepted fate.

The queen's role was different. She stood for the Earth Mother, whose fertilizing was her consort's duty. As the human queen passed child-bearing age, she would simply hand over to a daughter. There would be no question of sacrifice, because the Earth was irreplaceable

– only that which fertilized her was (and indeed must be) constantly renewed.

The queen or her heiress was thus (like Creiddylad, whom we considered in the last chapter) the focus of contest and challenge between possible successors to the king whose term was approaching its end.

It is this which underlies the constantly repeated theme of fairy-tales, in which the young hero successfully achieves the daunting tasks put before him, at which others had failed, and is rewarded with the hand of the king's daughter – post-medieval romance and the forgetfulness of centuries having obscured the fact that what really mattered was that she was the *queen's* daughter. However, hints do survive: sometimes the fairy-tale king does his best to frustrate the hero's efforts, and/or the queen or princess secretly aids him.

The actual duration of the king's term varied, but seven years is a frequently found figure. This would fit in both with the magical significance of the number seven (sum of the Heavenly three and the Earthly four) and with a reasonable estimate, in those days of more rapid ageing, of the duration of peak manhood.

The sacrifice itself tended to take place around one of the four main pagan seasonal festivals at the beginning of February, May, August and November, or at the midwinter or midsummer solstice. Evidence of this interweaves with that of the sacrifice of the Oak King and Holly King, and of the Corn King at harvest time; sometimes it is difficult to see which is involved, since the themes did tend to overlap.

The concept of the sacrificed king lasted a great deal longer than is immediately apparent. The first major scholar to investigate its survival in medieval England and France was Margaret Murray (1863-1963), in her controversial books *The Divine King in England* and *The God of the Witches*.

There can be very little doubt that William the Conqueror and his Plantagenet successors, whatever lip-service they paid to the church (which had become a politically convenient formality but had not yet established its monopoly dictatorship), were followers of the Old Religion.

One incident in support of this cited (among many others) by Murray is the founding of the Order of the Garter by Edward III. The accepted story goes that the Countess of Salisbury, during a dance at Court, dropped her garter and, to save her embarrassment, the King put it on his own leg and founded the Order. Now it is extremely unlikely that a medieval lady would have been embarrassed by the mere dropping of a garter. Murray's far more plausible suggestion is that the garter was recognizably that of a witch high priestess and that Edward's action at this unfortunate revelation (Church dignitaries being present) was to put her under his protection – his statement *'Honi soit qui mal y pense'*, usually translated 'Evil to him who evil thinks', actually meaning 'Any of you want to make something of it?'

And the Order which he founded was a further challenge – consisting of two covens of the traditional thirteen each, led by himself and the Heir Apparent, which is still its form to this day.

But to return to the sacrificed god/king element. Murray cites much evidence to show that this concept, too, persisted, including a tendency to seven-year terms or multiples thereof. Her outstanding example is William Rufus – the Conqueror's son and successor, as King William II – and his death by Walter Tyrrel's arrow in the New Forest on 2 August 1100. Much evidence points to this being a willing ritual sacrifice, including his recorded words to Tyrrel, the facts that he was approaching the fourteen year of his reign, that his age was forty-two (6 x 7) and that his death took place within a day of the Lammas festival. (He was also, it should be mentioned, a very capable and respected ruler, and a constant mocker of the Church hierarchy.)

By that time, the practice of sacrificing a substitute for the king had gained ground; often the chosen substitute would be honoured with high office until his time came. So it may be significant that Rufus's Archbishop Anselm fell out with him when Rufus had reigned for seven years, was charged with treason and fled to safety. This practice may also explain the initial friendship between Henry II and Thomas à Becket, first his Chancellor and then his Archbishop of Canterbury; their later rivalry and estrangement; and the final killing of Becket in 1170, fifteen years after he was made Chancellor and eight after he was made Archbishop.

Another of Murray's examples of the substitute sacrifice – in this case, a successfully self-appointed one – was Joan of Arc.

Anyone interested in more details of these significant survivals should read Murray herself – or, for an admirable summing-up of them, Chapter 9 of Janet and Colin Bord's *Earth Rites*. But they have been worth mentioning here to show how deep-rooted the concept of the divine victim, the sacrificed god/king, actually is in human attitudes.

It cannot be questioned that it has pervaded Christian thinking. It may well be that Jesus so saw himself, as the spiritual King of Israel whose death was a destined climax to his Messianic mission. But he was later exalted to divine scapegoat, whose sacrifice atoned for all the sins of the world. Thinking Christians, we find, tend to concentrate more on his actual teachings, as a guide to their own behaviour. But there are still many who focus their faith on his scapegoat role, in the belief that mere acknowledgement of him absolves them from personal responsibility.

And this is relevant to the question: what meaning has the sacrificed god/king for us today?

In his historic form, we would say he has outlived his role. We can no longer shift responsibility for communal well-being, or for the health and fertility of Mother Earth, onto the shoulders of a sovereign, a charismatic leader or even a government. This emphasis now must be increasingly on individual responsibility for these things, and for group responsibility exercised through the co-operation of individuals.

The sacrifice is our own – of outworn ideas, of tunnel vision, of gain at the expense of others. It is best symbolized by the Tarot card of the Hanged Man, whose sacrifice is not by death but by enlightenment.

And with our recognition of this, the sacrificial victims of our evolutionary development will at last rest in peace.

XI The Underworld God

For in that sleep of death what dreams may come
When we have shuffled off this mortal coil,
Must give us pause.

Shakespeare

The Underworld, Afterworld or Otherworld has meant many things
to many people. In its various aspects, it has been a shadowy Sheol to
the Hebrews, a happy Otherworld to the Celts, a golden Heaven or a
flaming Hell to the Christians, a peaceful duplicate-Egypt to the
Egyptians, a seven-walled prison to the Assyrians, and so on. And its
deities have differed accordingly.

So has its location, which was often ambiguous. To the Egyptians,
it was Amenti, which meant the West, but it was both the perilous
region through which the Sun travelled at night in his Boat of a
Million Years, and in which the dead faced judgement, and also
Sekhet-Hetepet or Tchesert, the Egyptian Elysian Fields, for those
who successfully passed that judgement; a mirror-image of the Nile
Valley life he or she had known, but without such drawbacks as
disease.

The unquestioned king of the Egyptian Underworld was Osiris, whom we shall consider in detail in Chapter XVIII. But he had many gods and goddesses to supervise the arrival and judgement of the dead – from Anubis, who conducted them, Ma'at, whose red feather of truth was weighed against their hearts, and Thoth, who recorded the verdict, to minor functionaries such as the goddess Tenemit, who refreshed them with ale.

The Greek concept was more élitist. The happy Elysian Fields, with their graceful white poplar trees, were for special heroes and their like; for ordinary mortals there was Tartarus, a place of black populars, willow and asphodel, inhabited by ghosts, pale spectres of their former selves. Only the outstandingly wicked suffered active punishment.

Elysium and Tartarus together constituted the Underworld or Afterworld. At first it was conceived of as lying beyond the ocean which encircled the flat world but, as Greek exploration expanded, this concept became less easy to maintain, and it became literally the Underworld, buried in the centre of the Earth. It was surrounded by the rivers Lethe (Forgetfulness) and Styx, across which one was ferried by the grim Charon; he demanded an obolus in payment, and this coin was accordingly always placed upon the mouth of the dead.

Hades, its ruler, was the god of that which lay under the surface of the Earth, but he also represented the resting-place of life – in particular of vegetation and crops – during the arid months of winter. The name Hades apparently means 'the Invisible', but he was also known as Pluto, from the word for 'riches'.

It was in this role, as winter guardian of the wealth of the soil, that he abducted Persephone, daughter of his sister the barley goddess Demeter, and made her his bride. This immediately resulted in the Earth's becoming sterile as Demeter mourned. Finally Zeus arranged a compromise: Persephone was to spend half of each year as Hades' consort in the Underworld, and half on Earth. She thus personified the vegetation itself, alternately concealed under the ground and flourishing above it. (The whole story is told in Chapter XIII of *The Witches' Goddess*.) Her underground phase was not merely a time of repose, however; there she shared Hades' other function, being his effective co-ruler of the Land of the Dead.

The Celts believed in reincarnation. (It is said that Druids used to accept IOUs from each other, payable in a future life, as security for loans.) So their Otherworld tended to be a happy place, rather like the Summerlands of modern reincarnation terminology.

It is typified by the Welsh Annwn, another name for which was Caer Feddwid, 'Court of Carousal', or by the Irish Tír na nÓg, 'Land of Youth', visited by such people as Oisin between two quite distinct experiences (i.e. lives) in the mortal world. Like the Elysian Fields, stories about it almost exclusively concern the visits of heroes, but this tendency can be ascribed to the aristocratic nature of Celtic mythology as it has reached us. The grass-roots beliefs of earlier days doubtless lingered among ordinary people.

The warrior-aristocracy attitude can also be seen in the Nordic Valhalla, another Court of Carousal, destination of those who died honourably in battle. The Nordic Tartarus was Hel, which was also the name of its ruling goddess; but although it gave us our word Hell, it was not thought of a place of punishment.

The Underworld of the Scandinavians' Finnish neighbours, Tuonela or Manala, was very different. It was governed by Tuoni and his wife Tuonetar, whose daughters were goddesses of disease, evil and suffering.

The Assyro-Babylonian Underworld seems to have become more sinister by a patriarchal take-over. Originally, under the rule of the goddess Ereshkigal, it was admittedly a strongly fortified and unattractive place, as it appears in the story of Ishtar and Tammuz (see Chapter XIX), but more a Tartarus of shades than a Hell in the modern sense. Later, however, it was besieged and captured by Nergal, god of mass destruction by war, plague or the heat of the desert Sun. The defeated Ereshkigal was allowed to remain only by becoming his wife and subordinate.

The Hindu Underworld had several levels, or Talas, with different associations, not necessarily unpleasant. Nor was it arranged in descending order of attractiveness, for its lowest level, Patala, was said to be a pleasant place, associated with the sense of smell.

Another concept underlies all these views of the Underworld: that it represents the Unconscious, a realm of danger to the unprepared but of richly expanded awareness to those who come properly to terms with it.

This concept can be seen in the Chaldaean goddesses Sabitu and Siduri, both of whom were not only Underworld but also sea deities – and the sea is time and again a symbol of the Unconscious, of the feminine intuitive aspect. Both these ladies warned the hero Gilgamesh and his companion Arad-Ea of the dangers they would be facing if they crossed the world-encircling sea which was the approach to the Underworld; and Siduri asked them if they would not be happier sticking to what was familiar, the natural pleasures of the conscious world. Yet when the men showed they were determined to take the risk, both armed them with helpful advice.

It is not surprising that this aspect – the dangerous but potentially rewarding challenge of the Unconscious – tends to be personified by goddesses rather than gods.

But this is, after all, a book about gods. And a key to the role of the god in this can be found in the witches' Legend of the Descent of the Goddess (see our *Eight Sabbats for Witches*, pp 170-3, or *The Witches' Way*, pp 29-30). It has a basic similarity to the legend of the descent of Ishtar to the Underworld, but its meaning is different. It concerns the god-function of intellect and analysis, and the goddess-function of intuition and synthesis, meeting and coming to terms with each other – a process which may involve initial suffering but without which neither can progress further.

The invisibility of Hades hides the riches of Pluto. The Underworld is there to explore – but we need both the Gifts of the God and the Gifts of the Goddess to meet the challenge.

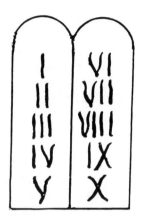

XII   The Monopolist God

Never mock the name by which another man knows his God; for if
you do it in Allah, you will do it in Adonai.

Old Hebrew saying

The first major god-form to claim a monopoly of Divinity was the
Hebrew Yahweh, from which in due course sprang the Christian and
Moslem forms. Over the centuries, as might be expected, it both
provoked the worst and inspired the best in human concepts of deity.

The name of the Hebrew god was only allowed to be whispered,
once a year, by the High Priest in the Holy of Holies in the Temple at
Jerusalem. Only its consonants were publicly known – the Hebrew
letters Yod, Heh, Vau, Heh, or YHVH, which came to be known in
Greek as the Tetragrammaton ('four-letter').

The vocalization of YHVH remained a closely guarded secret.

In fact, like all Hebrew words of any religious or mystical
significance, the Name was so composed that the Cabalistic meaning
of each letter, in order, constituted a formula or process. In this case
(to oversimplify considerably), Yod is that aspect of the genderless

Ultimate which stimulates manifestation; Heh is the feminine aspect which gives that manifestation form; Vau is the male fertilizing aspect to which Heh gives birth; and the second Heh (daughter where the first Heh was mother, so to speak) is the polarized partner of Vau, from which partnership all further manifestation arises.

Even without its vowels, then, YHVH is a formula of Creation.

The philosophy of the Tetragrammaton, however, is much later and more sophisticated than the origins of the Hebrew god himself. He was at first a tribal storm, fire, mountain and volcanic god.

The Hebrews (*Khabiru*, 'displaced people') were a confederacy of ethnic minorities who moved out of Egypt about 1225-1050 BC into Palestine, where they attracted kindred local tribes to form a distinct and more or less integrated community. (It should be noted here that, while the identification of the Hebrews with the *Khabiru* is majority scholarly opinion, it has come into dispute. The theory that the Hebrews had their origin in a Canaanite peasant revolt is, we understand, gaining some ground.)

It was still as a storm god that Yahweh had led them out of Egypt – guiding them as pillar of cloud by day and of fire by night (Exodus xiii:22), raising the flood which drowned their pursuers 'with the blast of thy nostrils' (xv:8) and descending upon Mount Sinai in fire, smoke and earthquake (xix:16).

The immigration (whether historical or not) engendered a memory of 'deliverance' from Egypt, doubtless crystallized into religious conviction by the inspired leadership known (again, whether or not with historical justification) by the name of Moses. If the Exodus was actual, it is still extremely doubtful that they were 'slaves in Egypt' as tradition maintains. One possibility is that they had been won over by the monotheism of the Pharaoh Akhenaton and in their fervour of conversion found the re-establishment of the rule of the priesthood of Amun-Ra intolerable.

Be that as it may, the concept was firmly established of the Divine Covenant which made them the Chosen People of God. But the actual forms of their religious practices, festivals and mythology they absorbed and adapted from the Near Eastern peoples who surrounded them.

The biblical Garden of Eden and Flood myths, for example, are transparent modifications of the Assyro-Babylonian ones. And the great autumn (New Year) Feast of Tabernacles took over the basic forms and liturgy of the Canaanite autumn festival, as did Passover that of the beginning of the barley harvest in April, and Pentecost that of the end of the wheat harvest seven weeks later.

The Hebrews' weekly Sabbath, too, was a direct adaptation of the Assyro-Babylonian *sabbatu* (from *sa-bat*, 'heart-rest') with its taboo on various activities at the New Moon, the menstrual time of the Moon goddess, later extended to the four Moon-quarters.

The devotion of the Palestinian peasantry (both Canaanite and Hebrew) to the Goddess was a constant headache to the thoroughly patriarchal Levitic priesthood, and it took centuries to get it under control, even in the holy precincts of the Temple itself.

Dr Raphael Patai, in his books *Man and Temple* and *The Hebrew Goddess*, shows that the goddess Asherah (after whom the tribe of Asher was named) was worshipped alongside Yahweh as his wife and sister in the Temple at Jerusalem for 240 of the 360 years the Temple complex existed, and her image was publicly displayed there.

And, as we saw in Chapter XIX, Hebrew women persisted in celebrating the festival of Tammuz and Ishtar, even in post-Exilic times, in spite of all attempts to suppress it.

The Jewish community at Elephantine in Egypt, who emigrated there from Judah during the reign of Nebuchadnezzar, acknowledged two goddess-wives of Yahweh, Ashima Baetyl and Anatha Baetyl, probably both Syrian in origin. The epithet *baetyl* seems to have referred to a holy meteoric stone.

In one passage (Ezekiel xxiii) Yahweh admits, if only metaphorically, to a pair of wives. He condemns the 'whoredom' of two sisters who 'became mine and bore me sons and daughters' (New English Bible). They were Ohola (personifying Samaria) and Oholibah (personifying Jerusalem). He rages against their lewd behaviour in Egypt and their infatuation with their Assyrian lovers – in other words, against the ineradicable sympathy of Hebrew women for the god-and-goddess worship, and free status of women, which they had seen in Egypt and still saw among their neighbours. Yahweh ordains their punishment in savage detail, culminating with: 'Summon the invading host; Abandon them to terror and rapine. Let the host stone them and hack them to pieces with their swords, kill their sons and daughters and burn down their houses.'

Death was the penalty for heresy, but there were limits to its practicability. In the confrontation between Elijah and the 450 prophets of Baal on Mount Carmel, recounted in I Kings, xviii, verse 19 (Authorised Version) there were also 'the prophets of the grove four hundred, which eat at Jezebel's table' – in other words, priests or priestesses of the goddess Asherah. The Mount Carmel confrontation was a public relations exercise; it achieved its purpose, and as its climax Elijah had all the 450 priests of Baal slaughtered, apparently with public approval. Yet the 400 priests of Asherah were untouched. That might have been too much for the ordinary people to stomach, and presumably Elijah knew just how much he could get away with.

Hebrew society, as ordered by the highly privileged Levite

priesthood, kept women in a totally subordinate position, as the property of their husbands or fathers. All this was justified theologically, of course. Man related to God; woman related to man. And to such a philosophy, goddess-worship was a dangerous threat.

Such an attitude to women, though admittedly without quite such brutal penalties, persisted into Pauline Christianity and continued to be held long after Judaism itself had abandoned it. 'For a man indeed ought not to cover his head, forasmuch as he is the image and glory of God; but the woman is the glory of the man. For the man is not of the woman; but the woman of the man. Neither was man created for the woman; but the woman for the man' (I Corinthians xi:7-9 – incidentally, one would think, contradicting Genesis i:27, in which God created mankind male and female 'in his own image'). Paul inherited this dogma from Levitic teachings, not from those of Jesus, who showed no such bias and seems to have treated women as fully human beings. Unfortunately, Paul's is an attitude still far from dead.

The pagan world on the whole was mutually tolerant, different pantheons being regarded as localized forms of each other, not as enemies. To the Hebrews, however, their god was the only true god. To begin with, they seem to have been prepared (or to have found it prudent) to regard other gods merely as lesser. 'God takes his stand in the court of heaven to deliver judgement among the gods themselves' (Psalms lxxxii:1 – NEB again). And the name Baal, which merely means 'Lord', was for some time often used for Yahweh – not surprisingly, for Yahweh absorbed many of the attributes of the Canaanites' Baal and El. El was the god who existed before all other gods, the divine principle itself; Baal represented the agricultural and environmental aspects, of greater importance perhaps to the ordinary people than to the privileged Levites.

The national hero Solomon, an expert in foreign diplomacy and dynastic marriages, was well aware of the political advantages of ecumenism and was too powerful to be prevented at the time. But much later King Josiah (c.630 BC) 'desecrated the hill-shrines which Solomon the King of Israel had built for Ashtoreth the loathsome goddess of the Sidonians, and for Kemosh the loathsome god of Moab, and for Milcom the abominable god of the Ammonites; he broke down the sacred pillars and cut down the sacred poles and filled the places where they had stood with human bones' (2 Kings xxiii:13,14, NEB).

Joshiah's purge was only temporarily successful; his successors Jehoahaz, Jehoakim, Jehoachin and Zedekiah all 'did that which was evil in the sight of the Lord' – which from other contexts we know meant they worshipped gods and goddesses unacceptable to the Levites.

As the Hebrews under Levite dictatorship became firmly established, so all other gods (and particularly goddesses) became anathema, heathen devils to be destroyed ruthlessly along with their shrines and worshippers.

Genocide of the heathen was the Will of God. Among many other examples, the people of King Og of Bashan were typical (Deuteronomy iii:6-7): 'And we utterly destroyed them, as we did unto Sihon, King of Bashan, utterly destroying the men, women, and children, of every city. But all the cattle, and the spoil of the cities, we took for a prey to ourselves.'

Even one's own family or friends were not to be spared: 'If thy brother, the son of thy mother, or thy son, or thy daughter, or the wife of thy bosom, or thy friend, which is as thine own soul, entice thee secretly, saying, Let us go and serve other gods ... Thou shalt surely kill him; thine hand shall be first upon him to put him to death, and afterwards the hand of all the people ... And all Israel shall hear, and fear' (Deuteronomy xiii:6-11).

It must be remembered that much of the earlier parts of the Old Testament is not so much history as late rewrites by the ultimately victorious Establishment. Such massacres, for example, may not actually have happened; they may well be what the rewriters believed *should* have happened. Forms of worship, even of Yahweh himself, were much more varied throughout most of Israel's history than the rewriters would like us to think.

Enough of the negative aspects of Yahweh, of the nationalist bigotry and extreme male chauvinism, and the attendant brutality, with which Levitic dictatorship invested him. Judaism, as we shall see in Chapter XV, evolved over the centuries a far more fruitful concept of him which embraced his essential feminine aspect, Shekinah.

The negative aspects survived all too terribly in centuries of Christian and Moslem monotheism (for Allah is the same god) and are still rampant from Northern Ireland to the Ayatollah's Iran, and in the Fundamentalist persecution of 'heretics' in Britain, America, Australia and elsewhere.

It would be equally bigoted of us to deny that there always has been, and still is, a positive side as well. In many parts of the Bible and among the finer minds in Christendom and Islam, this god has been not a jealous tyrant but a deeply spiritual concept expressive of the highest human ideals.

This is true of any god- or goddess-form; for there is only one ultimate Creator, to which all such forms are tuning-signals. They can be exploited to excuse the worst in us or developed to evoke the best in us.

At the tail end of ancient Israel's thousand-year existence, Jesus the Nazarene was a supreme spokesman of Yahweh's positive aspect. His merits as a great teacher shine through the four official Gospels, even though these were edited and amended by victorious political factions in the early Imperial Church, and in several apocryphal Gospels which were suppressed by those same factions.

He did not claim to be God; that would have blasphemed against everything in the spiritual environment in which he lived and taught. He called himself the Son of Man – an epithet which in Hebrew terminology meant the human channel of God's purpose; it was normally applied to the human king, who was expected to be Yahweh's executive on Earth.

Jesus's words and behaviour denied the negative aspects of Yahweh's official image. He was certainly not male chauvinist, and he blessed peacemakers as the children of God. He would weep at some of the things his name has been used to justify.

Skipping over the many true followers of his teachings of the past 2,000 years, to our own time, we would say that Mother Teresa of Calcutta is an outstanding example of one who lives entirely positively in the chosen terms of Christian symbology. So is the African Emmanuel Milingo, former Archbishop of Lusaka, who was forced to resign by the Vatican.

And if we may tell it – in our own personal experience, on an unpublicized level, Janet's father, Ronald Owen, was another example. He was a simple and devout Christian, one of God's holy innocents, who did much modest good and never harmed anyone in his life. He never wavered from his own faith, yet he lived with us and accepted ours as valid for us. Sometimes we would say, 'Ron, we're having a Circle tonight, to work for So-and-so. Will you work for him too, your way?'

Ron would retire to his room and do just that; and there were occasions when he asked the same of us. Many a time our joint efforts succeeded – and who are we to say which contribution was the more powerful?

Ron Owen died quietly in his sleep on 5 November 1987, while this book was being written. He was mourned by Protestant, Catholic and witch alike – and, at his funeral, side by side. It is in people like him (and there are indeed many) that Yahweh is justified of his children.

From many people's point of view, including our own, Yahweh as a Christian god-form, even at his best, suffers from only one human-imposed restriction: he is a grass widower, separated from his other half. When his consort, the feminine aspect of the divine polarity, is once again acknowledged, his worship will be able to reach its full potential.

And we know quite a few Christians who – some publicly, some privately – feel the same.

XIII   The Anti-God

Satan, so call him now, his former name
Is heard no more in heaven.

John Milton

The Judaeo-Christian Devil, as he is thought of today, is a comparatively modern invention, dating back to no earlier than about 300 BC, making his first biblical appearance in the Book of Chronicles.

Until then, Satan was not the arch-enemy of God but one of his civil servants. His duty was to try humans' worthiness by putting it under strain, as he did with Job. Not a very endearing function, perhaps, but an understandable one, exercised on God's orders and with his approval.

In Israel's monarchical period, up to 586 BC, evil and suffering were regarded as deserved punishments sent by God for wrongdoing. If Yahweh had enemies, the Levitic priesthood saw them as the gods of the neighbouring peoples, which had altogether too much appeal for the Israelite peasantry – as we saw in the last chapter.

An enemy which Yahweh shared with other Middle Eastern gods

was the primordial sea-chaos, symbolized as a dragon-like monster, which he had to subdue and organize – Tiamat to the Assyrians, Tehom to the Hebrews. This was in a sense also the 'serpent' of the Garden of Eden, who was condemned to mutual hostility with the seed of Eve but had not yet reached the stature of the Arch-Enemy of God.

That stature is reached in 1 Chronicles xxi, where 'Satan stood up against Israel, and provoked David to number Israel'. Satan's action here is for the first time described not as a God-ordained testing of David but as deliberately malicious.

But, remembering Satan's earlier function as an executive of Yahweh, he now had to be regarded as a fallen rebel angel, and this culminates in the famous passage in Isaiah xiv, from verse 12 onwards: 'How art thou fallen from heaven, O Lucifer, son of the morning!' Here Satan declares that, 'I will exalt my throne above the stars of God ... I will be like the Most High.' He is now the Anti-God, self-declared enemy and rival of the good God.

A strange result of the Authorized Version rendering of this passage into English is the identification of the name Lucifer – 'Light-bearer' – with Satan. In fact, the writer of Isaiah was merely using the Morning Star, the quickly obliterated dawn appearance of the planet Venus, as a metaphor; the New English Bible translates it more accurately as 'bright morning star'. An inappropriate metaphor, perhaps, because Satan had become the Prince of Darkness.

This was a new concept in Hebrew thinking – of Dualism, postulating two independent powers in perpetual conflict. On the one hand, Good and Light; on the other, Evil and Darkness.

The Koran was written in the seventh-century AD, so it treats Satan (Iblis) entirely as a fallen angel. Allah tells the angels to prostrate themselves before Adam, and only Iblis refuses, saying, 'I am better than he. Thou hast created me out of fire, while him thou didst create of mud.' So Allah banishes him, and Iblis declares that he will pursue mankind and 'lurk in ambush for them on Thy Right Path' (Surah vii:11-18).

The Zoroastrian theology which arose in Persia some twelve centuries before Mohammed was emphatically Dualist from the start, even ahead of Hebraism. The principle of Good, Truth and Light in this system was Ormazd (Ahura Mazda), who created Life. The principle of Evil, Falsehood and Darkness was Ahriman (Angra Mainyu), who created Death.

Everything which Ormazd thought into being was countered by Ahriman. Ormazd envisaged a world of warmth and light, and it came into being; Ahriman created one of cold where the winter was ten months long. Ormazd established a place where roses grew and colourful birds flew; Ahriman invented the insects which plague plants and animals. Ormazd spread out rich pastures, and Ahriman sent the beasts of prey which devour cattle. Into Ormazd's city of prayer Ahriman introduced doubt which gnaws at faith; into his city of rich craftsmanship he introduced sloth which breeds poverty. And so on.

One detail of Ahriman's activity is highly significant. one of his demonesses, Jahi, had the task of spreading the vices of women; and it was a kiss which Ahriman gave her that launched on humankind the 'impurity' of menstruation.

'Significant', because Dualism is essentially patriarchal. It replaces the creative polarity of God and Goddess, of the masculine and feminine principles, with the destructive confrontation of God and Devil.

As Robert Graves says (*The White Goddess*, p. 465): 'The result of envisaging this god of pure meditation ... and enthroning him above Nature as essential Truth and Goodness was not an altogether happy one ... The new God claimed to be dominant as Alpha and Omega, the Beginning and the End, pure Good, pure Logic, able to exist without the aid of woman; but it was natural to identify him with one of the original rivals of the Theme and to ally the woman with the other rival permanently against him. The outcome was philosophical dualism with all the tragi-comic woes attendant on spiritual dichotomy. If the True God, the God of the Logos, was pure thought, pure good, whence came evil and error? Two separate creations had to be assumed: the true spiritual Creation and the false material Creation.'

By 'the Theme' Graves means the twin-rivalry typified by the Oak King and Holly King which we discussed in Chapter IX – not a rivalry of good and evil but an expression of the rhythm of polarity which is in accord with nature.

The twins' cyclical rivalry is envisaged as being for the favour of the Goddess. But if you turn that rivalry into an eternal fight between good (which you identify with spirit) and evil (which you identify with matter) – in effect making the Oak King into God and the Holly King into Satan – then inevitably you force the Goddess out of her position as umpire and balance-holder, and into that of partisan.

And since the God is envisaged as pure thought, 'enthroned above Nature', with no need of the feminine principle for his creative activitiy, inevitably the feminine principle and all it stands for become identified with his opposite, his enemy. With Satan.

Pre-Dualistic paganism made no such mistakes; even in those cultures where patriarchal influence was beginning to distort the natural polarity, that polarity still operated.

The pre-Dualistic view of evil was pragmatic. Sinister deities existed, but they personified the various natural dangers which mankind faced. They were seen as elements in the total balance of Nature, not as total enemies to the forces favourable to mankind, and certainly not as creators of an evil material world which stood in opposition to the good spiritual one.

The Egyptian Set, for example, is often regarded as the origin of the Hebrew/Christian Satan and the Islamic Shaitan (Iblis). Etymologically he may have been, but essentially he personified one threat only – the constant danger of encroachment by the arid desert upon the fertility of the Nile valley. All his mythology, his conflict with Osiris, Isis and Horus, the transfer of his wife Nephthys's loyalty to the Osirian party, his outwitting by Thoth, dramatize this concept.

War gods, as we saw in Chapter VI, were ambiguous; sometimes (as mostly to the Romans) they represented the hope of victory, sometimes (as to the Greeks) pure destructiveness, and sometimes (as to the Celts) something of both, to be invoked or propitiated accordingly. But even at their worst, they personified only one aspect of the evils to be found in the world, not their totality.

The deification of evil as an Anti-God is a perilous step. Perhaps the most fruitful way of defining evil is as imbalance. To the Cabalists, the Qliphoth, evil counterparts of the ten Sephiroth of the Tree of Life, are not independent forces in themselves but the state of imbalance arising during evolutionary growth, before one Sephira's development has been matched by the maturing of the next. If all the Sephiroth are fully developed and balanced – in an evolutionary process, an individual or a situation – the Qliphoth lose their power.

Although not all pagans would use the same technical terms as the Cabalists, the healthy pagan attitude to evil is basically the same. Evil is a matter of context; what is evil in one situation (a knife in the hand, a thunderstorm, stubborn persistence, fire, acquiescence) may be entirely constructive in another. Evil is not a malignant god. It is an imbalance to be corrected.

Satan is man-made concept, which starts to create that imbalance the moment we accept it.

XIV   Some God Recipes

And he made the holy anointing oil, and the pure incense of sweet
spices, according to the work of the apothecary.

Exodus

There is no need to repeat here what we said at the opening of the
corresponding chapter in *The Witches' Goddess*, about the usefulness
of perfumes and incenses to create the appropriate atmosphere for
magical working, and about the ritual use of food and drink, so we will
go straight ahead with some suggested recipes – of which again some
are traditional and some designed by ourselves or our friends.

Perfumes, Oils, Incenses

Amun-Ra incense
   4 oz (120 gm) frankincense
   3 oz (90 gm) cinnamon
   1 oz (30 gm) mastic

2 drops olive oil
3 drops oil of rose
3 drops tincture of myrrh

Blend the three resins, and powder them very finely. Blend the oils and add them to the resins. This should be kept in an airtight jar in the dark for three months before use.

Fire of Azrael incense
½ oz (15 gm) sandalwood chips
½ oz (15 gm) juniper berries
½ oz (15 gm) cedarwood oil

Mash and chop the juniper berries, and add them to the sandalwood chips. Mix thoroughly. Add the cedarwood oil and again mix thoroughly.

We based this recipe on the Fire of Azrael which features in Dion Fortune's memorable novel *The Sea Priestess*. That fire was fuelled by a mixture of sandalwood, cedarwood and juniper wood. The fire was burned, she says, 'for vision as well as sacrifice ... Cedar is a lovely-burning wood, and sandal takes the flame well, too, but we soon saw why juniper was not recommended as fuel. It was fascinating, however, to watch the flame creep from twig to twig and see the flying shower of golden sparks as the sap-filled cells burst with the heat. But as the fire died down it cleared, and the juniper produced a curious pale charcoal of its own, the ashes of the twigs lying in fine golden lines among the redder embers of the other woods. It was a fire of great beauty.'

This is Azrael in his divinatory not his death aspect.

Sun God incense

Giant fennel	
Rue	
Thyme	Equal quantites
Chervil seed	
Pennyroyal	
Camomile	Half quantities
Geranium	

For an incense, these ingredients should be either chopped up small or dried and ground, before blending. If you find the mixture too quick burning, mix in a little gum mastic.

This recipe is, in fact, a combination of plants used as fuel for festival bonfires (especially at Bealtaine and Midsummer) in Co.

Donegal. It was given to us by Francis De'Venney, remembered from his Donegal childhood.

Herne incense

   ½ oz (15 gm) deer's tongue leaves
   ½ oz (15 gm) patchouli leaves
   ½ oz (15 gm) rue
   1 oz (30 gm) gum sandarac
   ⅓ oz (10 gm) gum guyicum
   26 drops vetyver oil

Make during the waxing Moon. Grind the deer's tongue, patchouli and rue extremely finely with pestle and mortar, and mix them. Grind the gum sandarac to gravel consistency, and the gum guyicum extremely finely, add them to the others, and mix. Finally add the vetyver oil, and mix well.

This recipe was given to us by Seldiy Bate (see list of suppliers below).

Pan incense

   4 oz (120 gm) dittany of Crete
   1 dried vanilla pod (2 if small)
   2 oz (60 gm) benzoin
   1 oz (30 gm) sandalwood
   ½ oz (15 gm) pine needles (better cypress if available)
   Half a dozen goat's hairs if available

Break up the dittany of Crete flowers with your fingers, powder the vanilla, and mix all the ingredients thoroughly.

We call this our 'Piper at the Gates of Dawn' incense (see p.78).

Dittany of Crete, incidentally, is an excellent herb for stews and casseroles, and for clearing the remnants of infection such as the common cold out of the system.

Kyphi incense

The ingredients of this important Ancient Egyptian incense are listed in the Ebers Papyrus (c.1500 BC), but not the proportions. Its preparation is a job for specialists, and we suggest you try one of the occult suppliers listed below; we have used those of Seldiy Bate, Paul Demartin and John Lovett and found them all good.

Witch Blood Anointing Oil

   ¼ oz (7 gm) artemisia (wormwood)
   ¼ oz (7 gm) valerian root
   ¼ oz (7 gm) vervain herb
   ½ oz (15 gm) madder root

½ oz (15 gm) English mandrake (white bryony) root
1 pt (570 cc) olive oil
9 drops oakmoss oil
7 drops elder oil
10 drops pine oil
5 drops mayweed or camomile oil
A pinch of sugar or sweet sap
A pinch of rock salt

This formula was given to us by Chris Bray of The Sorcerer's Apprentice (see list of suppliers below). He suggests that if it is for use solely by a High Priest one should leave out the vervain, or if solely by a High Priestess one should leave out the oakmoss oil. So for a specifically male-god ritual you may prefer it without vervain. But as it is difficult to make in small quantities, most people will find the complete recipe perfectly satisfactory for general use.

As Chris's method of preparation is rather complex, we give it in his own words:

'On the day of the Full Moon bruise and break the valerian root, madder root and English mandrake root into small pieces. Add to a large mixing-bowl or pestle and mortar. Mix in the wormwood and vervain. Add a palmful or two of the olive oil and beat to a mushy consistency (recite charm at this stage if you wish). Pour the mush into an oven-proof dish. Fit a lid and put in an oven for 15-30 minutes on a very low, gentle heat.

'Remove from the oven and allow to cool. Stir the mush (recite again) and scrape into a wide-necked glass jar (preserve jar, jam jar or the like). Stopper and leave on a warm south-facing windowsill (so that the mixture can soak up the sunlight and the moonlight) for about a fortnight. Shake well each morning and evening (recite charm if you wish).

'When you see the New Moon appear, shake the mixture and strain through muslin into a clean jar. Add the rest of the oils listed and the pinch of sugar and salt. Stopper and then agitate vigorously. Replace the jar on the windowsill and agitate vigorously morning and evening until the Moon reaches the First Quarter phase. Leave on the windowsill (untouched in order to allow the mixture to precipitate) until the night of the next Full Moon. Decant the clearest liquor off the precipitation and into the amphora/bottle you will use for ritual purposes.'

Some perfume and incense suppliers

There are many good suppliers of perfumes and incenses, and this list is certainly not meant to be exclusive; but we have used the products

of the following (listed in alphabetical order) and found them
excellent:

Seldiy Bate, Acca & Adda, BCM Akademia, London WC1N 3XX

Chris Bray, The Sorcerer's Apprentice, 4-8 Burley Lodge Road,
Leeds LS6 1QP

Paul Demartin, Anubis Books, 28 Bury Street, Heywood, Lancs

John Lovett, Occultique, 73 Kettering Road, Northampton NN1
4AW

Planetary perfumes and incenses

In *The Witches' Goddess*, we drew attention to Pat Crowther's helpful
suggestions for planetary-aspect ingredients from her *Lid off the
Cauldron*, and listed those for the feminine planets. Here are her lists
for the masculine planets:

Sun: Heliotrope, orange blossom, cloves, frankincense, ambergris,
musk, mastic, paliginia, sunflower oil.

Mercury: Sweet pea, lavender, mastic, cloves, cinammon,
cinquefoil.

Mars: Hellebore, carnation, patchouli, lignum aloes, plantain.

Jupiter: Stock, lilac, storax, nutmeg, henbane.

Saturn: Hyacinth, pansy, pepperwort, asafoetida, black poppy
seeds, henbane, lodestone, myrrh.

(Note that henbane is poisonous if eaten and that asafoetida is
highly unpleasant unless used in very small quantities.)

Crowley's attributions

Aleister Crowley, in his *777*, gives perfume correspondences for the
following male gods: Adonis, Aeacus, Agni, Amun-Ra, Anubis,
Apep, Apollo, Ares, Attis, Bacchus, Brahma, Buddha, Castor and
Pollux, Chandra, Ganymede, Hades, Hanumah, Helios, Hermes,
Horus the Elder, Horus the Younger, Iacchus, Indra, Janus, Jupiter,
Khephra, Loki, Mars, Maruts, Menthu, Mercury, Minos, Neptune,
Odin, Pan, Pluto, Poseidon, Priapus, Ptah, Ra, Rhadamanthus,
Saturn, Set, Shiva, Shu, Thor, Thoth, Tuisco, Uranus, Vishnu,
Vulcan, Wotan, Yama, Zeus. These perfumes are named in the gods'
alphabetical entries in Part III.

Food

Phallic cakes

For these you need cream-horn tins – metal tubes obtainable from
catering suppliers. Make ordinary short crust pastry, grease the tin
tube, and wind the pastry spirally in a flat strip around it, damping the
edges of the strip and pressing them together to make a continuous

pastry tube. Use your ingenuity to make the shape as phallic as you can by thickening one end.

Bake in a hot oven on a greased baking sheet until brown. Slide pastry off the tin, and fill it with thick cream.

Believe it or not, you are following a good Christian tradition here. In France, similar cakes called *pinnes* (penises) were carried in solemn procession to church at Easter and Corpus Christi, to be blessed by the priest. In the town of Saintes in Charente Maritime, Palm Sunday was known as *La Fête des Pinnes*.

Responsible witches, we find, are neither promiscuous nor kinky, but they are as unprudish in their symbolism as the good people of Saintes used to be. There are ritual occasions when such generative symbols are entirely appropriate – and doubtless some where they could be suitably accompanied by the Aphrodite cakes we described on pp 74-5 of *The Witches' Goddess*.

Apollo's golden coins

>1 tin or packet baby sweet corn cobs
>(obtainable from Chinese shops)
>8-10 medium sized carrots

Slice the cobs finely into discs. Peel the carrots, and slice them finely into discs. Boil together in salted water until tender (about 10 minutes). Drain, and add a large lump of butter to glaze. Turn into a dish, and squeeze on half a small orange and a little lemon. Garnish with freshly ground black pepper and a sprig of parsley.

If you like, you can add silver coins – finely sliced cucumber and white radish, with vinaigrette dressing.

This is another of Seldiy Bate's recipes. She finds it a great favourite with children – especially after a treasure hunt.

Heather Ale

>1 gallon (4.5 litres) heather in full bloom
>1 oz (30 gm) ground ginger
>4 or 5 cloves
>2 handfuls hops
>1 lb (450 gm) golden syrup
>1 lb (450 gm) malt
>1 oz (30 gm) yeast

Put the heather in a pan, add some water, and boil for an hour.

Strain off the liquid, and make it up to 2 gallons (9 litres) with plain water. Add the ginger, cloves and hops. Stir in the golden syrup and malt. Boil for 20 minutes, then strain into a 2-gallon (9 litre) jar.

When it drops to blood heat (about 98° F, 37° C,) take a little of the liquid and crumble the yeast into it. When fermentation has started, stir it into the bulk liquid. Cover the jar securely with a cloth, and leave in a warm place for two days. Then bottle and cork loosely for another day; then cork firmly and wire the corks to prevent blowing. (Screw-cap bottles may be less elegant, but they are more practical.) It will be ready for drinking in three weeks.

Heather ale was regarded as a drink of the gods by the Picts, aboriginal inhabitants of Scotland who in due course merged with the Gaels. There is a legend that three Danish warriors who had learned the recipe from the Picts were asked to give it to the Irish King Brian Boru after the battle of Clontarf in 1014, but preferred death to revealing it.

Francis De'Venney tells us that another version of the story gave Bloody Foreland in Co. Donegal its name. A local chieftain called Sweeny invited two Danish settlers, father and son, to his home and tortured them to give up the recipe. The father said he would if they killed his son, so that he could not go back with news of his treachery. Sweeny killed the son, and the father mocked him, saying that the secret was now lost because only his son had known it. He was then killed too.

Mead
    3 lbs (1.36 kg) creamy-white honey
    ⅓ pint (190 cc) cold weak tea
    Juice of 1 orange
    Juice of 1 lemon
    ½ oz (15 gm) baker's yeast
    Yeast nutrient
    ¼ teaspoonful tartaric acid
    1 lump of sugar per bottle

Add water to the honey to make up 1 gallon (4½ litres) and bring it to the boil, stirring until thoroughly dissolved. Simmer for 5 minutes. Add the cold tea, allow to cool to blood heat (about 98° F, 37° C), then add the orange and lemon juice and sprinkle on the yeast, yeast nutrient and tartaric acid. Strain through muslin into a fermentation jar. Plug the neck of the jar with cottonwool and leave for three days in a warm place, renewing the cottonwool and cleaning the jar-neck every now and then as the froth mounts. Siphon into another jar and fit a fermentation lock. Leave in a warm, dark place for up to three months, or until fermentation stops and the liquid clears. Bottle, with a lump of sugar in each bottle, and cork firmly. Leave for at least six months, and preferably a year, before drinking.

Mead is another drink with a long ritual tradition, and several deities are credited with having invented it. Zeus may well have been fond of it, having been reared in Crete as a child on the milk of the goat goddess Amalthea and the honey of the bee goddess Melissa.

May-bowl wine
½ oz (15 gm) dried woodruff leaves
1 sliced lemon
1 gallon (4.5 litres) inexpensive white wine (i.e. 6 standard bottles)
Add the leaves and the lemon (peel and all) to the wine and steep for
4-6 hours. Strain and chill.

This is the traditional German May Day drink. We are indebted for
the recipe to *Enchanted Forest Newsletter* (W.S. Adams, 201 Moneta
Avenue, Bakersfield, CA 93308, USA).

XV   The Grass Widower

So lonely 'twas, that God himself
Scarce seemed there to be.

S.T. Coleridge

No one has suffered more from the period of the patriarchal take-over, and from the banishing of the Goddess, than the God. Mankind's image of him has become less true to his essential nature, and contact and communication with that essence have become more distant and distorted. The call-signs are out of tune.

Pagan thinking and pagan religion were basically natural and organic. At first instinctively, later consciously, it acknowledged the polarized rhythms of the cosmos; the light and dark which were necessary to each other's existence; the Earth Mother's need for her fertilizing consort; the interplay of Moon-mystery and Sun-clarity. Heaven, Earth and Underworld were inseparable, at all the levels from spirit to matter, from the destiny of the soul to the ripening of grain.

This creative polarity was evident to them at a human level in the relationship between man and woman. They knew that this relationship perpetuated the race through child-birth, even when they still personalized the impregnator as a male god-form. They knew that the two sexes complemented each other and evoked the best from each other (as well as the worst, but that too was part of the rhythm) and that either was incomplete without the other. They knew the strange, inexorable magic of mutual desire, and the heights and depths of achievement which it inspired. They knew that communion with the gods required both priests and priestesses. They knew the secret of the Yin and the Yang.

Mankind creates Deity in its own image – and this is right and effective, because, in setting up call-signs to Deity, one must use concepts and symbols which are in tune with one's own nature. So since *homo* (and *femina*) *sapiens* knew that polarity was the source of all creation, all manifestation, they knew, too, that the Divine Source must be both male and female.

The wise ones (such as the priesthood of Ancient Egypt) knew that there was only one ultimate Source. But since that Source, too, must polarize before manifestation can begin, the Source could be known and communed with only in terms of that polarization.

Hence the God and the Goddess.

Hence, also, the many faces of God and Goddess which men and women conceived and invoked to attune themselves to the rainbow-spectrum of aspects of the great Two.

'All Gods are one God, all Goddesses are one Goddess, and there is but one Initiator' – the Initiator being oneself.

We firmly believe that this way of thinking and worship – condemned by later monotheism as heathen idolatry – was and is sound, healthy, fruitful and in accord with cosmic reality.

In the East it has largely retained that health. The god- and goddess-forms of Hinduism, for example, express a subtle understanding of cosmic truth from which the West could learn much. But in the West, religion contracted a chronic sickness with the onset of patriarchy.

This is sometimes presented as the result of an evolutionary leap in the development of the linear-logical, conscious mind, which is masculine-oriented. But this faculty had matured back in the mists of prehistory and had already achieved great things in co-operation with the intuitive-cyclical, feminine-orientated gifts of the Unconscious. Tool-making, building, boat-making and agriculture – to take but a few examples – would have been impossible without it. It had already evolved.

What had changed was the circumstances in which both faculties – what we have called the Gifts of the God and the Gifts of the Goddess –

were able to operate. As society became more complex, more class-divided and more highly organized, the linear-logical aspect not only became more important, it also began to have economic advantages to those who wielded it. Organization, and its attendant discipline, engendered efficiency, but it also engendered privilege and rigid books of rules. To those in charge, the Gifts of the God became of exaggerated importance.

The Gifts of the Goddess, on the other hand, tended to be unpredictable, difficult to discipline and unamenable to books of rules. They were thus regarded with increasing suspicion by the growing Establishment.

In the Western world, the incursion of the Indo-European peoples, who were already patriarchal in their organization and thinking, was a major factor in this development. Its effect on religion, and its attendant mythology, was particularly marked in Greece, as we shall see in Chapter XXV.

Another contributing factor was the firmly patriarchal and monotheist stance of the Levitic priesthood of the Hebrews, seed-bed of later Christian attitudes. This we considered in Chapter XII.

By the time Christianity became the official religion of the Empire, discipline was the prime consideration, and theology reflected it. Reincarnation had been taught in the early Church (as St Jerome and St Gregory testified) but discipline required the offer of eternal reward for obedience and the threat of eternal punishment for disobedience, so reincarnation was declared anathema by the Second Council of Constantinople in 553.

It proved impossible for the Church to banish the Goddess altogether; the acknowledgement of her is too deep-rooted and instinctive in the ordinary worshipper. But while an outlet had to be provided for this instinct (if only to counter the dangerous spread of Isis-worship to places as far apart as Asia Minor and York), it – or she – had to be denied the actual status of deity and firmly subordinated to the male God.

A symbol was ready to hand: the mother of that Jesus who had already been deified. The Council of Ephesus in 431 elevated Mary to *Theotokos*, Mother of God.

We have dealt with the subject of the Virgin Mary more fully in Chapter VII of *The Witches' Goddess*; here it is enough to observe that both the deification of Jesus and the semi-deification of his mother far outstripped the evidence of the Gospels, and would in any case certainly have struck both of them as blasphemous.

The masculine God, then, had been elevated to absolute sovereignty in the dogma of Christianity, and also in that of their Islamic neighbours; and these were two of the three acknowledged Western religions, even if they fought each other.

The third was Judaism, oppressed and persecuted, and it alone actually developed, and still retains, the principle of divine polarity. Judaism knows that God contains both male and female principles – Tiphareth ('Splendour') and Shekinah ('Brightness' or 'Dwelling'). Shekinah, the Brightness of God, is described in the *Zohar* as 'the consuming fire, by which they [humans] are renewed at night'; she is envisaged enthroned on the Mercy Seat in a cloud of fire, flanked by cherubim. Shekinah's day is Saturday, and the Jewish Sabbath is the Bride of Israel; it is considered a holy sacrament for man and wife to make love on Sabbath night. It is significant that, whereas a Catholic priest may not marry, a rabbi must, unwed, he would be distanced from the Shekinah aspect of the God he serves. Judaism does not share Christianity's deep-seated nervousness about sex, and in general regards the pleasures of this world, if responsibly enjoyed, as gifts of God.

It must be said, too, that the Hebrew Cabala is the subtlest and richest analysis of the operation of polarity, on all the levels, which is available to Western thinking.

What effect did the rejection of the feminine divine principle by Christianity and Islam have on God himself, as humanly visualized?

It banished polarity and natural rhythm from Creation, replacing both (as we saw in Chapter XIII) with arid Dualism. God was no longer Lord of the Dance, for the Dance did not fit in with the systemized logic of authoritarianism. Light and Dark were no longer partners, each the other's other self, but enemies. Matter was no longer the rich manifestation of Spirit, but its prison. Sexuality was no longer the urge to relatedness, to polarized creativity, but a bait of the Devil to drag man's disciplined consciousness into the treacherous waters of the intuitive female principle.

God, of course, was far above the prison of matter, or the deadly temptation of sexuality. He did not have to meet the challenge of the goddess's needs, because she did not exist. He was seen as having created Nature (even though matter was evil?) but was not himself involved in it.

Great Pan, as the early Christians claimed (see p.77), was dead.

A depolarized Father God is emasculated, remote from mankind and alienated from Nature.

Significantly, among Catholics who accept the Trinity plus a semi-deified Virgin, ordinary people's prayers tend to be addressed to her, as the humanly approachable channel to the rather coldly distant figure on the Cross or the even more distant Father. And among Protestants who have rejected 'Mariolatry' – in other words, who will not admit the Goddess even in a disguised form – there is great emphasis on the Son rather than the Father, because he at least was once human. To the ordinary Protestant, the Trinity is little more than a theological concept; the God who matters is the deified Palestinian.

One must be fair about this. Many people have an instinctive attunement to the Ultimate Source, and this even shines through the restricted god-form which patriarchy has imposed on them. To such people, God is Love indeed; and regardless of the theoretical evilness of matter, Nature is the smile on His face.

But how much easier would that attunement be for them – and in how many countless others would it be awakened – if the limitations of God the widower were removed?

Socially, politically and philosophically, patriarchy is dying on its feet. Even its scientific expression – mechanical materialism – has ceased to satisfy the advance guard of scientific thinking.

It is time for human religious concepts to catch up with the tide of change – by restoring to the shackled God his banished Consort. Men and women were not made to be one-parent children.

XVI   Restoring the Balance

Let me not to the marriage of true minds
Admit impediments

Shakespeare

Long ago (so the story is told, in many pagan and Christian forms) the Land of the Fisher King lay under a curse. The soil, and the wombs of women, and the minds of men, were dry and barren. The Fisher King himself lay sick in his Grail Castle, from a wound in the thigh – a wound of impotence.

His castle, nonetheless, contained the Grail and its promise of salvation, of release from the curse, and also a Lance which dripped blood. These treasures were guarded by mysterious maidens.

To break the spell, the Questing Knight had to come to the castle, eat and drink with the Fisher King and his maidens and then ask the right questions.

'What do these wonders mean?'
'Whom does the Grail serve?'
'Why does the Lance bleed?'

If his courage failed and he dared not ask the question, the castle would vanish from his sight and he would find himself back in the loneliness from which he had set out. But if he asked the questions bravely, the curse would be lifted, the Fisher King would be healed and the land and its people would come back to joyous life.

Few of the Grail Legend versions are precise about the answers. What matters, they seem to be telling us, is a readiness to ask the questions.

A grail or chalice is universally a feminine symbol – vividly enough, for it is both a womb and a receptive, nourishing breast.

A lance or spear is equally vividly masculine – phallic, penetrative and active.

For lack of communion with the Grail of the Goddess, the Fisher King is impotent, and the Lance weeps blood.

If the land – the totality of our life, our religion and our thinking – is to flourish again, Grail and Lance, Goddess and God, must be reunited in equal and complementary partnership.

Quite what form this reunion takes will vary. If Christianity, for example, is not to fossilize, we believe that it too will have to find ways of expressing the concept in terms of its own symbology.

For witches, the union and creative polarity of God and Goddess are basic to their outlook. In *The Witches' Goddess*, we considered some of the many faces of the Goddess which can help us to understand her totality. In the foregoing chapters, we have tried to do the same for the God. Now we will go on to look at some of the individual forms in which the peoples of various cultures and environments have envisaged him.

Part II
Invoking the God

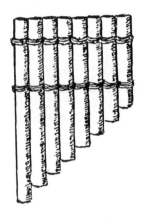

XVII Pan

Et in Arcadia ego (I too in Arcadia)
              Anonymous, often a tomb inscription

To modern popular knowledge (which has a strong classical bias, whether acknowledged or not), the goat-foot Pan is unquestionably the most familiar figure of the Horned God.

To the Greeks, he was primarily a god of shepherds, flocks and woods, and also of hunting. According to Frazer (*The Golden Bough*, p. 759), the Arcadians used to whip his image at festivals or when the hunters returned empty-handed, but this 'must have been meant, not to punish the god, but to purify him from the harmful influences which were impeding him in the exercise of his divine functions as a god who should supply the hunter with game.'

But Pan had much wider overtones than these purely pastoral and hunting aspects.

There is argument about what his name means. The simplest explanation is that it means exactly what it does in Greek, both ancient and modern – *pan* (τό πᾶν), 'all, everything'. The Homeric hymns so interpreted it, as centuries later did the scholars of Alexandria, who held that Pan personified the Cosmos. Many modern scholars prefer to derive it from *paon* (πάων) 'pasturer'.

For a long time, Pan was purely a local god of Arcadia in the Peloponnese, where he lived on Mount Maenalus or Lycaeus. Shepherd-like, he rested at noon, and could be angry if disturbed.

Appropriately, Arcadia was, and in poetic language still is, a synonym for idyllic rusticity.

The spread of Pan's worship beyond Arcadia was said to have arisen from the Battle of Marathon, before which he appeared to Philippides, an Athenian runner on his way to Sparta. Pan asked why the Athenians neglected him, and promised victory over the Persians if they would worship him. At Marathon, the Persians were routed and fled in panic; so, as honour and prudence required, the Athenians built a temple for him on the Acropolis, and his worship soon extended to all Greece.

The word 'panic' (Greek πανικόν) itself derives from Pan; as John Pinsent (*Greek Mythology*, p. 43) puts it: 'Pan causes irrational wild fear in the noonday silence of a deserted mountain side.'

Hermes, the god of wisdom, was also originally an Arcadian deity and was said to be Pan's father; in his Arcadian form, he too seems to have been goat-footed and horned. But with the absorption of both into the Olympian system, Pan acquired a variety of parents. He was said to be the son by Hermes of Dryope, whose father's flocks Hermes tended; or by Hermes of Penelope, wife of Ulysses; or of Penelope by all her suitors in Ulysses' absence; or by Zeus of Thymbris or Callisto. Another named mother was Amalthea, the Cretan goat-goddess who suckled the infant Zeus.

As his worship spread, he acquired many local forms. The Romans identified him with their own Faunus, whose characteristics and physical appearance were certainly very similar. He also tended to merge with Priapus, the ithyphallic fertility god who was an immigrant to Greece from Mysia in Asia Minor. Hermes and Pan were among Priapus's named fathers.

His loves were many, quite apart from his constant pursuit of the anonymous nymphs of his own woodlands. Caves were often dedicated to Pan and a nymph. Nymphs were very much his counterparts; often they were memories of primordial local goddesses, beings of the wild to be confronted with caution like Pan himself, rather than the coy, pretty creatures of Victorian art. The Greeks called (and still call) brides 'nymphs' (νύμφαι), which may mean that they possess magical power – a belief which persists in rural Ireland, where a bride is said to be able to calm a storm at sea.

Pan seduced the Moon goddess Selene by shape-changing into a white ewe or ram and tempting her to follow him into a wood. His successful wooing of the nymph Pitys ended sadly: he won her from Boreas, the North Wind, but Boreas in revenge threw her against a rock and crushed her. In pity, Earth Mother Gaia turned her into a pine tree.

Another unhappy ending was sometimes attributed to Pan's own anger. Echo, whom he desired, was a mountain nymph attendant on Hera. When she refused him, Pan had her torn to pieces by shepherds. Again Gaia stepped in, receiving Echo's mangled body but immortalizing her voice – which we still hear, particularly in her natural mountain surroundings. (In another version, Echo died of a broken heart when Narcissus spurned her love, and only her voice was left.)

Pan's pursuit of another nymph, Syrinx, was frustrated when she called on her father, the river god Ladon, for help. Ladon rescued her by turning her into a reed. Frustrated, Pan plucked some reeds and cut them into what we now call Pan-pipes, and he named these pipes the Syrinx after her (as we in due course named the voice-box, or lower larynx, of birds).

Beyond his pastoral, hunting and musical nature, Pan shared with his father, Hermes, the gifts of wisdom and prophecy. In this sense, he seems to personify the concept of wisdom through oneness with Nature, and through the recognition that Nature is the manifestation of all the other levels of reality, and our most immediate key to them. As Brewer (*Dictionary of Phrase and Fable*, Pan entry) puts it, Pan is 'the personification of deity displayed in creation and pervading all things ... He is also called the god of *hyle*, not of "woods" only, but "all material substance".'

His physical appearance reflects this concept of the total spectrum of reality. He had goat's feet, in touch with the Earth. His animal legs rose to his fertile energizing loins. His torso was purely human, culminating in his wise and prophetic head, with its power of creating music.

Pan as 'All' indeed.

One story told by Plutarch used to be quoted as confirmation of the victory of Christianity over paganism. At just about the time when Christianity was starting, in the region of Tiberius, a sailor called Thamus passing the Echinades Islands heard a voice calling out three times: 'When you reach Palodes, proclaim that the great god Pan is dead.' It is far more likely that what Thamus really heard was the ritual lamentation for the annual death of Tammuz (see Chapter XIX). That lament was 'Tammuz, Tammuz, Tammuz the all-great is dead' – and the word for 'all-great' is *pammegas* (πάμμεγας), which sounds very like *Pan megas* (πάν μέγας), 'great Pan'.

Perhaps the most moving modern tribute to Pan is our own favourite chapter from Kenneth Grahame's *The Wind in the Willows* – 'The Piper at the Gates of Dawn'. Through the eyes of Mole and Ratty, witnessing the god's rescue of a lost otter cub, Grahame powerfully conveys the quality of a genuine spiritual experience. We suggest that a study of that chapter should be part of every witch's training.

The Pan Ritual

Invoking Pan can be a fraught process. If you approach him correctly, the results can be wonderful and very beneficial. If you mess him about – beware. He can be a very chaotic god. We can remember some witches who summoned him carelessly and as a result ended up with their car stuck on a traffic island.

He can be a very helpful god to conservationists, as some friends of ours found out when they invoked him to protect a beauty spot from ruination by a mining company. The machinery which the company moved onto the site refused to work. The foreman was convinced that this was sabotage by 'hippies', because 'their blasted hippy-type pipe music kept on being heard' – though no one in the coven concerned could play the pipes. Mind you, he never found out how they were managing to affect the machinery, because no sabotage was found, and in fact no physical steps had been taken. In the end the project was dropped because the seam turned out to be uneconomic.

Good occultists do respect other people's property, even if they don't approve of what they are doing. The ordinary worker is not the commercial decision-maker, only a guy trying to feed his family; so don't leave any room for error which might harm him.

The ritual below is of the same nature – working for a specific conservationist purpose.

The Preparation
As with all magical working, the aim to be achieved must be exactly envisaged and carefully put into words which leave no loopholes or room for misinterpretation. It is as well to write these words down for everyone concerned to study and have clearly in mind.

If possible, the ritual should be performed out of doors – ideally, of course, on the site concerned. For such outside working, the minimum of equipment should be used.

It is also worth remembering that, if you are working on or near a controversial site, nothing that could be interpreted as a weapon (such as a sheath-knife or a sword) should be carried. Janet has a very nice wooden-bladed athame with a granite handle which is obviously only decorative. But a wand – or come to that, even a pointed finger – can cast a Circle just as well as an athame. It is the strongly envisaged intent that matters.

If this ritual is out of doors, and you have coven members who cannot join you for it, they too should have the wording of the purpose and know the time, so that they can give psychic support from home.

The Ritual

The Opening Ritual is as usual (see Appendix 1), though leaving out the Charge, to keep it short and simple.

After the Witches' Rune, the High Priest invokes Pan:

'Great Pan, Lord of the Arcadian paradise, inspire our hearts with your presence. Thrill our minds with your pleasant notes. Answer our wills with your perfect magic. Let the woods and fields, mountains and valleys, find protection in your footsteps. Let hare and hind, otter and badger, the vixen and her cubs, all the families of our brothers and sisters of the wild, find comfort in your touch. Let the birds of the air and the bats of the night dance freely to your piping, and the fish of the rivers and the great seas find peace at the echo of your call. Let all small things nestle secure against your mighty legs, protected by the goat-foot God.'

The High Priestess then addresses Pan, explaining the work to be undertaken and asking that no harm shall come either to the coven or to innocent people involved, yet firmly stating how the work must come to its conclusion.

Each member in turn then states what he or she intends to do about the problem in practice – anything from writing to the local paper or approaching the local Member of Parliament to spending so much time a week clearing up litter or raising a target sum for some such organization as Friends of the Earth. There is no environmental problem for which mundane, as well as magical, action cannot be devised.

When everyone has spoken, the High Priestess orders the Witches' Rune again, and the coven circle faster and faster until she cries *'Down!'* and the power raised is consciously discharged to fulfil the purpose.

Finally, after the Circle is banished, the entire coven scours the immediate area for litter or items of reparable damage. That is the best offering to Pan that one can make.

XVIII   Osiris

Praise be unto Osiris Un-Nefer, the great god who dwelleth in Abtu, King of eternity, lord of everlastingness, who passeth through millions of years in his existence.

Hymn of Ani the Scribe

The triad of Osiris, his sister/wife Isis and their son Horus the Younger were the most important and longest-lasting deities of Ancient Egypt; and Osiris was the most important and revered male god.

This was so in spite of the prominence of the Sun god Ra, or Amun-Ra, in Egyptian history (see Chapter XXVII). The Egyptian pantheon evolved from a complex process of compromise between, or absorption of, many local deities; and in this process, Osiris and Isis became known as the great-grandchildren of Ra. The family tree was as follows:

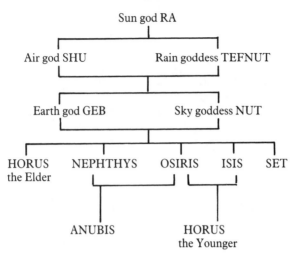

Ra was said to have produced Shu and Tefnut without female help, though, with the frequent ambiguity of such divine genealogies, a goddess Rait or Rat is sometimes mentioned as Ra's wife. Other legends make Nut the daughter of Ra, or even his mother, as the sky-cow who gives birth to the Sun each morning. But the above tree shows the concepts to which the key myths are related.

The great Egyptologist Sir E.A. Wallis Budge (*Osiris and the Egyptian Resurrection*, pp. xiv-xvi) argued that the religion of Osiris was indigenous to Egypt, while that of Ra was imported: 'It is well known that the cult of Ra, under one phase or another, was the form of Religion accepted by the Pharaohs, and the priesthood, and a limited aristocracy, from the middle of the Vth dynasty onwards. [c.2494-2354 BC] It is tolerably clear that the cult of the Sun-god was introduced into Egypt by the priests of Heliopolis, under the Vth dynasty, when they assumed the rule of the country and began to nominate their favourite warriors to the throne of Egypt ... Meanwhile, the bulk of the people clung to their ancient cult of the Moon, and to their sacred beasts and birds, etc., and worshipped the spirits which dwelt in them, wholly undisturbed by the spread of the foreign and official cult of the Sun-god ... It seems to me, then, that the existence of the cult of Ra in Egypt does not affect the enquiry into the indigenous Religion of Egypt in any way.'

We shall consider the Moon-god aspect further in Chapter XX, Thoth, and the Sun-god aspect in Chapter XXVII, Amun-Ra. Here let us accept the supremacy of Osiris and his family, as the ordinary Egyptian did for two or three thousand years, and look at Osirian mythology as it finally matured.

Osiris had two primary aspects. He was a vegetation god, similar to the Near Eastern Tammuz, with an annual cycle of birth, death and rebirth. He was both the Nile, whose annual inundation fertilized the rich soil of Egypt (which was Isis), and the crops and trees to which that soil consequently gave birth. But he was also the god of the Afterlife, who both judged and cared for the dead, assuring the immortality of the righteous.

Osiris and Isis became husband and wife in Nut's womb, as did Nephthys and Set.

Tradition says that Osiris was the fourth Pharaoh of Egypt, taking the throne when his father, Geb, retired. Isis was his Queen, and Thoth his Grand Vizier.

Osiris was a wise and civilizing ruler. He persuaded his people to abandon the cannibalism to which they had been addicted. He taught them how to make agricultural implements, and how to plant and harvest grain, make bread and brew beer (Isis meanwhile introducing wine-making). He built temples and laid down the forms of religion. (There may, of course, be a foundation of truth in this tradition. Many god and goddess forms have been deifications of great leaders, teachers and rulers revered in popular memory.)

Once he had Egypt organized, Osiris wanted to spread civilization abroad. So, leaving Isis at home as regent, he set out into Asia, accompanied by Thoth and Wepwauet ('Opener of the Ways'). He abhorred violence and needed no military conquest; he won other nations by the ideas he brought and charmed them with his music and singing.

When he returned, Isis had kept things running smoothly, and for a time all went well. But his brother Set, envious of his Kingdom, plotted against him.

Set personified the arid and constantly threatening desert by which the fertile Nile valley, on which life depended, is surrounded. His sister/wife Nephthys may be seen as personifying the fringe land between valley and desert, won for fertility by wise management – a process symbolized by the story of Nephthys' abandoning Set in favour of the Osirian party, in disgust at his treachery. The desert (Set) is sterile; only the Nile (Osiris) could fertilize her. So it is not surprising that she bore Anubis to Osiris, nor that Isis seemed unoffended. Isis and Nephthys appear thereafter as co-operating sisters, watching lovingly over birth and death.

Set and his fellow-conspirators murdered Osiris in the twenty-eighth year of his reign and threw his coffin into the Nile. It floated downstream and across the Mediterranean to Byblos on the Phoenician coast. Set found the body again and cut it into fourteen parts which he scattered around Egypt.

Isis would not give up; she roamed Egypt and found every part but the phallus, which a crab had eaten. At each place where she found a part, she engraved a funeral inscription, so that Set should think the part was buried there. In fact, she reassembled the body, magically fashioning a replacement phallus. She then, with the help of Anubis and Nephthys, performed the first-ever embalmment, symbolizing deathlessness.

Osiris, now immortal, entered his new phase as ruler of Amenti, the land of the dead. This was by his own choice; he could have returned to Earth if he had wished.

Amenti means 'West', and the Afterworld was considered to lie in that direction. It was not an Underworld, except in its negative aspects, such as the dangerous land through which the Sun travelled at night; the abode of the blessed, of those who had led a good life, was generally conceived as being in the starry heavens. In a sense, the West, the place of sunset, was the entry to both.

Osiris, except when he is symbolized by the djed-column (a stylized tree-trunk with horizontal bars at the top), is always portrayed in a winding-sheet, but with his face and hands exposed and greenish in colour. He either stands or sits enthroned, grasping the crook and scourge of royalty and wearing the crown of Upper Egypt, flanked by two ostrich feathers.

Isis bore his posthumous son, Horus the Younger, who became his father's avenger. A council of the gods ruled in his favour as Osiris's heir and banished Set back to the desert. Pharaohs identified themselves from their mothers' wombs with Horus as Lord of the Living.

As Lord of the Dead, Osiris was central to Egyptian thinking. He was both divine and human, and therefore intimately aware of human problems, hopes and sufferings.

The process of judging the dead – the weighing of the heart against the feather of truth and so on – was the responsibility of several deities, including Anubis, Thoth, Horus and Ma'at, but the final word rested with Osiris.

In many ways, Osiris was to Egyptians as Christ is to Christians (though, one may add, without the obsessive emphasis on celibacy and maternal virginity). By his divine parentage, his life on Earth, his suffering and death at envious hands, and his resurrection, he was the ordinary worshipper's own guarantee of immortality if one sincerely strove to emulate his goodness, in the knowledge that he should be compassionately understanding of human frailty.

In funeral rites, the dead human (whether man or woman) was identified with Osiris. The ritual statements written and spoken, for example, on behalf of a scribe called Ani would be worded: 'Osiris the scribe Ani answereth ...', 'The Osiris Ani declareth ...' and so on.

The ancient cult of the Sacred Bull very early merged with that of Osiris. The bull was for the Egyptians a supreme symbol of strength and virility, and in the cult as celebrated at Memphis, Heliopolis, Hermonthis, Saqqara and elsewhere actual bulls were selected and given divine honours, and splendid funerals and mummification on their death. The Apis Bull was identified with Osiris, as his living image or incarnation; but he was also the son of Osiris – and Horus, by the same token, was known as 'Bull of his Mother'. For Horus is, in a sense, his father's reborn self.

The Osiris Ritual

For once, something specifically for the children. Not a Circle ritual – there are strong feelings in the Craft about whether or not children should take part in working Circles as distinct from festivals. But they do have a natural sense of magic which should be encouraged.

Also, like many witches, we feel that children should be brought up to understand that there are and have been many different religions in the world, all with something to say, and should not be encouraged to believe that one is 'right' and all the others 'wrong'.

A witch friend of ours who is a school governor was asked: 'Should children be taught religion in school?' She replied: 'They should be taught *about* religion. They should not be *taught* religion.' We thoroughly agree with her. The better they understand the various paths, the better they will be able to choose, when they are mature, which path will suit them.

So here is an opportunity to do two things at once: to give them a basic idea of how the Ancient Egyptians worshipped, and to give them some practical magic to work.

Just how it is presented to them will depend of course on the age, mental sophistication and knowledge of the children concerned; but here is an outline of the idea.

Tell them the story of Osiris and Isis. That the Egyptians believed that they had ruled Egypt well and wisely a long, long time before history was written down. That Osiris's bad brother Set was jealous and invited Osiris to a party at which he killed him and chopped him to bits, scattering the bits all over Egypt. That Isis hunted till she found all the bits, put them together again and, with the help of their friend Thoth, used powerful magic to bring him back to life, and that they had a son, Horus. That the Egyptians looked on Osiris, Horus and Thoth as good gods, Isis as a good goddess, and Set as a wicked god.

Osiris's job was to look after people who had died and to see that they had a happy afterlife. Horus looked after this world and kept Set from doing harm. Isis, as the perfect wife and mother, did a bit of both. And Thoth was the god of wisdom, knowledge and magic.

In a way, Isis stood for the fertile Nile valley where all the people lived. Osiris stood for all the crops and fruit that grew there. And Set stood for the desert which was always threatening it.

Just as Osiris was brought back to life by Isis and Thoth's magic after Set had killed him, so the crops and fruit were reborn every year for the harvest. The Egyptians saw this as magic, too – and they were right. They used to celebrate it every year with special festivals.

Today, as the children know, we've had Self Aid, Band Aid, Comic Relief and so on, to help the people living in places where there isn't enough food to eat. So why not some Magic Aid?

For this, the children can work a spell themselves. Cut out a piece of flannel (green, if possible, because green is his colour) in the shape of Osiris, the right size for the bottom of a dinner-plate, and tell it its name is Osiris. Then put it on its plate and carefully spread mustard-and-cress seeds all over it. Put it in a place where it won't be disturbed, and pour just enough water in the plate to soak the flannel. Check on it two or three times a day to make sure the flannel is still damp, but not swimming in it.

After a few days the seeds will sprout, and Osiris will grow a coat of little green leaves. In his crops-and-fruit form, he has been reborn. The children will know that, by working this spell, they will have given more strength to all the people who are working to get food to the hungry countries.

Which, if you believe in psychic power, they may well have done.

XIX Tammuz

For Tammuz, lover of thy youth,
Year after year thou hast mourned.

Epic of Gilgamesh

Tammuz is perhaps the clearest and most dramatic example of the
dying and resurrecting vegetation god we considered in Chapter V. He
was Assyro-Babylonian, the beloved of the supreme goddess Ishtar,
but his story extends both before and after that.

Originally, up to the beginning of the second millennium BC, he
was the Sumerian Dumuzi, beloved of Inanna. As Inanna evolved into
the Assyro-Babylonian Ishtar, he became known as Tammuz. To the
Phoenicians he became Adoni (Semitic for 'Lord'), and his goddess
Astarte or Ashtoreth. And finally, for the Greeks the pair became
Adonis and Aphrodite, and for the Romans Adonis and Venus. All
this development took well over a thousand years and is described in
greater detail on pp. 113-14 of *The Witches' Goddess*.

The story at each stage was much the same, though in the Greek one
the vegetation theme and its accompanying ritual were overshadowed

Honduras maize god. 8th century AD

Bacchanalian Revel before a Term of Pan by Nicolas Poussin

Mithras sacrificing the bull. 2nd century AD

Thoth in his baboon form. 18th
Dynasty

Ganesa, Hindu god of good fortune, wisdom and literature. *c.*AD 800

Hermes, from the Temple of Artemis, Ephesus. *c.*340 BC

The power of the God balances that of the Goddess – a balance purposefully symbolized in Wiccan ritual. (Coven of the Enchanted Forest, Berkeley, California)

Assyro-Babylonian seal impression: Sun god Shamash rising behind mountain, with attendant gods. *c.*2300 BC

Hercules. Hadrian's Wall, 2nd-3rd century AD

Pan, from Jacob Epstein's *Family of Man* group, Hyde Park, London

Mercury instructing Cupid before Venus by Antonio Allegri da
Corregio

by the love-tragedy – not because the Greeks were insensitive to the annual fertility cycle but because that was already more than adequately dramatized in the story of Demeter and Persephone (*The Witches' Goddess*, Chapter XIII), and the ritual aspect by the profound Eleusinian Mysteries.

The actual legend is best seen in that of Tammuz and Ishtar; and it is from Phoenician practice that we have the most evidence of the seasonal ritual which expressed it.

Ishtar, in her youth, loved Tammuz, god of the harvest. He returned her love, but he was killed by a boar. There is a hint here – for the sow is an archetypal goddess symbol (compare Cerridwen and others) – of older harvest sacrifice rituals, in which the sacred victim mated with the goddess-priestess, who then slew him (see Chapter X). The boar who killed Dumuzi/Tammuz/Adoni/Adonis may thus be a masculinization of the goddess herself.

Be that as it may, Ishtar was devastated by his death. As told in tablets discovered at Nineveh, she determined to go to the Underworld, ruled over by her sister Ereshkigal ...

To the house which none leave who have entered it,
To the road from which there is no way back

... in an attempt to recover him.

This, of course, is a constant theme of vegetation myths. The Earth Mother, made barren by the departure of the loved partner who makes her fertile, strives to recover what has been lost – as Demeter did for Persephone, Isis for Osiris, and so on.

To reach Ereshkigal, Ishtar had to pass the seven gates of the Underworld, at each gate surrendering some of her jewellery or a garment, until finally she stood before her sister naked, unadorned and completely vulnerable. (Witches will recognize in this story elements of their own Legend of the Descent of the Goddess – though that has a rather different meaning – see p.46).

Ereshkigal was unmoved. Not only would she not surrender Tammuz; she ordered her servant, the plague-bringer Namtar, to imprison Ishtar and afflict her with threescore illnesses.

In the absence of both Ishtar and Tammuz, the Earth was a barren waste, and the gods were seriously alarmed. Ishtar's father, Sin, the Moon god, and the Sun god Shamash appealed for help to Ea, god of wisdom and magic. (Ea was also the water god, an appropriate ally in times of terrestrial aridity.)

Ea sent a messenger, Asushu-Namir, to the Underworld with a spell to secure Ishtar's release. Erishkigal tried to resist, but the magic words were too powerful for her, and she had to release her two prisoners. Ishtar, purified with Ea's water, was whole again and retrieved her adornments as she passed through the seven gates back to freedom; and with the return of Tammuz, the Earth was fertile again.

The celebrations of the death and rebirth of Tammuz/Adoni, every year just after the harvest, was a very important occasion for the women of the Near East. Identifying themselves with the bereaved Ishtar, they mourned his loss with the lament we have already quoted on p.77: 'Tammuz, Tammuz, Tammuz the all-great is dead!'

They planted little gardens of quickly fading species, such as lettuce, and when these died after a few days, they threw them into springs, rivers or the sea. After that, sorrow was transformed to rejoicing, as they hailed the god's rebirth.

It was the custom of planting 'gardens to Adoni' which Isaiah (xviii:9-11) condemned: 'Because thou hast forgotten the God of thy salvation, and hast not been mindful of the rock of thy strength, therefore shalt thou plant pleasant plants, and shall set it with strange slips: in the day shalt thou make thy plant to grow, and in the morning shalt thou make thy seed to flourish; but the harvest shall be a heap in the day of grief and of desperate sorrow.' Ezekiel too (viii:13-14) frowned on the practice, in Jerusalem itself: 'He said also unto me, Turn thou yet again, and thou shalt see greater abominations that they do. Then he brought me to the door of the gate of the Lord's house which was towards the north; and, behold, there sat women weeping for Tammuz.'

According to Graves (*The White Goddess*, pp. 302-3), post-Exilic Hebrew women covered up their custom by pretending that they were mourning for 'the daughter of Japhthah the Gileadite' each year (Judges xi:39-40) – and Carmarthen women in the last century used the same excuse for their August mourning for Llew Llaw Gyffes.

Women tend to be more instinctively aware of spiritual continuity, regardless of official dogma, than men.

In fact, there was more of the barley god Tammuz in the make-up of the Israelite 'God of their salvation' than Isaiah and Ezekiel would have cared to admit. Plutarch maintained that the Hebrew ban on eating pork was because it was a boar that killed their Adoni.

The Tammuz Ritual

There would be two possible ways of celebrating a Tammuz vegetation god ritual – one centring on the Underworld, the other on the Earth. But in an Underworld approach, the active characters would be Ishtar and her sister Ereshkigal, so, since this is a God book, we have chosen the Earth theme, which involves the Sun god Shamash, the Moon god Sin (Ishtar's father) and Ea, the god of wisdom and magic, as well as Ishtar.

The Preparation

Witches are chosen to enact Shamash, Sin, Ea, Tammuz and Ishtar. Tammuz should if possible be young and good-looking.

Food and drink of kinds which clearly represent the products of the Earth and its creatures – such as bowls of fruit, of cereal-based food such as barley cakes, of hard-boiled eggs, a bottle or two of wine and fruit juice, and perhaps a flask of milk – are placed ready round the perimeter of the Circle but covered with cloths. A vase of flowers is concealed behind or near the altar. None of these things should be visible during the first part of the ritual.

The Ritual

Tammuz lies supine in the centre before the Circle is cast, his head to the west, motionless and with his eyes closed until the moment of ritual awakening.

The Opening Ritual (see Appendix 1) will proceed as usual, omitting the Witches' Rune. After the summoning of the Watchtowers, Shamash kneels by the South candle and Sin by the West candle. The rest of the coven seat themselves around the perimeter. The usual 'Hail, Aradia' invocation is replaced with the following:

'Hail, mighty Ishtar! Queen of woods and fields,
The crops that flourish, and the herds that roam –
Queen of the blessings that the good Earth yields,
Queen of the sowing, and the harvest-home!
Without thy bounty, all is dark and cold;
Nothing will grow, however hard we strive.
Therefore we kneel before thee, as of old;
Renew thy blessing, that the Earth may thrive!'

The 'Great God Cernunnos' invocation is the same, except that it is addressed to 'Great God Tammuz'.

After the *'Akhera goiti ... Akhera beiti'*, Ishtar suddenly looks alarmed, points at Tammuz and cries: *'Great Tammuz is dead!'*.

She goes and kneels at Tammuz's head, mourning for him. Ea goes and kneels at his feet. The whole coven take up the lament: *'Great Tammuz is dead!'*

They fall silent when Ishtar looks up at Sin and asks (pronouncing his name 'Seen'): *'Sin, my father – what shall we do? Without my love Tammuz, the Earth's womb is sterile. The fields will bear no crops, and my creatures will bear no young. Help me, my father!'*

Sin replies: *'What can I do, my daughter? I am the Moon who lights up the night. I can bring rest, but not fruitfulness; visions, but not deeds; understanding, but not action. Such things belong to Earth. What can I do?'*

Ishtar turns to Shamash, and pleads: *'Shamash, my brother – what shall I do?'*

Shamash replies: *'What can I do, sister? I am the Sun who lights up the day, shining upon your Earth to bring it heat. I can call forth your crops once they are sown, and warm your young once they are born; but I cannot sow the grain, or fertilize the womb. Such things belong to Earth. What can I do?'*

Ishtar appeals finally to Ea (pronouncing his name 'Eh-ya'): *'Ea, my brother, help me! You are wisdom, you are magic – you are the air which my creatures breathe. Help me!'*

Ea does not reply for a moment; then he stands up, as Sin and Shamash also do when he commands them. (Ishtar remains kneeling, but watches Ea hopefully.) Ea says: *'Be upstanding, my brothers. Despair and resignation will not help our sister, nor bring Tammuz to life ... What is wisdom, and what is magic? Wisdom is knowledge of the laws of the universe, which are greater than each of us alone. And magic is the courage to call upon them. So let us call! It is a law of being, that fruitfulness is a great wheel which never ceases to turn; and in that turning, death follows life, and rebirth follows death. Tammuz may seem to die, but his rebirth must follow as the great wheel turns.* [Raising his voice and throwing up his arms.] *We call upon the laws of being – we call upon the wheel of rebirth!'*

Sin and Shamash also throw up their arms, Ishtar takes Tammuz's hands, and all three (and the rest of the coven) take up the cry: *'We call upon the wheel of rebirth!'*

Tammuz opens his eyes and sits up. Ishtar stands and pulls him to his feet. All surround him joyfully, and everyone, including Tammuz himself, joins hands and circles for the Witches' Rune.

When it is over, Ishtar says: *'Great Tammuz is reborn, and the fruits of the Earth are ours once more. Bring them forth, and let us enjoy them!'*

The food and drink are uncovered and brought into the centre, and the flowers are put on the altar.

The feast begins.

XX Thoth

I am Thoth, the perfect scribe, whose hands are pure, the lord of
the two horns, who maketh iniquity to be destroyed, the scribe of
right and truth.

The Book of the Dead

Among Egypt's masculine gods, the supreme personification of the
spiritual, compassionate and immortality aspects was Osiris, whom we
have already considered. The knowledge, science and wisdom aspects
were above all the province of Thoth. And both were closely involved
with morality and justice.

Thoth's Egyptian name was actually Tehuti or Djehuti (as with
Osiris, Isis and others, modern usage seems stuck with the Greek
form). He is portrayed in two ways – either as an ibis (or ibis-headed
man) or as a baboon. Both symbols have pertinent meaning.

He was a very ancient god, worshipped from predynastic times. His
principal cult centre was in Middle Egypt at Hermopolis (Egyptian
Khemnu, modern el-Ashmunein), but he had shrines elsewhere.

Every major Egyptian deity, at least within his or her own temples,
was credited with a creator role, and Thoth was no exception. As ibis,

he was said to have hatched the World Egg from which everything came. The sound of his voice alone produced four gods and four goddesses. The gods had the form of frogs, the goddesses of serpents. These eight continued the work of creation by voice, singing morning and night to keep the Sun moving.

Thoth's baboon form seems to have derived from the baboon's habit of talking to greet the rising Sun – perhaps a memory of the Eight?

There were various stories of Thoth's parentage, according to the pantheon into which he was being fitted. He arose spontaneously out of Nun, the Primordial Chaos (though Nun and his wife Naunet were also said to have been the first pair of the Eight); or he was the son of Geb and Nut, and thus the brother of Osiris, Isis, Nephthys, Set and Horus the Elder; or he was the eldest son of Ra.

Three different wives were attributed to him. One was Sefkhet-Seshat, a Moon and stellar goddess with characteristics very similar to those of Thoth himself. Another was Nahmauit, 'She who Removes Evil'. The third – and in many ways the most convincing – was Ma'at, goddess of justice, truth and the natural cosmic order to which her husband gave practical expression.

Thoth was at first a Moon god and time-measurer (see Chapter II). So Thoth, like other Moon gods, ruled over the first piece of precise, scientific observation. And as mankind's knowledge grew and became recognized as wisdom and recorded with increasing sophistication, it was natural that he should acquire the characteristics which came to be more important for him than their starting-point: those of god of wisdom, of knowledge, of science, mathematics and architecture, the inventor of writing, scribe of the gods and patron of human scribes, keeper of archives, and arbiter of disputes.

It is almost ironic that, although the Moon-time-measuring gift started Thoth off as a god of wisdom, it was that same wisdom that led him to realize that a lunar calendar cannot be neatly fitted into a solar year, to devise a cunning solution and thus to distance himself from his own lunar origins; all of which, of course, is a mythologizing of mankind's own process of realization.

The legend which embraced this solution is as follows.

Nut, the sky goddess, had married her brother Geb, the Earth god, against the will of their grandfather, the Sun god Ra. Furious, Ra ordered their father, the air god Shu, to separate them, and ordained that Nut should bear no children in any month of the year.

Thoth pitied Nut's distress and planned a way round Ra's ban. He played draughts with the Moon and won a seventy-second part of the Moon's light, which he turned into five intercalary days belonging to no month. These, added to twelve approximately lunar months of thirty days each, made a year of 365 days – the most accurate solar calendar until the Gregorian one which we now use. Nut was thus able to give birth to her five children – in order: Osiris, Horus the Elder, Set, Isis and Nephthys – during the intercalary days.

Thoth remained titular master of the Moon (for old times' sake, so to speak) but left the Moon itself in the hands of a caretaker goddess by the name of Woman-Light of the Shadows – a charming description of the feminine function we mentioned above, of illuminating the secrets of the Unconscious. She looked after Thoth whenever he visited the Moon.

Thoth remained a loyal ally of the party of Osiris, Isis, Nephthys and Horus the Younger.

He had a great reputation as a healer and magician, and time and again worked as Isis's magical partner.

He also continued to co-operate with Osiris in the admission of the dead to Osiris's realm. It was Thoth who presided over what George Hart (*A Dictionary of Egyptian Gods and Goddesses*, p. 216) describes as the 'Ancient Egyptian equivalent of the lie detector' – the balance in which the human heart was weighed against the red feather of the goddess of truth, Thoth's wife Ma'at.

Most Egyptian deities except Osiris and Thoth seem to have had their moments of anger, of what may be called human weakness. But as J. Viau puts it (*Larousse Encyclopaedia of Mythology*, p. 269): 'During three thousand two hundred and twenty-six years Thoth remained the very model of a peaceful ruler.' And perhaps today, when more and more people are taking a less rigid attitude to god-forms than they used to, Thoth once more has a role to play.

The Thoth Ritual

Our suggestion here is a ritual for a working partnership, with the man taking the role of Thoth and the woman that of Woman-Light of the Shadows. It involves Thoth in his wisdom, lunar and scribe aspects; with these, he inspires and records the divinatory abilities and experiences of his partner. For simplicity, we refer to the partners in the ritual below as the Man and the Woman.

The Preparation
Collect the materials for making two things: a scrying mirror and a blank recording book.

A scrying mirror is a black concave mirror, suitably mounted. For this you need a clear convex clock-glass at least five inches (12 cm) across, obtainable from any clockmaker. You also need some matt black paint; aerosol paint is simplest, but for ecological reasons most witches will want to make sure the aerosol is of the type which does not harm the ozone layer. The mount or frame is according to taste. Making and mounting the mirror is the Man's task.

Materials for the book are an adequate number of blank sheets of good-quality paper (or, even better, parchment), suitable front and back covers the same size or slightly larger, a tool for punching and thongs for binding. Leather would be ideal for the covers and thongs, but whatever the materials, the finished book should be as handsome as possible. Making the book is the Woman's task.

The Ritual
For making the two objects, the Man and the Woman work separately – preferably in an Egyptian temple (set up as in Appendix II) or at least within a simply cast Circle (Appendix I). They may perform the setting-up or casting together if they wish, but once that is done the maker of the object should be left alone.

The Man makes the mirror by painting the convex side of the clock-glass (after cleaning it thoroughly) with the matt black paint – preferably two or three coats. When the paint is dry, the concave side becomes a dark mirror. It can then be securely placed in its mount or frame.

The Woman makes the book by punching the pages and covers along the left-hand edge and binding it with the thongs.

Both should use their imagination and skill to make their objects as neat and attractive as they can.

The Man should also have for presentation with the mirror a large black velvet cloth, and the Woman a suitable pen.

When all is ready, the couple wait for the night of the Full Moon. They then set up the Egyptian temple as in Appendix II, with the two objects ready on the altar.

The opening invocations complete, the Man and Woman face each other in front of the altar.

The Woman says: '*Greetings to thee, O Thoth, god of wisdom, god of the Moon, and scribe of the gods.*'

The Man says: '*Greetings to thee, Woman-Light of the Shadows, seeress, unraveller of mysteries.*'

The Woman takes up the book and pen and says: '*Take thou this book and pen, scribe of the gods. In it you shall write whatever visions I may see.*'

The Man takes up the mirror and cloth and says: '*Take thou this mirror, seeress. In it thou shalt find the visions which I shall write down.*'

They exchange their gifts. The Woman seats herself comfortably and cups the mounted mirror in the velvet cloth in her palms, arranging them and herself so that no candle-lights or other bright spots are reflected in the mirror; it should look dark and misty.

The Man seats himself to one side of her, where he can watch and listen to her easily without intruding on her vision.

(Note: unless the Man is a quick, confident and neat writer, he may prefer to record what the Woman says in a rough notebook first and transcribe it carefully to the book itself afterwards – but still in the temple.)

The Woman then relaxes, breathes naturally, clears her mind and watches the mirror, reporting what she sees.

Scrying is an art which cannot be hurried, and it comes more easily to some than to others. Neither partner must be disappointed or discouraged if nothing happens for a while – or even at all on the first session; they may set up the temple again on later nights and use the objects which they have already ritually exchanged.

When images do appear in the mirror, the Woman should describe them spontaneously without any attempt to interpret or pass judgement on what she sees; and the man should record them in the same way. Attempts at interpretation of what has been seen and written can be a joint effort later.

XXI Herne/Cernunnos

Hh-errrn!... Hh-errrn!... Hh-errrn!

The hind's call to the stag

Celtic knowledge and legend, in pre-Christian centuries, was not written down by the Celts of the time, because they had no written script (apart from the late Ogham script, used only for brief epitaphs etc on stones). Their history, mythology and wisdom – and very rich it was – was handed down by word of mouth, by druids and bards who had years of training in the method.

Our own knowledge of that verbal tradition is derived from Christian monks who did write it down. The richest source of all is Irish, because the early Irish monks recorded it with remarkable faithfulness. Admittedly, the gods and goddesses were transformed into racial heroes and heroines, but their stories survived with little more than the occasional formal nod in the direction of Christian requirements, easily detected.

From such written sagas as the *Lebor Gabála Érenn* (*Book of the Taking of Ireland*, usually called the *Book of Invasions*) and the *Táin Bó*

Cuailnge (*Cattle Raid of Cooley*), and from the folk-legends attached to such saints as Bridget, we can harvest a pretty reliable idea of the gods and goddesses of pre-Christian Ireland.

With Welsh sources, we are less lucky. The main substantial source is the *Mabinogion* but, as Matthew Arnold observed, 'The very first thing that strikes one, in reading the Mabinogion, is how evidently the medieval story-teller is pillaging an antiquity of which he does not fully posses the secret.'

As for England and Scotland, we have not even a *Mabinogion*, only folklore, the evidence of artefacts such as hill-cut figures, of Romano-British statuary, place-names and what is known of the pagan traditions of the Celts, Saxons and others who contributed to the final synthesis; and by the time that synthesis had settled down, Christianity (the disciplined Roman kind, not the freer early Celtic kind) was firmly in control.

Which brings us to the surprising fact that we cannot be certain of the actual original name of the Celtic Horned God. All we have is the Herne of British folklore, and the happy accident of a single, partially mutilated, Gaulish altar on which his name is inscribed as Cernunnos.

That he existed cannot be doubted. He is portrayed in many Celtic artefacts, from a rock-carving at Val Camonica in northern Italy (c. fourth-century BC) to the famous Gundestrup Cauldron which was found in a peat bog in Denmark.

The nearest ones to our own home are on the medieval market cross in the centre of Kells, Co. Meath, and a few miles farther off, on a stone in the churchyard on Tara Hill (see Plate 10 of *The Witches' Way*). Most people probably think the market cross one is meant to be the Devil but, as he is flanked by two wolf-like creatures, he is quite evidently the Horned God of Animals; medieval carvers had few inhibitions about pagan subjects, as everything from Lincoln Imp to Sheila-na-Gigs to countless foliate masks testifies.

He is usually portrayed with horns and accompanied by animals. He usually either wears or has looped on his horns the torc (circular necklet) of Celtic nobility. Often, as on the Gundestrup Cauldron, he holds a serpent with a ram's head or horns.

If he is so widespread and so similar in his various portrayals, why does he not appear in the preserved body of legend which names everyone from the Dagda, Lugh and Dana in Ireland to Arianrhod, Llew Llaw Gyffes and Cerridwen in Wales?

The most likely explanation is that, while the deities of recorded legends are those of a warrior aristocracy, the Horned God of Animals, Nature and fecundity was primarily a god of the ordinary people. Mother and Earth goddesses would tend to be common to both, but male gods would be rather more class-conscious. Peasant gods would be unlikely to find their way into the songs which bards sang to warrior kings.

As Prionsias MacCana puts it (*Celtic Mythology*, p. 48): 'The deity's evident concern with fecundity may have influenced the form of his cult and the content of his myth, and this in turn may explain why artists of the early Christian period tended to assimilate him to Satan and why only residual elements of his myth survive. In such circumstances the Cernunnos cult would probably have survived longest among the lower orders of society, where custom died hard and orthodoxy was not easily imposed. Unfortunately this is virtually unknown territory, for it is only in recent times that the usages and beliefs of the common people received conscious recognition in written literature.'

Reasonably enough, students of pagan mythology have used the name Cernunnos, the only contemporarily recorded name of the Celtic Horned God, as a general label. But being from Gaul, it is likely that 'Cernunnos' is a latinization or hellenization of the native Celtic one. And the survival in British folklore of an equatable god under the name Herne suggests that the real name had the root H-RN or K-RN.

There are other hints of this. For example, the Ulster hero Conall Cernach in *Táin Bó Fraich (The Driving of Fraich's Cattle)* goes to attack a fortress guarded by a terrible serpent – and the serpent submits to him tamely, jumping into his girdle, where Cernunnos's attendant serpent is often found. Was this a memory of a Cernunnos story? Irish Gaelic being Q-Celtic, the K-RN form would be expected.

More K-RNs are among the Irish saints, those semi-legendary figures who (like Bridget/Bríd) absorbed wholesale the characteristics of similarly named pagan deities. Kieran or Ciaran was the name of two fifth- sixth-century saints, both of whom have animal legends attached to them. St Kieran of Clonmacnoise had a tame fox who used to carry his writings for him. Other saints were so jealous of him that they prayed for his early death – except for Columkille (Columba), which is significant, for Columkille had druidical sympathies and was himself a leading member of the Guild of Bards. Just before he died, Kieran asked for his bones to be left on a hilltop 'like a stag', and for his spirit to be preserved rather than his relics. St Kieran of Saighir built his hermit's cell with the help of a wild boar, his first disciple, to which he soon added a fox, a badger, a wolf and a stag, which obeyed his every command.

There is a St Kieran's Well near our home, to which within living memory horses used to be taken on his feast day for a ritual blessing.

Another Irish saint, Cainnech, had a stag which let him use its antlers as a book-rest.

As for the H-RN form, Herne the Hunter is an established figure in

British folklore. His best-known legend is associated with Windsor Great Park, where he is said to appear at times of national crisis. Crowned with stag's antlers, he leads his Wild Hunt of red-eared hounds at a furious pace across the sky. In Wales, the leader of the Wild Hunt is called Gwyn – not so very different.

One of the most famous hill-cut figures in Britain is the Cerne Abbas giant in Dorset. He is not horned (though perhaps he was once), but with his great erect phallus he is unquestionably a fecundity god; and can the place-name (which is also the local river-name) be pure coincidence? We doubt it.

There are several places in England incorporating Herne or Hern – including Herne Hill in South London, which is often interpreted as meaning Heron's Hill. But since when did herons, which are river-fishers, live on hills?

A final interesting thought from Francis De'Venney, a member of our coven with much experience of deer. The call of a hind to her stag sounds like a deep throaty 'HH-ERRRN'. Could our ancestors, hearing him so addressed, have decided reasonably that that was his name?

The Herne/Cernunnos Ritual

This ritual, which was devised by Francis De'Venney, is not a coven one or even a working-partnership one. It is a personalized initiatory experience for one male witch, in which the Earth herself becomes his working partner – a direct communion with the Goddess without the intervention of a human representative.

It is admittedly a difficult one to arrange, because it is done outdoors, preferably in natural country, where a small fire can be lit and there is no danger of being overlooked or interrupted, and in weather mild enough for skyclad working. But it is well worth the trouble of achieving these conditions.

We have written this ritual in terms of Celtic symbology and of the stag which is important to it; witches of other traditions can excercise their brains and their knowledge to devise equivalents. The Song of Amergin, for example, which is declaimed in the ritual, is a treasured piece of Celtic tradition. Amergin, in Irish legend, was the bard and spokesman of the Gaels when they took over Ireland from the Tuatha Dé Danann, and is said to have uttered his Song when the Gaels landed. It is analysed in depth in Graves' *The White Goddess*.

The Preparation

We will call the witch undergoing the experience the Man. Two other people are present as helpers, neither of them being his working partner, though one or both of them should be a woman. They should be experienced and sensible people, used for example to simple first aid and to standing by when someone may go into a state of altered consciousness. They remain clothed throughout.

The Man must have prepared himself by learning by heart the Song of Amergin (below) till he can declaim it without hesitation. For the ritual, he is completely skyclad (for non-witches: this means ritually naked) without even jewellery, but his warm clothes should be handy for putting on afterwards.

A small fire is lit, with enough fuel within hand's reach to keep it going. The helpers should have a hot drink ready, either by way of a kettle on the fire or in a vacuum flask.

The Ritual
The helpers sit facing the fire, and the Man sits slightly apart with his back to it. He focuses his eyes on the shadows in the darkness.

The helpers talk quietly and appropriately to him, perhaps telling Celtic stories and singing Celtic songs.

When he feels ready, he stands (still with his back to the fire and the helpers) and declaims the Song of Amergin:

> I am a stag of seven tines
> I am a wild flood on a plain,
> I am a wind on the deep waters,
> I am a shining tear of the Sun,
> I am a hawk on a cliff,
> I am fair among flowers,
> I am a god who sets the head afire with smoke,
> I am a battle-waging spear,
> I am a salmon in the pool,
> I am a hill of poetry,
> I am a ruthless boar,
> I am a threatening noise of the sea,
> I am a wave of the sea,
> Who but I knows the secret of the unhewn dolmen?

When he has finished, he repeats seven tines the first line, '*I am a stag of seven tines*' – each time more forcefully, convincing himself that the statement is personal and that he means exactly what he says.

Finally he sits down, still facing the darkness, and expands his consciousness, feeling the boundaries of his awareness move outwards from him.

The helpers continue with their quiet stories and songs.

The Man ceases to label what he becomes aware of, the sights and sounds and smells around him; the only distinctions he must make are those which represent danger, safety or food. He must raise himself to the state where he is still aware of the voices behind him as friendly, not no longer of the meaning or of the fact that what he hears are words.

Then he must know (not just believe) that he is a stag. At this stage he must follow his own instincts.

The helpers should not interfere unless he is endangering himself. If he moves away, the 'stag' should be followed only at a discreet distance – and for this one of the helpers should preferably have woodcraft experience.

When cold or discomfort to his human body draws him back to his normal consciousness, he returns to the fire and puts his clothes on. He should take a warm drink, but not alcohol.

A final tip: if you feel you have had a genuine experience from this ritual, do not be in a hurry to communicate it to others. It is very personal and likely to be so incommunicable that any attempt to do so may distort it for you.

XXII Shiva

When one sees Eternity in things that pass away, and Infinity in
finite things, then one has pure knowledge.

The Bhagavad Gita

Shiva or Siva means 'benevolent' or 'favourable' – an epithet which is
mainly propitiatory, for he has his terrible aspects. But like Kali (who
is one form of his wife Parvati), he is among the Hindu deities most
misunderstood in the West.

In fact, he is the supreme example of the Lord of the Dance and is
often portrayed dancing. He is a god of the cosmic rhythm, of
birth-death-rebirth, of the metabolic and katabolic cycle without
which development, and life itself, could not exist.

He was a pre-Aryan god, evolving from the more primitive Rudra.
Like most such, he tended to be looked down upon by the Aryan
conquerors. But he was too popular to be pushed aside – as was the
more obviously benevolent Vishnu.

So the Brahmanic caste personalized their abstract principle
brahman (a neuter noun) into Brahma (masculine), to form with these

102

two the Trimurti (triad) best summed up in the declaration: 'For I, the supreme indivisible Lord, am three – Brahma, Vishnu and Shiva; I create, I maintain, I destroy.'

Vishnu lived through nine avatars (incarnations), with one still to come (see his entry on p.242) – always, incidentally, with the same wife, the lovely goddess of fortune Lakshmi, in nine different forms and under nine different names. Vishnu can thus be said to represent the actual experience of living, while Brahma personifies its eternal essence, and Shiva the cyclic processes which carry it onward.

Shiva is known as Bhudapati, 'prince of demons'. But in many episodes, he summons, or even temporarily creates, minor demons to fight and destroy the major demons who are the real menace. And often his intervention is in fact a rescue operation.

On one occasion – the Churning of the Milk Ocean – he actually saved the world.

The Churning is a mixture of creation, Deluge and disaster myth. It occurred during Vishnu's second, or tortoise, incarnation. He descended to the ocean bed to recover the lost treasures of the Vedic tribes. The Devas (positive forces) and Asuras (negative forces), using the serpent Vasuki in a spiral tug-of-war, churned the ocean and brought up many treasures, including Amrita, the ambrosia of the gods, the goddesses Lakshmi, Sura and Rambha, Surabhi the Cow of Plenty, Parijata the Tree of Knowledge, and Uccaihsravas the first horse.

Unfortunately, a deadly poison, Visha, also appeared, from the head of Vasuki which the Asuras were tugging. This venom spurted forth onto the Earth in a flood, which would have destroyed everything, even the gods.

The gods begged Shiva for help, and he swallowed the poison. The world was saved, but Shiva's throat was burned, leaving a permanent blue mark which earned him the epithet Nilakantha ('blue-throat').

The Devas are often defined as 'gods' and the Asuras as 'demons', but this is an over-simplification. The Asuras are, rather, raw natural forces like the Titans, often in conflict with the Devas, yet given their powers by them. The concept seems to be that they are dangerous only when uncontrolled, being (like Shiva's katabolic destructive aspect) a necessary part of the overall cosmic process.

On one occasion the Asuras actually battled with the gods and threw them out of Heaven. It was Shiva who led the counter-offensive. He took the mass of flame which was the gods' burning anger, adding the rays of his own deadly third eye, and spun it to produce a brilliant disc which even blinded the gods and singed Brahma's beard. With this disc Shiva cut off the head of Jalandhara, the Asuras' leader.

But Jalandhara had the power to restore his severed head again and again. So Shiva called on all the goddesses, who joined the battle and drank Jalandhara's blood, finally subduing him. Thus the Asuras were evicted from Heaven, and the gods and goddesses reoccupied it.

Brahma himself was occasionally vulnerable to Shiva, as his singed beard reminds us. Once Brahma, drunk, pursued the twilight goddess Samdyha, he in the form of a stag, she as a hind. Shiva shot off the stag's head with an arrow, and Brahma apparently afterwards acknowledged that he had been right to intervene.

On another occasion, Brahma created the goddess Satarupa (Savitri, Brahmani, Sarisvati, Gayatri – all the Trimurti's wives have many names) out of his own body and fell in love with her. She dodged around him, and he grew four extra heads to keep watching her. She stopped dodging and married him, but Shiva, with the rays of his third eye, burned off Brahma's fifth head.

Thus the essence of life is never destroyed but is constantly modified in its development, by the dance of Shiva.

Shiva's own wife was Parvati, who also has many names and aspects. He married her as Sita, daughter of Daksha, one of the lords of creation, against her father's violent opposition. Sita means 'power' – and Sita/Parvati indeed personfies the power of Shiva. Sita is still worshipped by millions in northern India, the Himalayan foothills; our friend Dr Ashok Singh comes from there, and the village where he was born is called Sheohar, after Shiva, while the nearest town is Sitamarhi, named after Sita and regarded as her birthplace.

As Parvati herself, Shiva's consort is portrayed as young and beautiful. She had to use all her charm to overcome Shiva's initial ascetic indifference, but eventually she won him over, and their embrace made the whole world tremble. During this wooing phase, she was known as Uma.

To be complete, Shiva must have as his dancing partner the feminine aspect. For Shiva also personifies the male generative principle, as Parvati does the female; his symbol is the lingam, and hers the yoni.

Under the name Durga, Parvati is a mighty Amazon who destroys demons. Her face is still beautiful, but she has ten arms, each with a weapon.

In another guise she is Kali, like her husband a necessary devourer – Kali Mor, the 'black mother', the womb who is also the tomb. Once, when she had slain the demon chief Raktavija, Kali's victory dance was so wild that she did not notice Shiva begging her to stop and trod him underfoot. She realized her mistake and was duly remorseful, but she is often portrayed with her feet on the supine Shiva's chest.

At the other end of the scale, Parvati is Ambika the Generatrix (*amba*, 'mother'), who must be a very ancient fertility goddess.

The offspring of Shiva and Parvati include the elephant-headed god of wisdom and literature, Ganesa, the war god Karttikeya (Skanda, Kumara) and the wealth god Kubera (Kuvera).

Shiva is portrayed as white or silver-coloured, with the blue throat mentioned above. He is often dancing or riding the sacred white bull Nandi, calf of the Cow of Plenty. He has four arms. He usually has one head, sometimes as many as five; each has the formidable third eye in the forehead. He wears a necklace of skulls, and snakes as ornaments.

His annual festival, Mahashivatri ('The Great Night of Shiva'), stresses his benevolent aspect. It is particularly an occasion for married couples, families or groups of friends. It is preceded by a twenty-hour semi-fast, during which only a little, non-rich food is taken, and vows and promises are made to Shiva. The night itself is devoted to ritual worship, which is continuous but with the groups of worshippers coming and going.

No one is barred, for Shiva is a forgiving god, whom even sinners may approach.

The Shiva Ritual

We showed this chapter to our friend Dr Singh, whom we mentioned above, since he is a very well-informed Hindu himself, and he was good enough to approve it. But as far as ritual practice is concerned, he pointed out that the Western mind can have great difficulty in grasping the Hindu inner mysteries: 'Our Yoga, our Tantra, just do not gel with the Western way of thinking.' Far too many Westerners try to use the outer forms of these systems without even beginning to understand their inner meaning.

He saw no reason, though, why a European should not invoke a Hindu deity who personified an aspect with which he or she wished to be in tune. So we devised this simple Shiva ritual to help a solo worker to attune to the Cosmic Dance. As the worker is assuming a god-form, we suggest that this is suitable only for a man – just as it would not be suitable (for example) for a man to assume the form of Shiva's consort, Parvati. If a woman feels like working out an equivalent Parvati ritual, she should study her carefully first and keep it as simple as this one.

No meat should be eaten during the day leading up to this ritual.

The Preparation

Have ready on tape or record some suitable Indian music for the dance.

On the altar, put small containers of spring water, uncooked rice, milk and wine, and an item of fruit, a separate goblet of wine for drinking and two golden yellow candles. There should also be images of a tiger and a serpent, and a black wand or stick, piled together – symbols of demons sent against Shiva by rebellious Rishis, which he defeated and on whose bodies he danced. Little statues of the dancing Shiva can be bought in Indian shops (see Plate 21), so if you have one, stand it between the candles, with these symbols at his feet. Burn sandalwood incense or joss sticks.

The candles at the cardinal points should also be golden yellow.

You should be skyclad except for a golden yellow loincloth or jockstrap; but you should have a warm cloak handy for after the dance.

The Ritual

Start the music, and cast the Circle in the usual way (see Appendix I), up to the summoning of the Lords of the Watchtowers.

Sit comfortably facing the altar (lotus position if you can), compose yourself and spend a little time breathing in *prana*, the all-pervading energy of the cosmos.

The technique is to breathe in for a count of ten, first using the diaphragm and then expanding the rib-cage, completely filling your lungs; hold your breath for a count of five; breath out for a count of ten, first collapsing the rib-cage and then using the diaphragm till the lungs are completely empty; hold this for a count of five; and repeat the whole process. Breathing in, envisage *prana* as tiny golden specks swarming in the atmosphere, being absorbed into your body not only through your lungs but through every pore; holding your full breath, envisage *prana* spreading throughout your body; breathing out, envisage impurities being expelled; and while holding your lungs empty, prepare yourself for the next intake of *prana*.

With practice, you will be able to slow down this technique quite comfortably to two or three breaths a minute, with the counting becoming unconscious.

When you feel ready, invoke: '*Great Lord Shiva, destroyer of illusions, beautiful dancer of cosmic laws, guide my hands with your touch, free my feet from their bondage, that intoxicated with your splendour I may join your dance, and feel the fire of creation coursing through my veins.*'

Stand up, drink the whole of the goblet of wine and begin to let the music move through your body. When you feel ready, start to dance, more and more energetically until you have become a channel for Shiva himself and are bursting with the joy of your own part in the cosmic dance. At the climax, fall to your knees before the altar and wrap the cloak around yourself for warmth as your body temperature cools, never letting yourself be distracted from the elation you feel.

When you are ready, rise and say: '*Lord Shiva, creator and destroyer, dance master of the stars, as you return to your heavenly realm I offer you these gifts for guiding me in my cosmic dance with you.*'

Hold up in turn the rice, the wine, the milk and the fruit, replacing them on the altar.

After banishing the Circle, we suggest you eat a hearty meal to earth yourself and replace all the calories you have burned up during the dance.

That night or next morning, take the four offerings outside and scatter them, saying, '*I thank you, Lord Shiva*' as you do so.

XXIII   The Dagda

He is called the Dagda, i.e. 'good for everything' – a leading
magician, a redoubtable warrior, an artisan – all powerful,
ominiscient.

Myles Dillon and Nora Chadwick

Dagda, in Irish Gaelic, means 'the Good God' (*dagh* – prefix 'good',
dia 'god'), and he also has the titles Eochaid Ollathair ('Eochaid,
Father of All') and Ruad Ro-fhessa ('Red One of Perfect Knowledge').
   He is the unquestionable king and father-figure of the Tuatha Dé
Dannan, full of strength, wisdom and sexual potency, terrible in
battle, a god of fertility and abundance, and a skilled musician to boot.
Yet there is something paradoxical and ambivalent about him. He
seems to have inspired both respect and mockery; he is portrayed as
gross and pot-bellied and dressed like a peasant. We shall consider this
ambivalence further in a moment.
   The Tuatha Dé Danann ('People of the Goddess Dana') were the
last-but-one occupiers of Ireland in the mythological cycle. They
defeated their predecessors the Fomors and were in turn defeated by

the Sons of Mil (Gaels), whereupon they retreated, under the armistice agreement, into the sidh-mounds or hollow hills, leaving the surface to the Gaels. They still live there, a magical people, the aristocracy of the *sidhe* or fairy-folk.

The heroes and heroines of the Tuatha are the pagan Irish Celtic gods and goddesses as they were envisaged in immediately pre-Christian times, only thinly disguised in the process of monastic transcription.

The Dagda played a leading part in the defeat of the Fomors at the Second Battle of Magh Tuiredh (Moytura); and at the other end of the Tuatha's reign, it was he who decided the allocation of sidh-mounds among the various Tuatha chiefs.

He was a formidable warrior. His club was so huge that it took nine ordinary men to lift it, and when dragged along the ground it created a furrow like the boundary between provinces. With one end he could slay nine men at a time – yet with the other he could restore them to life. He was thus also an archetypal Celtic Otherworld god of death and rebirth.

His other famous possession was his cauldron of abundance, called Undry, 'from which no company went unsatisfied'. It was one of the Four Treasures of the Tuatha, the other three being the Lia Fail (Stone of Destiny) which cried aloud when the rightful King of Ireland mounted it and which may still be seen on Tara Hill (Plate 9 of *The Witches' Way*); the Sword of Nuada, a Tuatha king; and the Spear or Lance of Lugh.

The Dagda was thus both the defender of his people and their nourisher; he received them on death and assured their rebirth.

Both Dana and the often triple Bríd/Brigid were said to be his daughters, though this is probably an effect of the patriarchalization process; Graves (*The White Goddess*, p. 143) says that Bríd was once his mother. Boann, goddess of the River Boyne, is sometimes referred to as his wife, but his mating with her does not seem to have been a marital one. The name of their son, the love god Aengus mac Óg, means 'Aengus, son of the Virgin', in the old sense of a woman of independent status, mating with whom she chose but subject to no man; and Boann appears to have been just that.

His other goddess mate was the war goddess, the Morrigan. With her, too, he coupled on a river – in her case the Unius in Connaught. Both matings were at Samhain and were doubtless divine prototypes of a royal or chieftainly Samhain mating ritual.

Boann represents the fertility aspect (as anyone who knows the rich Boyne Valley could appreciate), while the Morrigan, who had magical and precognitive powers to supplement her warrior nature, stood for the battle aspect.

Aengus mac Óg, offspring of the Dagda and Boann, lived in Brugh na Boinne, which looks down on his mother's river; he won it from his father by a cunning legal technicality. Brugh na Boinne is Newgrange, one of the finest neolithic structures in the world, which has today been skilfully restored and is visited by thousands of people every year; its magic can still be felt. (See p.13.)

The repeated theme of the river-mating of the tribal god may be another confirmation of his antiquity. The neolithic peoples who predated the cattle-raising Celts, in Ireland and elsewhere, were cropraisers, vitally dependent upon rivers. Newgrange, which was built about 3,000 BC, is the focus of the Boyne Complex, an astonishingly rich concentration of mounds and dolmens all within easy reach of the river. Perhaps the Dagda's mating with Boann, and his ownership of Brugh na Boinne, in Celtic legend, derive directly from the mating of a neolithic tribal god with that same river-mother on whom their lives depended.

Back to the battle aspect. Before the Second Battle of Magh Tuiredh, the Dagda went to the Fomors under a flag of truce, ostensibly to discuss a possible compromise but in fact to spy out the land. The Dagda had a fondness for porridge, so the Fomors dug a pit into which they poured eighty measures each of milk, meal and fat, and added some sheep, goats and pigs. They then told him he must eat the lot or be slain.

He accepted the challenge and consumed the whole pitful. Before leaving, he seduced one (or, in other accounts, several) of the Fomorian maidens, persuading her to use her magic skills against her own people.

This story is told as a humorously clownish episode and would appear to be an example of the buffoon treatment we have mentioned. On the other hand the Dagda, with wry one-upmanship, certainly emerges from it as the victor, both gastronomically and sexually.

This apparently irreverent attitude to an important god seems puzzling. But it must be remembered that the deities of late Celtic paganism were the sophisticated pantheon of a warrior aristocracy and their dependent highly skilled craftsmen.

They were deities such as Lugh Samhioldánach, 'Equally Skilled in All the Arts', Bríd the patroness of healers and craftsmen, and Oghma of the Sunlike Countenance, god of wisdom and learning and inventor of the Celt's only native script. To quote Anne Ross (*Pagan Celtic Britain*): 'It has often been suggested that the Dagda was a sort of amiable fool, but there is no real evidence of this. Hostile or humorous *literati* bent on reducing a powerful tribal god to a good-natured buffoon could be responsible for such an impression.'

Ancient deities, revered by the common people – such as the mighty

All-Father, ancestor, protector and sustainer of the tribe; or the Horned God of Animals we considered in Chapter XXI, whose very name was half-forgotten; or the Great Mother herself, who had been subdivided into specialities – these might be regarded as somewhat crude concepts by the sophisticated in a culture of high achievement. But they were too real and numinous, and too much loved by the peasantry, to be dismissed altogether, whether by mocking or by ignoring them.

And are they not still?

The Dagda Ritual

Anyone who knows Newgrange, the Dagda's palace of Brugh na Boinne, will recognize in the following ritual the symbolism of the Triple Spiral (a design, unique in these islands, inscribed on the wall of the central recess of the inner chamber) and the incoming light (the Winter Solstice sunrise). But we hope that even those who have never been there will find the ritual drama effective.

The Preparation

The Circle is prepared in the normal way, plus a cauldron just to the south of its centre. Inside the cauldron is a bowl filled with red wine, large enough to dip hands in. In an adjoining room is a candle in a candlestick, ready for lighting. The altar must be strong enough for the High Priestess to sit on it, and carry the bare minimum of tools, as these have to be removed at the appropriate moment.

This ritual may be performed either skyclad or robed – though skyclad would be more symbolically appropriate (and also more practical in view of the way the wine is taken). But whether skyclad or robed, all the men are completely without jewellery or adornments of any kind – with the exception of the High Priest, who wears round his neck a torque or serpent-necklace, both symbols of the Dagda and of Cernunnos.

The Celts probably inherited the serpent-symbol from the Picts, to whom it was particularly sacred. It was often associated with winding rivers, bringers of fertility and mating-places of the God. Two snakes intertwined, as in the caduceus, also appear in Celtic symbology; they represent polarity – in particular, of the male and female aspects which are within each of us, regardless of sex, and which must be brought into harmony for spiritual and psychic health. And that – in this case, for men – is the meaning of the present ritual.

Since this ritual is specifically for the benefit of the men, it looks at first sight as though the women, with the exception of the High

Priestess and the Maiden, have little part to play. In fact, they should be concentrating on giving all the psychic support they can to the men – in particular, of course, to their own working partners. Their effort, even though silent, can greatly strengthen the exercise.

The Ritual
The Opening Ritual is as usual (see Appendix I). When it is over, the altar is cleared and the High Priestess is enthroned on it, holding a lit candlestick in each hand.

The women seat themselves around the perimeter of the Circle.

Fig. 3 – The triple spiral of the Dagda ritual.

The High Priest then leads all the men in a Dance of the Triple Spiral, following the path shown in Figure 3 – first two or three turns outwards deosil in the West, then two or three turns inwards widdershins in the East, and finally two or three turns inwards deosil around the cauldron. Her and the men then sit close around the cauldron, facing inwards.

The High Priestess says: '*Welcome, my brothers, to the House of the Dagda, who is the Good God. I am Grian, the living Sun; priests of the Horned One know me well. My rays light the path to knowledge, and my heat burns within your bodies. I am the glory of the Dragon Fire, the Rainbow Path to Inner Treasures. Drink from the Dagda's Cauldron, and turn your true sight inwards.*'

The High Priest dips his hand in the wine, bringing out some cupped in his palm and drinks it. (He should lean over the cauldron to do so.) Each man in turn, deosil round the group, does the same.

When all the men have drunk, the High Priestess says: '*Close your eyes, my brothers – close your eyes, and seek what your inner vision has to show you.*'

When all the men have their eyes shut, the coven Maiden goes round and blows out all the candles except for the two the High Priestess is holding. She then takes her athame and quietly leaves the room – of course, opening the normal Gateway in the Circle (widdershins athame sweep, step through, and deosil athame sweep to re-close it) to do so.

The High Priestess then blows out her two candles, leaving the room in complete darkness.

In the other room, the Maiden lights her candle, turns off any lights which might cast a glow through the door when it is reopened, and waits, listening for her signal.

The men do as they have been told – seeing with their inner eyes and listening to their own inner voices.

The women concentrate on identifying themselves with Grian, the Sun, to give support to the High Priestess and Maiden and to the men.

When the High Priestess decides that the men have meditated long enough, she knocks three times slowly with her knuckles on the altar and says: '*Open your eyes, my brothers.*'

Hearing this signal, the Maiden takes up her candle and athame, opens the door and walks in. Her candle must be the only light visible, even when the door is open. In a slow and stately manner, and without turning round, she closes the door behind her, opens the Gateway with her athame, steps through and re-closes it. She then walks to stand beside the High Priestess and hands the candle to her. The High Priestess holds the candle out in front of her with both hands.

The High Priest stands, walks over to the other side of the High Priestess and says: '*I am the Dagda – father, protector, provider, leader and inspirer. And all of this is within each of you, for you are sons of the Dagda. But hear this: within me also, and within you, is the light of my sister Grian – and it is this which you have been seeking with your inner vision. Seek it now and always, that the twin serpents of your being may work together in harmony.*'

The High Priestess says: '*So mote it be!*', and all the women repeat it after her.

The High Priest says: '*Let us now eat and drink together.*'

All rise. The High Priestess gets off the altar, and the tools are restored to it. All the candles are relit, and the food and drink brought out. (At this stage, it may be avisable to pour the wine left in the bowl into a jug!)

XXIV   Loki

When in doubt, win the trick.

Edmond Hoyle

The Nordic Loki was a trickster god, quick-witted in speech and cunning in action. He could be everything from a helpful ally (particularly to the strong, courageous but not very cunning Thor) to a disastrous saboteur (again, including Thor) – though, when he provoked disaster, he usually found a way of cancelling its effects after a cliff-hanger or two.

He was totally unpredictable.

Unpredictability, contrary perhaps to popular belief, is a male-polarity aspect, one of the God functions. The Goddess, and woman, can be mysterious, but there is a subtle difference between unpredictability and mystery.

In Cabalistic terms – the first three Sephiroth (spheres) of the Tree of Life are Kether, pure existence without activity or form; Chokmah, the Supernal Father, who is raw directionless (or omnidirectional) energy without form; and Binah, the Supernal Mother, who takes the

114

fertilizing energy of Chokmah and is both the confining womb which gives it form and the breast which nourishes it.

The energy of Chokmah, in action, is unpredictable because it is omnidirectional. In any given situation, one cannot always tell in which of his infinity of possible directions the effect will manifest.

The form-giving action of Binah is mysterious in its complexity; and the mystery includes the fact that each of the myriad forms which she produces is individual, and yet at the same time true to its own nature (of its species, for example).

One factor does give the unpredictability of Loki a bias, so to speak, and that is his historical development.

He was essentially Scandinavian, entering into German mythology only by later adoption. He was originally a fire demon, who developed into a mainly benevolent god. His father was Farbauti, who gave birth to fire, and his mother was Laufey, 'Wooded Isle', who provided fuel for that fire.

Loki was one of the Aesir, the company of principal gods and goddesses living in Asgard; though, unlike other major deities, there is no evidence of his having been independently worshipped or having his own shrines or rituals. Early on he became the blood brother of the supreme god Odin by exchanging vows, but gradually his stories presented him more and more as the trickster, the provocateur; the gods never knew whether he would solve crises or cause them, or even both.

And there can be little doubt that the advent of Christianity pushed him into an increasingly devilish role.

His very loyal wife was Siguna (Signy, Sigyn), who may be the same as Sin, goddess of truth, who was similar to the Egyptian Ma'at (an interesting parallel, because Ma'at's husband Thoth was also a god of cleverness, though unlike Loki he never used it irresponsibly).

Siguna bore him the twins Vali, god of justice, and Vidar, the Silent One, who was almost as strong as Thor; though another version makes Vali and Vidar the sons of Odin and Rinda.

Loki himself, being by nature a charmer and seducer (and handsome with it), was anything but faithful to Siguna; he boasted openly of having enjoyed the favours of most of the goddesses. By the giantess Angurboda he fathered the death and Underworld goddess Hel (Hela), the monster Midgard Serpent which coiled itself round the Earth at the bottom of the sea, and Fenrir, the Fenris Wolf, enemy of the gods, who finally consumed Odin at Ragnarok, the Twilight of the Gods (see below).

In one of his co-operative moods, Loki helped Thor to win back his famous hammer, Mjolnir ('Destroyer'), when it was stolen. Loki borrowed Freya's magic robe of feathers, which enabled the wearer to fly anywhere, and was able to seek out and identify the thief as the giant Thrym.

Thrym said he would give the hammer back only if he was given Freya as his wife. Freya was so furious that her neck swelled till it broke her golden necklace. But Thor's hammer was of great importance to all the Aesir, being concerned not only with fighting but also with the sealing of oaths, contracts and marriages, so the gods decided on a trick. Thor disguised himself as Freya, with a bridal veil and Freya's mended necklace, and Loki disguised himself as 'her' servant. They went to Thrym's Court, where the delighted giant ordered the wedding feast.

The 'bride's' appetite amazed everyone: 'she' ate and drank everything that had been prepared for all the women, including a whole ox and three barrels of mead. Loki covered this by explaining that 'Freya' had been so eager for the wedding that she had eaten nothing for eight days. Thrym then tried to kiss his bride and glimpsed the ruddy cheeks and flashing eyes; Loki explained hastily that she had not slept for eight nights and was feverish with anticipation.

Thrym fell for it and, in accordance with ritual, sent for the hammer to be placed in the bride's lap.

Thor seized the weapon, threw back his veil and easily demolished Thrym and his fellow giants. He and Loki returned in triumph to Asgard.

On another occasion, a giant called Thjazi who had taken Loki prisoner demanded as the price of his release the goddess Idun, owner of the magical apples which kept the gods young. Again by trickery, Loki managed to fulfil the bargain but, deprived of Idun and her apples, the gods found themselves ageing and forced Loki to get her back – which he succeeded in doing, as always by cunning instead of force.

Loki's cunning was often very useful to his fellow gods. Once they rashly agreed with a giant who was building a stronghold for them that his price should be Freya, the Sun and the Moon, provided the work was completed within a year (which they believed he had no chance of doing). The giant worked with his horse Svadilfari, who helped him to do it so fast that he was about to meet the deadline. Loki saved the situation by shape-changing into a mare and tempting the stallion away, so that the work was held up and the deadline missed. Thor slew the giant, and Loki, in his mare form, birthed a grey foal with eight feet – Odin's mount Sleipnir, whom none could overtake.

When Loki cut off the lovely golden hair of Thor's wife, Sif, Thor nearly killed him. Loki stopped him by swearing to get the dwarfs to make her new hair of pure gold, which would grow on her head like natural hair. The dwarfs did so, at the same time making a magical ship and spear for Odin. Loki had escaped Thor's anger but nearly spoiled things by betting another dwarf that he could not fashion similar marvels – which the dwarf won by making three treasures including Thor's hammer. The stake had been Loki's head but, typically, he saved himself on the legal technicality that the dwarf could cut his head but must not damage the neck. (Did Shakespeare know this story when he wrote *The Merchant of Venice*, one wonders?)

The crime which offended the Aesir most was Loki's responsibility for the death of Baldur, the handsome and popular son of Odin and Freya. Freya had made all things, animate or inanimate, swear that they would never harm Baldur – but she had missed out the mistletoe, which seemed to her too young to take an oath. Loki discovered this and, out of jealousy, when the gods were playfully pelting Baldur with things which could not harm him, he persuaded the blind god Höd to throw a mistletoe branch. Unsuspecting, Höd did so; it hit Baldur, who fell dead.

The desolated gods sent Baldur's brother Hermod, mounted on Sleipnir, to the Underworld to plead with Hel to send Baldur back to life. She was willing to help but could do so only if everything in the universe wanted Baldur back. The gods asked every being and every thing, and all agreed – except one aged giantess named Thokk, who refused to mourn Baldur; so he had to stay in the world of the dead.

Thokk was, in fact, Loki in disguise, his jealousy unabated.

The gods realized that Loki was responsible for Baldur's death and bound him to a rock with a snake dripping venom above him. But the faithful Siguna stood by him catching the drops, and Loki was able to escape. From then on he sided entirely with the gods' enemies, the giants and monsters.

It was Baldur's death which led to Ragnarok, the Twilight of the Gods, known in German as *Götterdämmerung*. Odin led forth his army from Asgard to save the Earth from the tempest of fire which threatened it, and the situation escalated till all the gods and goddesses were fighting all the giants and monsters, including Loki and the Fenris Wolf. The war ended with both sides, and the Earth and mankind, being destroyed.

But from it all, eventually a new Earth, with new gods and goddesses and new men and women, came to birth. The only divine survivors were a resurrected Baldur, Höd, Vali and Vidar and possibly one or two others, but it has been suggested that some of these were titles of divine aspects, rather than the names of individual deities.

The Ragnarok legend seems to be a mixture of prophecy and the possible memory of a great natural disaster – perhaps the advance and retreat of the polar cap in the Ice Age, of which Scandinavia was a total victim. But mythology agrees that in the dim past gods and men alike were honourable and peaceful and that both honour and peace were gradually eroded, until things deteriorated to the point where Ragnarok was inevitable.

The stories of Loki also seem to follow this pattern of degeneration. To begin with, and in some ways throughout his development, he represented constructive cleverness – and that stimulating joker-in-the-pack for which gods and humans must always be prepared, lest they become complacent and static. But he also represented the danger that mere cleverness can lapse into unscrupulous cunning, finally self-destructive.

And maybe the same threat hangs over us today, when technical brilliance is all too often indifferent to the real needs of the community and of Mother Earth. Loki's cleverness, which is that of mankind, can be useful and life-enhancing – but if it becomes mere cunning for selfishly dodging responsibility, for getting out of immediate trouble or for making a quick profit, it could hasten our own Ragnarok.

The Loki Ritual

Our suggestion for this is simple. We suggest putting Loki on trial.

The essence of Loki is singularity – the joker in the pack, the element of unpredictability, sometimes humorous, sometimes 'unfair' – the currents and whirlpools of the river of life which we must learn to navigate even if there is no reliable way of charting them. The man chosen for Loki should be articulate and witty, difficult to pin down and good at making out a case for his own function in the universe.

The charge which Loki faces is that he is a 'destructive influence which the universe would be better without'. Quite how complicated or formal you make the proceedings is up to you – though, to avoid excessive preparatory study, we suggest you confine the actual legends cited to those given in this chapter.

We have found that these occasions, when roles are assumed and cases argued, can be educative as well as enjoyable.

Zeus-Ammon. AD 150-200. An example of the equivalizing of
Greek and Egyptian pantheons

Krishna with Radha, cowherd girl said to be an incarnation of
Lakshmi. Rickshaw painting

Achilles in Hyde Park, London

The Mouth of Truth, Rome

Osiris. *c*.100 BC

Hindu Sun god Surya. 11th century AD

Centaur battling with Lapith, from the Elgin Marbles

Assyro-Babylonian Su
god Shamash with Kir
Hamurabi

The High Priestess 'Draws Down the Sun' to invoke the essence
of the God into the High Priest

Antlered god statuette by Philippa Bowers and the dancing figure
of Shiva

XXV Zeus

O Zeus, that art not subject to sleep or time,
Or age, living for ever in bright Olympus!

Sophocles, Antigone

Every culture's mythology and its god- and goddess-forms are
determined by its history, and this is particularly true of the Greeks.
Classical Greek imagination and creative thinking were a major
foundation-stone of European civilization, and their body of myth was
rich and dramatic. But that mythology's actual form and its dominant
themes reflect an earlier fundamental change in the nature of Greek
society.

Greek-speaking peoples came to the Aegean about 1900 BC. They,
and indigenous pre-Greeks such as the Minoans of Crete, were
essentially matrilinear in royal succession, and this was the dominant
pattern until the Dorian Greeks overran the area about 1000 BC. The
centuries before this invasion included the heyday of Crete (which
may be called the first European civilization), the flourishing of
Mycenae and its take-over of Crete, and the legend-creating Trojan
War.

The invading Indo-European Dorians were patrilinear and patriarchal and, as they established dominance, this became the pattern of Greek life. They inherited the mythology, and many of the deities, of pre-Dorian Greece and transformed them – but the transformation was often transparent, revealing the themes on which it was built.

Time and again, for example, a classical (i.e. Dorian) Greek story is like the fairy-story we considered in Chapter X – a tale of the young hero who survives many challenges to win the hand of an old king's daughter. The old king does everything he can to frustrate him, and often the daughter schemes to ensure her suitor's success. In the end the old king is killed, or dies by accident, and the young hero wins through to the throne and the daughter's bed.

Classical Greece told such stories in terms of personal drama and near-Freudian psychology. But the original story would have been an accurate description of ancient matrilinear succession. Title to the throne belonged, as we have seen, to the queen and passed to her daughter. A king served for a set term, at the end of which a young challenger would prove his worth by undertaking tasks and defeating his rivals. The old king would then be killed by his successor in combat, or ritually sacrificed, and the successor would marry either the queen herself or her daughter if the queen retired to dowagerhood.

(Matrilinearity persisted in Ancient Egypt to the end, even though the Pharaoh stayed on the throne till his death; which is why so many Pharaohs married their sisters or daughters, to legitimize their own status.)

The Olympian deities, too, were patriarchalized in the Dorian mythology (of which the earliest written version, which became accepted as more or less definitive, was Hesiod's *Theogony* in about the eighth century BC). But the story of Zeus's parentage and his succession to kingship of the gods recalls this same ancient pattern.

Gaia, the Earth Mother, had many offspring by Uranus, including Rhea and Cronus. Uranus hated all his children, as threats to his continued sovereignty, and hid them away from the light as soon as they were born. Gaia, outraged, persuaded her youngest son, Cronus, to hide in her bed with a sickle which she had made; when Uranus came and mounted her, Cronus reached out and castrated him.

By this ritual sacrifice, Cronus, in traditional manner, had become the dominant male deity. He had children by his sister Rhea: Demeter, Hades, Hera, Hestia, Poseidon and finally Zeus. But Cronus in his turn feared replacement, so he swallowed each of the first five at birth. But when Zeus was about to be born, Rhea hid in a cave on Crete, bore him there and tricked Cronus into swallowing a stone in his place.

The baby Zeus was reared on the milk of the goat goddess Amalthea. When he was old enough, his first wife, Metis ('Wisdom'), helped him to subdue Cronus and compel him to vomit up the other children.

Rhea was originally the Cretan mother-goddess, and Zeus one of her dying-god consorts; Cretans still point to a hill range which looks remarkably like a recumbent man and tell you it is the dead Zeus. (They will also, incidentally, take you into the deep mountain cave, on the edge of the high Plain of Lassithi, where Zeus was born.)

But after the Mycenaeans, and then Greece as a whole, had adopted Zeus as their supreme father-god, and his brothers and sisters as Olympians, his legend was modified by the Dorians so that he was not actually guilty of killing or mutilating his father. Such crude details were left to a generation earlier.

He led his fellow gods first against the Titans, offspring of Gaia and Uranus. After they had been defeated, the Olympians had to subdue the Giants, who had sprung from the blood of Uranus's castration.

Angered by the defeat of her children, Gaia sent against Zeus the fearful monster Typhoeus, her offspring by Tartarus. Typhoeus overwhelmed Zeus and imprisoned him in Cilicia, but Hermes rescued him to fight again, and this time Zeus defeated Typhoeus with his thunderbolts.

From then on, Zeus was the unquestionable master of the gods on Olympus and the humans on Earth.

Nevertheless, hints survived that Zeus, too, was wary of replacement. For example, when Metis was pregnant by him, Gaia warned him (i.e., reminded him of the matrilinear principle which she represented) that his children would supplant him. So he swallowed Metis, and in due course the child, Pallas Athene, was born fully armed from his head – patriarchy even commandeering the female function of childbirth.

'Athene' simply means 'the Athenian', and Pallas Athene, patron goddess of that city, was unquestionably originally the pre-Dorian, and possibly pre-Greek, regional form of the mother-goddess. She was demoted to be the virgin warrior offspring of the father-god, but such were Athenian pride and Greek creativity that even in this form she became a vivid and powerful figure.

But it was Hera, as Zeus's final consort, who suffered most from the patriarchalization process. She, like Athene, was a form of the indigenous mother-goddess, and her independent worship did survive in places such as Argos, where she had five or six temples. She was also particularly honoured in Crete.

Something of her ancient status survived, too, in her traditional patronage of young heroes such as Jason and Herakles (which means 'glory of Hera'), but in general she appears merely as the jealous wife, trying with varied success to frustrate her husband's many amours, or to take revenge on the ladies concerned.

Zeus's amours were indeed many. As John Pinsent points out (*Greek Mythology* p. 23), they sometimes represented the take-over by the Indo-European monogamous divine family of existing gods who already had mothers and fathers of their own. The mothers were retained, but Zeus replaced the fathers.

Or a hero might be the son of a *hieros gamos* (sacred marriage) between a woman or priestess and a priest personifying a god. Zeus in these cases simply replaced the god concerned as divine father. Often he was said to put the woman into a deep sleep before possessing her, which may recall a ritual use of drugs for a *hieros gamos*.

'The amours of Zeus thus reflect either ritual or genealogy or both. But in the monogamous Indo-European family a wife was not expected to tolerate her husband's concubines or bastards, and when this social structure was projected upon heaven it produced a shrewish Hera' (Pinsent, *ibid.* p. 30).

Zeus had other wives between Metis and Hera: Themis (Law), daughter of Uranus and Gaia, who bore him various appropriate children, such as Dike (Justice) and the Fates; the Titaness Mnemosyne (Memory) who bore him the nine Muses; and the Oceanid Eurynome who bore him the three Graces.

As for his lovers – Zeus became the father of Artemis and Apollo by Leto; of Hermes by Maia; of Dionysus by Semele; of Perseus by Danaë; of Helen and Pollux by Leda; of Minos by Europa; of Epaphus by Io; of Persephone by his sister Demeter; of Herakles by Alcmene; of Argos by Niobe; of Aeacus by Aegina; of Arcas by Callisto; of Locir by Mera, and so on. Among these sons, Minos was king of Crete, Argos founder of the city of that name, Arcas ancestor of the Arcadians, and Locir of the Locrians – the stories thus claiming divine origin for the royal houses or peoples concerned. Others of Zeus's offspring, too numerous to list, served a similar function for their own localities.

Before the Olympian take-over, gods and humans had lived in harmony with each other. 'In those days,' Hesiod wrote, 'meals were taken in common; men and the immortal gods sat down together.' But Zeus had a more élitist attitude and soon clashed with mankind as represented by Prometheus, who stole fire from Heaven. He punished the human race by sending them Pandora with her box of disasters – a kind of Greek Eve, a first woman bringing the Fall to mankind.

Even this was not enough for Zeus; he sent a flood to wipe out mankind. But Prometheus warned his son Deucalion, and Deucalion's wife Pyrrha, who was Pandora's daughter, to build an ark. they did so and survived the flood, landing either on Mount Othrys or on Mount Parnassus. There they prudently offered sacrifice to Zeus, who was moved to grant their wish to restart the human race. Thereafter, of course, mankind was firmly subjected to the gods.

And firmly in charge of the gods was the supreme patriarch, Zeus.

The Zeus Play

Here we have done what we did with Lilith and Eve in *The Witches' Goddess* (pp. 133-8): offered, for a change, a little play instead of a ritual. Once again, you can either read it or perform it, with any degree of realism you like.

Cast:

Zeus	Poseidon
Hera	Demeter
Hermes	Persephone
Athene	Aphrodite

Scene: Olympus, today
Zeus and Hera are fast asleep, side by side, face upwards as though lying in state, under a rich coverlet. Off to one side is Zeus's empty throne. Demeter (comfortably motherly) and Persephone (young) enter together.

Demeter: *That's all very well, Persephone, but you have not been yourself recently.* (Lightly pinching Persephone's bicep.) *Not the same muscle tone – and you're definitely paler ... Is Hades ... er ...*

Persephone: *No, honestly, mother – you mustn't listen to all these hellfire stories about him. He's a darling, really; no problems down there. It's when I come up to Earth and start sprouting ... All these nitrates and things in the soil.*

Demeter: (Sighs) *I know – Gaia's always on about it, and threatening to do something drastic ... Will humans never learn?*

Persephone: *I hope they don't drive her to it. Push Gaia too far, and she can be a bit ... well, wholesale. Then there'd be no one left to plant me ...* (Gesturing at Zeus) *Time he woke up. His thunderbolts are more selective.*

Demeter: *Zeus and Hera have been asleep for nearly 2,000 years now. I sometimes think* nothing *will ever wake them.*

Hermes: (Entering) *I wouldn't bet on that.*

Demeter: *Ah, Hermes. Good morning ... What's the matter? You look flustered.*

Hermes: *Morning, Demeter ... Persephone ... Trouble, I'm afraid. Can't you feel it?*

Demeter: (Sniffing the air) *There is something ... Like a tidal wave in the distance.*

Persephone: (Pointing at Zeus) *Mother! Look!*

(Zeus sits up, yawns, and stretches. Then Hera sits up, pats her hair, gets out of bed, pulls off the coverlet and starts folding it neatly.)

Hera: *Come on, Zeus, get up. You can't idle all day. There are things to attend to. You were going to deal with the Persians, remember? And that priest in Sparta who's been getting above himself ... I've told you several times ...*

Zeus: (Standing up and resuming his dignity, he goes to his throne and sits down.) *Stop nagging, woman ... Demeter – Persephone – Hermes – who's first?*

Hermes: *Er ... Zeus ... And Hera too, for that matter ... I'm afraid we must bring you up to date, and it may be a shock to you. You have both been asleep for nearly 2,000 years.*

(Zeus and Hera both stare at Hermes unbelievingly. Hera drops the coverlet, then hastily picks it up and re-folds it. Zeus shakes his head as though to clear it.)

Hera: *I don't believe you.*

Zeus: *No, my dear, he means it ...* (Laughing) *Oh, well, what's a couple of thousand years to the gods? At least it'll have fixed that Spartan you were worrying about.* (To Hermes,) *And the Persians too, I imagine?*

Hermes: *Well, not entirely – but leave that for the moment ... What do you think woke you?*

Zeus: (Pausing, frowning, and suddenly angry) *A thunderbolt! By Myself, a thunderbolt! Who has had the audacity? Thunderbolts are my prerogative only!*

Hermes: *Humans, I'm afraid.*

Zeus: (Leaping to his feet) *HUMANS!*

(Athene, Poseidon and Aphrodite hurry in. They are all talking at once, interrupting each other and trying to get Zeus's attention)

Athene: *Father – you're awake ...*

Poseidon: *Zeus, I need your help ...*

Aphrodite: *Everything's wrong – even my lipstick's changed colour ...*

Athene: (Scornful aside) *Is that all you can think of?* (To Hera) *Tell him to listen ...*

Poseidon: *Dead fish, and living ones the wrong shape ...*

Aphrodite: (To Athene) *You could do with some colour yourself!*

Athene: *Father – for Your sake ...*

Zeus: (Thunderously) *SILENCE!* (They all subside, and he sits down again, taking his time, then, speaking quietly:) *That's better. Now, Hermes – I think you should put us in the picture.*

Hermes: *Thank you, Zeus ... Well, for many centuries after you and Hera went to sleep, everything proceeded more or less as normal. Kingdoms rising and falling, Hephaestus thinking up new techniques, Ares stirring up his usual trouble ...*

Athene: *Bloodthirsty oaf.*

Aphrodite:(Smugly) *He has his nicer moments.*

Demeter: *Burning crops, for instance?*

Zeus: *Order, order!*

Hermes: *They discovered America ...*

Zeus: *Damn. I had hoped we could keep that to ourselves.*

Hermes: *Well, they do call it God's Own Country.*

Zeus: *Gratifying.*

Hermes: *Except that they don't mean you. It's been taken over by Yahweh – as indeed has what is now called Europe.*

Hera: (Muttering) *Named after that hussy Europa, I suppose.*

Hermes: *...and much of Africa and the Near East.*

Zeus: *That doesn't worry me too much. Keeps it in the family, at least. Inter-pantheon relations work fairly smoothly.*

Hermes: *Not any more, they don't. While you've been resting, there's been a marked tendency to monopolization.*

Zeus: *H'mm. I think I'll call a Council of the Gods about that.*

Athene: *And Goddesses, if you please. We've been declared redundant wherever Yahweh's in charge.*

Hera: *What?*

Zeus: *But Yahweh has a wife himself! What's happened to Ashtoreth?*

Athene: *Divorce and oblivion.*

Hermes: *To be fair, I think it's the priesthood to blame, more than Yahweh himself. You see ...*

Athene: (Vehemently) *And that's the trouble. Men have taken over entirely. Which makes things easier for Ares, for a start. Men have had things more and more their own way ever since you fell asleep. Women are their property, denied power ...*

Aphrodite: (Chuckling and taking out her compact) *Who says?*

Athene: (Turning on her) *Yes, they can simper and seduce and pull strings, sacrifice their self-respect ...*

Aphrodite: (Starting to make up her face) *You're just a radical feminist.*

Zeus: *And what in Hades is 'a radical feminist'?*

Hermes: *Please – let's not be sidetracked. We were talking about thunderbolts.*

Zeus: *Indeed we were. Go on, Hermes.*

Hermes: *Thank you. A century or two ago, man discovered electricity. The simple principle of your thunderbolts. At first he used it fairly sensibly, for lighting and warmth and ingenious engines for making things move ...*

Zeus: (Shaking his head) *Clever little creatures we made.*

Hermes: *Perhaps too clever. Just before Ares' worst orgy, called the Second World War, they discovered the real secret.*

Zeus: (Aghast) *You don't mean ...*

Hermes: *Yes.*

Zeus: (After a pause) *As I slept, I dreamed. I dreamed of Helios gone mad, of cities wiped out in an instant. I dreamed ...* (Groans) *Even Gods have nightmares ... Then, today ...*

Hermes: *Men tried also to harness your thunderbolts for peaceful use. But they were too greedy, too careless. Today, in a place called Chernobyl, the power broke loose. It was that which awakened you.*

Poseidon: *I did not have to be awakened.* (Coughs as though bringing up phlegm) *My realm has been sick for years.* (Patting his chest) *I caught this offshore from Sellafield ... And it's not only your thunderbolts.*

Demeter: *The dryads come weeping to me, as man destroys their trees.*

Persephone: *The creatures of the wild call to me, as man shrinks their boundaries.*

Athene: *My builders of old cry out to me, as acid rain eats away our temples.*

Aphrodite: *The ordinary people call to me, as wealth outweighs love.*

All: (Looking at Zeus) *What shall we do?*

Zeus: (Pauses, then rises) *I think it is time to call that Council of Gods and Goddesses – by whatever name they are known. And to call upon all men and women of good will – whatever Beings they worship. Otherwise Gaia may take matters into her own hands ... Are we agreed?*

All: *We are agreed.*

XXVI Eros

Eros is a mighty daemon.

Diotema to Socrates

Eros, the Greek God of love, was even more affected by the Dorian transformation which we described in the last chapter than most of the other deities of Greece.

Originally, according to Hesiod's *Theogony* (see p. 120 above), he had been one of the very first gods, brother of the Earth Mother, Gaia, of Erebus, god of the Dark, and of Nyx, goddess of Night. All four arose spontaneously out of the primordial Chaos.

The Phoenicians, who largely shared their first Creation myth with the Greeks, held Eros to be the son of Cronus by his sister Ashtart, who also bore him Eros's brother Pathos (Desire).

The Phoenician version is interesting, because it helps us to define the archetypal Eros more exactly. He was the original raw sexual force, certainly, but if he had been merely that, a brother called Desire would seem to have been superfluous.

Eros is Love in the broader sense – the urge to relatedness from which, given the prior emergence of Earth and Darkness out of Chaos, all other categories spring.

Hesiod's account of Eros was in these terms, as he who 'brings harmony to chaos' – unlike his accounts of most of the other deities, which were in terms of the Dorian, patriarchal transformation.

Perhaps there is something about love, about that urge to related-ness, which even patriarchy cannot entirely sweep under the carpet.

Nevertheless, Eros himself became gradually demoted to an irresponsible if charming child, winged, with a bow and arrows which he aimed on impulse, often at inappropriate targets, sometimes even divine ones. This accords with patriarchy's view of love and emotion in general, and of sex in particular, as a factor which cannot be denied but which has a habit of upsetting intellectual logic and tidiness.

In his new form, the original story of Eros's birth was pushed aside. He became the son of Aphrodite by Ares, Hermes or Zeus himself. Other versions said he was the son of Zeus's and Hera's daughter Ilithyia, goddess of childbirth, or of Iris, rainbow messenger of the gods, by Zephyrus, the West Wind.

But it was as the son of Aphrodite that he became generally accepted (a relationship of which that of their Roman counterparts Cupid and Venus was, as in so many other cases, a mere carbon copy). He was her constant companion, helping with her toilet and travelling with her wherever she went. Sometimes his irresponsible choice of targets annoyed even his mother (herself not renowned for responsibility) and she impounded his arrows. But he always soon got them back.

While Aphrodite was committing her famous adultery with Ares, Eros amused himself beside the bed, playing with the war god's armour. He seems to have been too quick-witted, though, to be caught in the net of Hephaestus as the lovers were.

Only one substantial Eros legend carries anything of his earlier and deeper significance: the story of Eros and Psyche.

Psyche (Soul) was a king's daughter of such beauty that Aphrodite herself was jealous and sent her son to humble her by making her fall in love with someone hideous. But Eros fell in love with her himself and had Zephyrus carry her gently to a wonderful palace.

There Eros came to her at night when she could not see his face. He did not reveal his identity, only telling her that he was the husband destiny had ordained for her. He would visit her only at night, and she must promise never to try to see his face. She promised and for a time was more than content with her mysterious husband's lovemaking.

But, for all the palace's luxury, she found herself bored during the day and asked her husband's permission to have her sisters live with her.

The sisters were both mystified and envious and kept suggesting to

Psyche that her husband would not let her see him because in fact he was hideous. In the end their nagging wore her down and she broke her promise, taking a lamp to look at him while he was sleeping.

She was delighted with what she saw, but the light woke him. Eros sadly reprimanded her, and then both he and the palace vanished. Psyche found herself sitting alone on a barren rock.

Aphrodite's anger pursued her, forcing her to undergo many unpleasant tasks. But, helped invisibly by Eros, who still loved her, she survived all these ordeals.

Finally Eros went to Zeus and begged him to let Psyche rejoin him. Zeus agreed and made Psyche immortal. Aphrodite relented and forgave her, and the two were married on Olympus in appropriate style.

The theme of this charming story (a favourite subject for Greek artists) is self-evident: the human soul coming to terms with love and learning its lessons on the way – including the one that you should not analyse it too minutely but should live with it on its own terms.

'Eros' has come to be used as a philosophical term to define Relatedness, the emotions, in polarity with Logos, the Word, the intellectual process.

The key word here is 'polarity' – not opposition. The real conflict lies elsewhere. As Jung points out: 'Logically, the opposite of love is hate, and of Eros, Phobos (fear); but psychologically it is the will to power. Where love reigns, there is no will to power; and where the will to power is paramount, love is lacking' (*Collected Works* Volume VII, p. 53).

And on Eros again: 'We shall never get the better of him, or only to our own hurt. He is not the whole of our inward nature, though he is at least one of its essential aspects. Thus Freud's sexual theory of neurosis is grounded on a true and factual principle. But it makes the mistake of being one-sided and exclusive; also it commits the imprudence of trying to lay hold of unconfinable Eros with the crude terminology of sex. In this respect Freud is a typical representative of the materialist epoch, whose hope was to solve the world riddle in a test-tube' (*ibid.*, p. 28).

Yet even Freud (as Jung points out) in his later years recognized this lack of balance and wrote: 'After long hesitancies and vacillations we have decided to assume the existence of only two basic instincts, *Eros* and the destructive instinct ... The aim of the first of these instincts is to establish ever greater unities and to preserve them thus – in short, to bind together; the aim of the second is, on the contrary, to undo connections and so to destroy things ... For this reason we also call it the death instinct' (*Standard Edition of the Complete Psychological Works*, Volume XXIII, p. 148).

So by acknowledging Eros's true stature as the urge to relatedness, in complementary partnership with Logos and in opposition to the urge to power and destruction, we establish Love in its true creative role and revalue sex as one essential aspect, though not the whole, of that total relatedness.

The Eros Ritual

This is a simple dramatization of the loneliness and sterility of intellect and power-seeking on the one hand, and emotion and instinct on the other, when they are divorced from each other. We have called the one Law and the other Love, for simplicity – though, as Eros (who works to bring them together) points out, both names are over-simplifications.

Law is played by a man, and Love by a woman, preferably, of course, by working partners. Eros should obviously be a man.

None of the three should be played by the Priest and Priestess conducting the Circle, because by the nature of the Opening Ritual (especially Drawing Down the Moon) their mutual integration has already been affirmed, whereas the ritual which follows should, so to speak, start from scratch.

The Preparation
One goblet of white wine and one of red are ready on the altar.

The Ritual
The Opening Ritual is as usual (see Appendix I). When it is over, Law takes the goblet of white wine and sits with his back to the East candle, while Love takes the goblet of red wine and sits with her back to the West candle. Eros sits with his back to the altar.

Eros: (To Law) *Who are you, brother?*
Law: *I am Law. I am quite sufficient unto myself. I organize my affairs logically so that everything shall proceed in an orderly and predictable manner.* (He sips his wine.)
Eros: (To Love) *And who are you, sister?*
Love: *I am Love. I listen to what my heart tells me – and that isn't predictable.* (She sips her wine.) *I don't need him.*
Eros: (To Law) *You call yourself Law. But doesn't her intuition also follow a cosmic law?*
Law: *Only at a primitive stage of evolution. It has been superseded and must be firmly disciplined.*
Eros: *So you demand the power to do that?*
Law: *Of course. Logic requires power, to enforce its rule.*

Love: *You see? He calls himself Law, but he loves power. I call myself Love, but mine is a deeper law than his.*

Eros: *So really you need each other.*

Law: *NO! She's a disruptive influence.*

Love: *And wear his handcuffs? NO!*

(Law and Love both clutch their goblets and drink.)

Eros: *How does that wine taste?*

Law: *Mine is clean and fresh, and I have its exact vintage on record. I know precisely what it will taste like before I drink, and it never makes me intoxicated. Would you care for some?* (Holds out goblet.)

Eros: (Accepting, tasting and returning) *H'mm. A bit sharp, on its own.*

Law: *Not to a trained palate.*

Love: *Mine is warm and exciting, and I couldn't care less about the label. And if it gets me a little drunk, where's the harm in that? Here, try it!* (Holds out goblet.)

Eros: (Accepting, tasting and returning) *Somewhat heady, isn't it?*

Love: *That's what it's for.*

Law: *See what I mean? No restraint, no respect for licensing hours, no thought for others ...*

Love: *And have* you *thought for others, you with your rules and regulations?*

Law: *I know best what is good for them.*

Love: *Power, again! Pretending to be so detached! Really you enjoy ordering them about!*

Law: *Not at all. It is you who enjoy disruption and chaos.*

(Both are getting angry)

Eros: (Raising his hand) *May I make a suggestion?*

Law: *If it will restore order.*

Love: *If it stops him bossing.*

(Both look at Eros expectantly)

Eros: *Why don't you taste each other's wine?*

(A pause)

Law: *No. I might lose control of the situation. I have managed to get things orderly and disciplined, to my own satisfaction. One taste of that stuff, and chaos would be let loose again. There'd be no order in the world.*

Love: *No. One taste of his and everything that's natural would be cramped and starved. What my heart tells me would have to be censored by a book of rules. There'd be no warmth in the world.*

Eros: *Aren't you both forgetting one thing?*

Love: *What?*

Eros: *That you're both part of the same world.*

(Eros rises and goes and changes over the goblets, so that the red is in front of Law and the white in front of Love. Then he returns to his place.)

Law: (Staring at the red goblet) *I'm afraid.*

Love: (Staring at the white goblet) *So am I.*

Eros: *Fear is a denial of both your natures. Law should have the courage to handle fear, and Love the strength to challenge it.*

(A pause)

Law: *He has a reasonable point, you know.*

Love: *I've got a hunch he's right. Let's take a chance, eh?*

(Love grabs the goblet of white and drinks. After a moment's hesitation, Law takes the goblet of red and sips cautiously. They both pause, considering.)

Law: *It has a certain ... body to it, I must admit. Perhaps if one took it in reasonable quantities, now and again ...*

Love: *It does add a bit of variety ...*

Law: *With properly agreed licensing hours, of course ...*

Love: *It might help me to understand my hunches, sometimes ...*

Eros: (Smiling, rising and taking both goblets) *Your health, both of you.* (He drinks from each and returns them.)

Law: (Rising to give the red back to Love) *I think you'd better take charge of this one, my dear. I wouldn't entirely trust myself with it, and your hunches might tell me when I'd had enough.*

Love: (Still seated, accepts the red and gives him the white) *And you hang on to this one for us. I wouldn't want to get too hooked on it.*

Law: (Sitting down beside her) *Now then, my dear. I have one or two suggestions for future co-operation ...*

Love: (Taking his hand with a slightly mischievous smile) *And I might have a few myself.*

Eros: (To the rest of the coven) *Shall we leave them to it?*

XXVII Ra and Amun-Ra

Homage to thee, O Ra, when thou risest! I adore thee when thy
beauties are before mine eyes, and when thy radiance falleth upon
my body.

Papyrus of Ani

The development of Greek gods and goddesses, as we saw in the last
two chapters, was determined largely by the patriarchal take-over.
This was only a minor factor in the development of Egyptian deities;
the principal ones were the integration of many local deities during the
unification of Egypt, and the relative importance of various seats of
royal or priestly power during her long history.

The tidy-minded Dorian Greeks liked to arrive at definitive
answers. Zeus, or Apollo, or Artemis, or Athene was so-and-so, and
that was that. Not so with the Egyptians. If in the early stages one
nome (local tribal area) conquered another, the god of the defeated
nome would not be eliminated; he would be assimilated, perhaps with
a hyphenated title, as an aspect of the victors' god.

Or if, after unification, two important centres had differing pantheons, similar hyphenations and rationalizations would be arrived at. This was not difficult for the Egyptians, because the more thoughtful of them recognized that there was one ultimate divine creative essence, of which all gods and goddesses were aspects – a concept much less noticeable in Greek thinking.

But the mythology of the Egyptian deities was vivid, poetic and full of meaning, so its complexity and its parodoxes can be confusing to the modern mind, which tends to work in the Greek manner. The Egyptians took the paradoxes in their stride.

Let us look, then, at the development of their Sun god.

In the beginning, according to the version at Heliopolis (the main theological centre for many dynasties after unification), the Sun's disc, which was known as Aten (Aton, Atum, Atmu,) lay hidden with his eyes shut in the bud of a lotus in Nun, the primordial waters. From there he finally emerged, by his own will, and revealed his splendour. His name was then Ra (Re), sometimes called Aten-Ra.

He bore, unassisted, the air god Shu and the rain goddess Tefnut, who in turn gave birth to the Earth god Geb and the sky goddess Nut. Against Ra's will, Geb and Nut produced Nephthys, Osiris, Isis and Set. These were the Ennead (Nine) of the Heliopolitan pantheon, into which Horus the Elder and Horus the Younger became integrated. (See p.81 for this family tree.)

This integration was set in train by the earliest Pharaoh of whom we have written records – Menes (Narmer), founder of the First Dynasty about 3100 BC. He came from Upper Egypt and worshipped the sky falcon god Horus. He set up his unifying capital at Thinis on the border between Upper and Lower Egypt, near Abydos, which was the cult-centre of the fertility god Osiris, who was popular throughout Egypt. Later he built a new capital at Memphis, which was close to Heliopolis, centre of solar worship. So from this political unification emerged the integration of the sky, fertility and solar cults into one pantheon and its mythology.

Later on, a wife of Ra appears – Rait or Rat, the feminine form of his name. She is a vague and ill-defined figure, and many scholars think she is merely a memory of much earlier times when the First Creator, Ra, was envisaged as feminine.

For Ra, at Heliopolis at least, was regarded as the Creator. All living creatures, including men and women, came from his tears – which may be a pun, since the words for 'tears' and 'men' sound alike in Egyptian.

Ra initially created a First Universe, which he ruled from Heliopolis. Every morning he would set out to spend an hour in each of of his twelve provinces.

While he remained young and vigorous, all went well. But, alone among the Egyptian gods, he gradually became old and decrepit. When he reached this stage, Isis tricked him into revealing his Secret Name and thus acquired his magical powers.

When Ra discovered that mankind was plotting against him, he ordered the goddess Hathor (or Sekhmet, regarded as Hathor in her vengeful aspect) to devour them. The goddess went berserk, but before all mankind were dead, Ra relented, and she was deceived into drinking beer coloured with red ochre, which she thought was human blood, and she became too drunk to continue. Humanity was reprieved.

Ra now withdrew to the sky, across which he sailed daily in his Boat of a Million Years. During each night his boat bore him on a perilous journey through the Underworld, avoiding in particular his arch-enemy the serpent Apep, to reach the eastern place of his daily rising. Sometimes (as at solar eclipses) Apep even attacked him during the day, but he was always fought off.

Ra's most formidable weapon was his eye – overlapping with that of Horus as the other major sky god, whose right eye was the Sun and his left the Moon.

One of Ra's symbols, particularly at dawn, was the Khephra beetle, with the solar orb in its claws – an image inspired by the actual dung-beetle, which determinedly rolls its ball of egg-containing dirt across all obstacles.

Ra was especially a god of the Pharaohs, each of whom was known as 'son of Ra'. This was meant literally; in the official belief, Ra was held to visit and impregnate the queen disguised in the person of her husband. This of course tallied with the matrilinear principle that the right to the throne came from the mother, not the father.

From the Twelfth to the Eighteenth Dynasties (c.1991-1320 BC) Thebes, the modern Karnak and Luxor, grew steadily in importance to become the royal and priestly heart of the kingdom. The god of Thebes was Amun ('Hidden'), a fertility deity. He and his consort Mut ('Mother') and their son Khons ('Sky-Navigator', originally a Moon god) formed the Theban Triad.

When Thebes became the capital, the usual integration ensued: Amun and Ra were identified under the name Amun-Ra, and he and Mut became predominantly solar. The fertility aspect remained, typified by the festival of Opet, the annual visit on 19 July (the heliacal rising of the goddess star Sirius) of Amun-Ra from his great temple at Karnak to Mut in her Luxor temple a few miles upstream, dramatized by the ritual mating of a priest of Amun-Ra with a selected one of the priestesses of Mut, who were regarded as the god's concubines.

Pharaohs naturally became 'sons of Amun'. A princess would often be named as Divine Consort of the god.

The priesthood of Amun-Ra became rich and politically and theologically powerful. As Veronica Ions puts it: 'The high priest of

Amon-Ra ruled the priests of all the other cults, and himself became a kingmaker in the Eighteenth Dynasty, supporting Hatshepsut, the first woman to reign as pharaoh, and her successor Thuthmosis III' (*Egyptian Mythology*, p. 20).

But less than a century after Thuthmosis's death came one of the most remarkable events in Egyptian history. The Pharaoh Amenhotep (Amenophis, 'Amun is Satisfied') IV, 1379-1362 BC, changed his name to Akhenaton ('Glory of Aten'), left Thebes, built a new capital called Akhetaten (the modern Tel-el-Amarna) and introduced a hitherto unheard-of system – monotheism.

Only one deity was to be worshipped, symbolized by the Sun's disc, Aten. No images of him in human or animal form were displayed; only the disc and rays, each ray ending in a tiny hand holding the ankh, hieroglyph of life (Figure 4), the gift which Aten dispensed.

Fig. 4 – The Ankh, Egyptian hieroglyphic for 'Life'.

Along with this, Akhenaton encouraged a revolution in art from formalized to naturalistic. The murals of him, his wife, the lovely Nefertiti, and their children are among the most charmingly domestic in Egyptian art – and unflattering to him, because he was pot-bellied and had a long distorted head, but even for himself he decreed naturalism.

Such a revolution, both theological and cultural, was too much for priesthood or people to swallow, for it was out of tune with the whole nature of Egyptian civilization. And unfortunately for Akhenaton, however dedicated his ideas, he was an incapable ruler. Egypt became economically and militarily threatened.

Under his three successors, whose reigns totalled a mere sixteen years and who included his young son Tutankhamun, things returned gradually to normal; it is significant that the boy Pharaoh had originally been named Tutankhaten ('Living Image of Aten') and changed it to Tutankhamun ('Living Image of Amun'). The power behind the throne, keeping that return as smooth as possible, was the shrewd Horemheb, who had been military commander under Akhenaton and who eventually became Pharaoh himself (1348-1320).

One change, however, remained: the Pharaohs were no longer the puppets of the Amun-Ra priesthood, which they had been in danger of becoming. Seti I (1318-1304) and his son Rameses II (1304-1237) continued Horemheb's work and became two of Egypt's most renowned rulers. Among other things, the first built and the second continued the great temple of Osiris at Abydos, with its chapels to six other gods and goddesses; but both contributed substantially also to the Theban temple of Amun-Ra.

Such essentially Egyptian ecumenism must also have helped to strengthen the bonds between Pharaoh and people, for while the patronage of royalty had always been solar, the heart of the ordinary Egyptian, as we saw in Chapter XVIII, was with Osiris, Isis and the child Horus.

Amun-Ra, like all god-forms, was capable of symbolizing everything from the best to the worst of humanity. At worst, he was identified with priestly wealth and political power-seeking. At best, as the Hidden Sun, which is the meaning of his name, he represented the spiritual essence behind the outward symbols; and to the ordinary worshippers, he and his family stood for the fertility on which their everyday survival and prosperity depended.

No one can visit his wonderful temple at Karnak (still in area the largest religious building in the world), and that of his consort Mut nearby, without feeling the magic which still electrifies them, 2,000 years after their official function ceased.

The Amun-Ra Ritual

The Festival of Opet was a three-day event of great popular rejoicing. The god's image was brought with great ceremony upstream from his temple at Karnak to that of the goddess at Luxor, for this was their honeymoon. And the whole population, from Pharaoh and queen and their family to the humblest farmer and his wife and theirs, were the divine couple's wedding guests.

Our suggestion here is that the coven should recapture the spirit of the Festival of Opet.

The whole ritual takes three days. In modern conditions, this is probably most practicable from Friday night to Sunday; and if it can be in July (remember that 19 July was the day) so much the better. It will mean as many as possible of the coven spending at least two nights in the same house, but in our experience sleeping-bags are regular items of most covens' equipment.

The arrangement of an Egyptian temple and the opening procedure for an Egyptian ritual are given in Appendix II on page 255.

First Day

A room is prepared for an Egyptian temple, with the altar in the East and the appropriate objects in place. (If you already have a room which you use exclusively for Craft rituals, this will be easier.)

It is thoroughly cleaned and aired, and all iron objects are removed from it. It is kept locked overnight. The appropriate robes are made ready, cleaned and ironed.

Second Day

The whole coven is up before dawn. They go out of doors and greet the sunrise. As the Sun makes its first appearance (or in the weather conditions of these islands, as soon as they know that it has actually risen!), the High Priest declaims: '*Hail to thee, Ra-Harakhte, Ra of the Horizon! We welcome thee in thy Boat of a Million Years. We welcome thee back from Amenti, where thou hast conquered the serpent Apep. We welcome thee, returned to light up the world. So let it be, day by day forever!*'

The coven say: '*So let it be!*'

The High Priestess says: '*We greet thy consort, Mut the Mother. May you come together this day, that the Earth may be fruitful!*'

The coven say: '*So let it be!*'

The coven then return to the house, robe themselves and unlock the temple. The Opening Ritual (Appendix II) is then conducted.

During the day, fruit and flowers are brought into the temple and suitably arranged.

At noon, the coven assemble out of doors, and the High Priest declaims: '*We greet thee, great Amun-Ra, at the height of thy power. Bless this Earth and light it with thy radiance. Draw forth the flowers and fruit, that thy people may live in beauty and plenty. So let it be, now and forever!*'

The coven repeat: '*So let it be!*'

The High Priestess says: '*Hail to thee, great Mut, mother of us all! Bless this Earth on which thy consort sheds his light, that it may be fruitful.*'

The coven say: '*So let it be!*'

The coven return to the house.

At sunset, they come out again, and the High Priest declaims: '*Hail to thee, great Amun-Ra! The hour of thy union with Mut approacheth. Join with her in love, that the Earth may be fruitful!*'

The coven say: '*So let it be!*'

The High Priestess says: '*Hail to thee, great Mut, mother of us all! The god approacheth. Welcome him in love, that the Earth may be fruitful!*'

The coven say: '*So let it be!*'

The coven return to the house. All are present while the High Priest locks the door of the temple, and says: '*This now is the place of the coming-together of the God and the Goddess. No man or woman may enter it for this their night of union, that the Earth may be fruitful.*'

The coven say: '*So let it be.*'

Third Day

In the morning, the temple is unlocked and the fruit is removed. The temple is left tidy, with the flowers still in place, for as long as possible.

The day is given up entirely to human celebration. If possible, for example, the coven should enjoy a picnic out of doors. In any case, the minimum of work should be done; the entire coven should enjoy relaxed happiness in the company of each other and the Earth.

XXVIII   Wayland the Smith

Where now are the bones
of Wayland the wise,
that goldsmith
so glorious of yore?
Who now wots of the bones
of Wayland the wise
or which is the low
where they lie?
Attributed to King Alfred

The folk-roots of England and her old gods and goddesses are a blend
of Celtic and Nordic. Once, in the brave days of Arthur, indigenous
Celt fought immigrant Saxon for possession of the land; but by the
time the Normans seized it, the two together formed its ordinary
people, equally exploited by their new lords. For better or worse, the
marriage had been consummated.

And underlying it all – marriage-bed to this sometimes turbulent
mating – were the mysterious ways of the neolithic peoples, whose

brooding megaliths bear witness to a culture which is still part of Albion's chromosomes.

Nowhere, perhaps, is this triple ancestry so clearly manifest as at Uffington in the Vale of the White Horse in Berkshire.

Brooding over it is the famous hill-cut figure of the running horse, 374 feet from nose to tail, who is probably Epona herself, one of the forms of the great Celtic Mother Goddess. On the ridge can be seen the ramparts of a chalk hill-fort which some say is Mount Badon, battleground of Arthur's key victory over the Saxons about AD 518. A mile or so away are the huge stones of a neolithic long barrow, erected at least 5,000 years ago, which has been known since long before the Norman Conquest as Wayland's Smithy.

To the Anglo-Saxons (as to the Celts before them) such wonders could only have been built by gods or giants. So, just as the Celts saw Newgrange as the home of the Dagda and his son Aengus mac Óg, the Anglo-Saxons attributed the Uffington stones to Wayland, farrier and goldsmith of the gods.

It is said that if you leave a horse there overnight, with a silver coin laid on the stones, when you return in the morning you will find that Wayland has shod it for you. When Wayland's Smithy was excavated in 1921, two Iron Age money-bars were found there, so the tradition may be very ancient.

Wayland the Smith has been an ineradicable part of English folklore for a millennium and a half, in spite of Church attempts to suppress him along with other pagan heresies. But his origins are far older than that.

Wayland (Weyland, Weland) is his Anglo-Saxon name; to their Nordic ancestors he was Volund. His father was Wade (Wada), King of the Finns, who possessed a magic boat, and his grandmother was a sea-witch called Wachilt.

He had two brothers, Egil and Slagfid. One day the three of them were walking by the lake at Wolfdales when three swans flew in from Murkwood. They turned into maidens, Allwise, Swanwhite and Olrun, and were spinning flax on the shore when the brothers met them. They fell in love at once. Olrun joined Egil, Swanwhite joined Slagfid, and Allwise chose Volund.

For seven years the three couples lived happily, but during the eighth the three maidens became increasingly homesick for Murkwood, and in the ninth year they disappeared.

Egil and Slagfid went off in search of their lost loves, but Volund stayed in Wolfdales, working at his craft as a smith and jeweller.

Nidud (Nidhad, Nidung), King of the Niars, heard of the master smith alone in his forge at Wolfdales and sent armed men who stole his sword and one of his gold rings while Volund was out hunting, and then hid. When Volund returned, he saw that a ring was missing and thought Allwise had come back to him. He fell asleep waiting for her and woke to find that the king's men had bound him.

He was taken to Nidud, who had kept the sword and given the ring to his daughter Bodvild (Beadohild). Nidud accused Volund of stealing his gold, to cover up his own theft. But the queen warned him that Volund had recognized both the sword at Nidud's belt and the ring on Bodvild's finger and would be out for revenge.

So Nidud had Volund hamstrung, and imprisoned the lame smith on the island of Saevarstod, where he was to work only for the king, and only the king was allowed to see him.

Volund bided his time, plotting his revenge. His chance came when Nidud's two sons, breaking their father's orders, visited Volund secretly and demanded the key to his jewel-chest. Volund cut off their heads, buried their bodies in a dung-heap and made two silver-mounted drinking-cups out of their skulls as a gift for the king. He also carved two brooches for Bodvild out of their teeth.

The princess was curious, so she broke the gold ring which had been stolen from Volund and in her turn went secretly to the smith to ask him to mend it, on the excuse that she dared not tell her parents it was broken. Volund agreed and gave her beer to drink while he was working. When she was drunk and half asleep, he raped her.

His revenge complete, Volund flew away from his island prison on wings which he had fashioned for himself.

This legend contains some interesting elements – including the fact that only the king was allowed direct access to the smith. It was, in fact, the early custom that only royalty had personal contact with sword-makers; anyone else would leave a block of iron and a sum of money near the forge and collect the finished weapon a few days later. This may well have been the origin of the tradition at Wayland's Smithy.

Smiths and farriers, from the earliest times, were regarded with awe as natural magicians, as we saw in Chapter VII. And among them, the 'fairy sword-makers' such as Wayland were a special class. The difference was a practical one. The earliest iron swords, like their bronze predecessors, wounded chiefly by the sheer weight of the blow. But some sword-makers had mastered the complicated art of tempering, so that their swords wounded much more effectively, by actual cutting.

Two of the necessities for proper tempering are high-carbon iron and a ready supply of good charcoal, and these were not obtainable everywhere. So the 'fairy sword-maker' was often a foreigner (hence perhaps Weyland's 'sea-witch' grandmother?), and the iron he used was a special import. It was hardly surprising if kings wished to keep a royal monopoly of both.

Wayland/Volund fashioned the sword Mimung for the Aesir, the gods of Asgard, and the one with which the Anglo-Saxon hero Beowulf slew his dragon. He also made Beowulf's coat of mail: 'This best of corselets that protects my breast ... the work of Weland.'

A special feature of Wayland is that, as we have seen, he is lame – as was his Greek equivalent, Hephaestus. And the craftsmen who fashioned everything from Thor's hammer to Freya's necklace were dwarfs. Are all these features, again, a memory of imported foreign specialists – perhaps of the swarthy, thickset ironworkers of the Black Forest, who were among the first such?

In every pantheon, craftworking gods are given special respect. Their consorts are Beauty (as with Hephaestus and Vulcan) or Wisdom (as with Wayland). Craftsmen gods tend to stay outside the personal dramas of their fellow-deities, impartially supplying all of them. But if those dramas impinge on their own lives, the carefully planned and devastating nature of their counter-measures is typified by Hephaestus's revenge on Ares, and Wayland's on Nidud.

The gods of craftsmanship are to be revered, and emulated, never to be treated casually.

The Wayland Ritual

The sword is an important ritual tool of witches and magicians. In the Wiccan initiation, it is the first of nine tools to be shown and explained to the new witch, who is told that, with it, 'Thou canst form all Magic Circles, dominate, subdue and punish all rebellious spirits and demons, and even persuade angels and good spirits. With this in thy hand, thou art the ruler of the Circle.'

It is essentially a symbol of psychic and spiritual power, and of authority. That is why we, like many other witches, associate it with the element of Fire, and the wand with Air.

Wiccan tradition (see *The Witches Way*, p. 78) insists that, while a man may never enact the ritual role of a woman, a woman may in certain circumstances enact that of a man; she symbolizes this role-change by buckling on a sword (like Joan of Arc) and is treated ritually as masculine as long as she wears it.

Gerald Gardner's ritual for consecrating a sword (*ibid.*, pp. 44-5) is based, largely word-for-word, on that in the medieval grimoire (magical textbook) *The Key of Solomon* (see Bibliography under Mathers). Many people feel that it is more suited to ritual magic than to the Craft. For them, and for anyone who feels like trying an alternative, who better to invoke than Wayland the Smith?

The Preparation

No special preparations are necessary; the pentacle, water, candle and incense found on the normal Wiccan altar are the only other tools needed.

A sword may of course belong to a man, a woman, the partnership or the coven as a whole. The consecration should be done by a man and a woman together. In the ritual below, we have assumed that the man is the owner; if it is the woman, 'I, me, mine' become 'she, her, hers' at the appropriate places, and 'he, him, his' become 'I, me, mine'. If the sword is group property, everything is 'we, us, our'. It sounds complicated, but the changes are obvious in practice.

The parts of the sword referred to are shown in Figure 5.

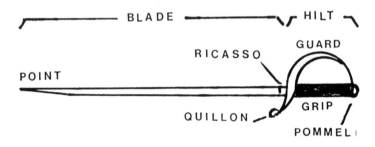

Fig.5 – The parts of a sword. If the guard is a plain crosspiece with two quillons, the names are the same. If the blade has a groove, it is called the 'fuller'.

The Ritual

The Opening Ritual is as usual (see Appendix I), but the god-name used should clearly be Wayland. The goddess-name should be that of a Celtic or Nordic one associated with the inspiring of craftsmen or with weapons, such as Bríd, the Morrigan, Freya or Gunnlauth.

The Man and Woman stand facing the altar, holding up the drawn sword together.

The man says: '*Wayland, Swordmaker of the Gods, we call on you to bestow your strength upon this my sword.*'

The Woman says: '*Wayland, Swordmaker of the Gods; we call on you to bestow your wisdom upon this his sword.*'

They carry the sword to the altar and lay it across the pentacle, each placing the right hand on it.

The Man says: '*We consecrate this sword with the element of Earth. May my hand ever grasp its hilt in firmness and strength.*'

The Woman dips her fingers in the water bowl and sprinkles the sword, saying: "*We consecrate this sword with the element of Water. When patience is called for, may his hand rest in peace upon its pommel.*'

The Man lifts the sword from the pentacle and passes its blade through the flame of a candle, saying: *'We consecrate this sword with the element of Fire. May its power be always at my command.'*

The Woman takes the sword and passes it through the smoke of the censer, saying: *'We consecrate this sword with the element of Air. May its guard allow no evil influence to touch him as he wields it.'*

They face each other in front of the altar, positioning the sword point downwards between them, and embrace and kiss, holding the sword in place by the pressure of their bodies. Then they separate, being careful not to drop the sword.

The owner (or both together if it is a group sword) holds the sword by the hilt and points upwards, saying:

'Forged of steel [iron, bronze] on the craftsman's anvil,
By this rite Wayland the Smith has honed thy blade.
Wrested from the earth and birthed by fire,
Blade, hilt, guard, quillon and grip,
By this rite has Wayland wedded thee to my hand [our hands].
Protect me [us] upon the paths of the seen and unseen,
Give strength to the hand[s] that wield[s] thee.
In the name of Wayland the Smith!'

The consecration is complete.

If the sword has a scabbard, this can be consecrated separately and simply by Earth, Water, Fire and Air and with the embrace.

Part III
Gods of the World

Gods of the World

As with Part III of *The Witches' Goddess*, this is a 'selectively comprehensive' list of the gods of the various cultures of the world, both past and present. The remarks we made in that book on the nature and use of goddess-forms apply equally well to god-forms.

Here, too, our purpose is threefold: to fill out our picture of the overall nature of the God; to provide material for finding the exact aspect one wishes to work with; and to offer a useful work of reference.

Again, we have been flexible in our interpretation of the word 'god'. Our list includes the Adams (first men) of many cultures, some semi-deified culture heroes, and some on the borderline between legendary men and unquestioned gods.

In some entries there is a sentence beginning '777: ...'. These are the Tarot and other correspondences given in Aleister Crowley's *777* for the god concerned.

With the gods who are equatable to Sephiroth on the Cabalistic Tree of Life (Chokmah, Chesed, Geburah, Tiphareth, Hod, Yesod), the correspondences given are those in Dion Fortune's *The Mystical Qabalah*.

A name in CAPITALS in the body of an entry means that he has his own entry in his alphabetical place.

We would welcome any additions or corrections which readers can suggest for future editions.

AAH, AH, IAH: Egyptian. An early Moon god, later assimilated by THOTH.

ABONSAM: Ghana. An evil spirit who used to be banished annually, first with four weeks of communal silence to lull him, followed by dramatic din-raising to frighten him away.

ACAT: Mayan, Yucatan. God of life, who shaped children in their mother's womb.

ACHELOUS: Greek. A river god, eldest son of OCEANUS and Tethys, or of HELIOS and Gaia. During a wrestling match with HERAKLES for the hand of Deianeira, he changed first into a serpent, then into a bull, and Herakles tore one horn off, which became the Cornucopia. Defeated, Achelous threw himself into the river (the largest in Greece) which thereafter bore his name. Father by the Muse Melpomene of the Sirens.

ACHILLES: Greek. Grandson of AEACUS and son of PELEUS and the Nereid Thetis. She dipped him in the River Styx to make him invulnerable but held him by the heel, which remained vulnerable. He led the Myrmidons (see AEACUS) in the Trojan War, of which he was one of the greatest heroes and in which he died from an arrow shot by PARIS hitting him in the heel.

ACMON – see DACTYLS, THE.

ADAD – see HADAD.

ADAPA: Assyro-Babylonian. Created (or fathered) by EA to rule over the human race. He lost the chance of immortality for man by refusing the food of life offered by ANU.

ADAM: Hebrew first man, his wife being Eve. The Garden of Eden story is a patriarchalization of an earlier one, in which he had a first wife, Lilith, later demoted to a demoness.

ADAR – see NINIB.

ADDANC, AVANC, ABAC: Welsh. The monster who caused the Flood which DWYVAN and his wife Dwyfach escaped in their ark Nefyed Nav Nevion. He lived near Lake Llyon Llion, the Lake of Waves. Eventually killed by the oxen of HU GADARN, or in other versions by PEREDUR.

ADDU – see HADAD.

ADIBUDDHA: Hindu, Buddhist. Personification of the ultimate masculine principle, essence of all the BUDDHAS.

ADITYAS: Hindu. Twelve month gods, sons of the original ultimate mother goddess Aditi ('Free from Bonds').

ADONI: ('Lord') Phoenician annually drying vegetation god, lover of Astarte/Ashtoreth. See Chapter XIX.

ADONIS: Greek. Stemming from DUMUZI/TAMMUZ/ADONI. See Chapter XIX. 777: Tarot: Sixes, Emperors or Princes, Hermit; gems: topaz, yellow diamond, peridot; plants: acacia, bay, laurel, vine, snowdrop, lily, narcissus; animals: phoenix, lion, child, virgin, anchorite, any solitary person or animal; perfumes: olibanum, narcissus; magical weapons: Lamen or Rosy Cross, Lamp and Wand, Bread.

AEACUS: Greek. Son of ZEUS and the nymph Aegina, and ruler of the island named after her. Father of PELEUS, Telemon and Phocus. The jealous Hera sent a plague against the island, and Aeacus appealed to Zeus for help. Zeus changed a colony of ants into men, the Myrmidons, who repopulated the island and fought successfully under Aeacus's grandson ACHILLES in the Trojan War. Because of his integrity, after his death Zeus made Aeacus one of the three judges of the Underworld. 777: Tarot: Justice; gem: emerald; plant: aloe; animal: elephant; perfume: galbanum; magical weapon: Cross of Equilibrium.

AEGIR: Scandinavian sea god. Accepted as equal by the AESIR, but not one of them; he seems to have been a pre-Nordic culture hero too firmly established to be forgotten or absorbed. He lived with his wife, Ran, 'the Ravisher', and their nine daughters on the Danish island of Hlesey – or in an underwater palace illuminated by the gold of sunken treasure. Ran stirred up the waves to capture ships, and the daughters held out seductive arms to tempt young sailors to their doom.

AENEAS: Roman. Son of Aphrodite by the mortal Anchises. He escaped from burning Troy with his father and son and, after wandering via Sicily, Carthage and the Underworld, reached Italy and founded the Roman nation. His story is told in Vergil's *Aeneid*.

AENGUS (ANGUS, OENGUS) MAC ÓG: Irish. The Young God of Love, son of the DAGDA and Boann, goddess of the River Boyne. 'Mac Óg' means 'son of the virgin' – in the old sense of an independent woman or goddess whose status is in her own right, not as a mere consort. Aengus tricked his father into possession of Brugh na Boinne (Newgrange). He repeatedly helped DIARMAID and Gráinne to escape the vengeance of FIONN MAC CUMHAL. He abducted Étain, the wife of MIDIR.

AEOLUS: Greek and Roman. Originally guardian, later father and in Roman mythology god, of the Winds, which he kept chained in deep caverns on the island of Lipara. Said to have invented sails. Son of POSEIDON and Arne. His wife was Gyane, daughter of King Liparus.

AESCULAPIUS – see ASCLEPIUS.

AESIR: Scandinavian. The fellow-gods of ODIN, living in Asgard. They seem to be a memory of actual invaders of Scandinavia, arriving soon after the VANIR, whom they first fought and then accepted as allies.

AESMA: Persian, Zoroastrian. A demon of wrath and vengeance, 'with a terrible spear'. The ASMODEUS of the Book of Tobit. Modern name Khasm.

AF: Egyptian. A form of RA in his nightly Underworld journey.

AGANJU: Nigerian, Yoruba tribe, and Brazilian Voodoo. Son of ODUDUA. His sister and wife Yemaja bore him the midday Sun god ORUNJAN and sixteen other gods, including OGUN, OKO, OLOKUN, SHANGO, SHANKPANNA, the Moon and several river goddesses.

AGAO: Haitian voodoo. The LOA of thunder.

AGAROU TONERRE: Haitian voodoo. Thunder god of the Sky Pantheon, associated with DAMBALLAH.

AGASSOU: Benin and Haitian voodoo. In Africa, panther god and divine ancestor of the royal house. In Haiti, guardian of customs and traditions, and god of springs. Said to be son of AGWE.

AGATHADAIMON: ('Good Spirit') Egyptian, Graeco-Roman period. A popular serpent-god of fortune at Alexandria. See also SHAI.

AGLOOLIK: Eskimo. Helps hunters to find game. He lives in a cave under the ice and is the tutelary spirit of seal caves.

AGNI: ('Fire') Hindu fire god. Son of sky god DYAUS and Earth goddess Prithvi. As ruler of the Earth, to which his lightning brought fertilizing rain, he was a benefactor of mankind. He formed a triad with INDRA (Air) and SURYA (Sky). Also a trinity in himself, said to have three bodies and three births: (1) as born of water, a calf who grew yearly to a bull; (2) as born of a fire-drill, a glutton with a fiery tongue; and (3) as born in highest Heaven, an eagle. One of the eight VASUS. His wife is sometimes the fire goddess Agnayi, sometimes his sister the dawn goddess Ushas. Horses used to be sacrificed to him annually. Said to be 'born in wood' or in the embryo of plants. 777: Tarot: Judgement, (Wands) Kings or Knights; gem: fire opal; plants: red poppy, hibiscus, nettle; animal: lion; mineral: nitrates; perfumes: olibanum, all fiery odours; magical weapons: Wand or Lamp, Pyramid of Fire.

AGWE: Haitian voodoo sea god, of major importance. His wife is the love and beauty goddess Erzulie in her sea aspect, La Sirene. In frequent conflict with war god OGUN because of his affairs with her.

AHI (1): Hindu. A serpent god killed by TRITA, or in later versions by INDRA.

AHI (2) – see IHY.

AHRIMAN, ANGRA MAINYU: ('Agonized or Negative Thought') Persian, Zoroastrian. Leader of the powers of evil, constantly at war with AHURA MAZDA (according to one version, his twin brother, their father being ZERVAN AKERANA). May have been a god (or goddess – the name is feminine in old Persian) of the early Persians, turned into a devil by their Indo-European conquerors. See pp.55-6.

AHSONNUTLI: Amerindian, Navajo. Bisexual divinity, known as the Turquoise Hermaphrodite. Believed to have created Heaven and Earth.

AHTO, AHTI: Finno-Ugric water god. His wife was the water goddess Vellamo. Overlaps with the hero LEMMINKÄINEN.

AHURA MAZDA ('Lord of Knowledge'), ORMAZD: Persian, Zoroastrian. Leader of the powers of good. Originally the god of the Achaemenian dynasty of kings (c.550-330 BC). Depicted as a bearded man with wings and a plumed body. The Asha (universal law) was born of him, and in one version the world was created from his body. See AHRIMAN.

AIPALOOKVIK: Eskimo. An evil spirit who lives in the sea and tries to bite and destroy boatmen.

AIZEN MYOO: Japanese Buddhist. One of the MYOOS, he has a ferocious face with three eyes, topped by a lion's head, but is full of compassion for mankind.

AJI-SUKI-TAKAHIKONE: Japanese thunder god, son of O-KUNI-NUSHI.

AKA-KANET: Chilean, Araucanian Indian. Grain and fruit god, presiding over harvest festivals. See also GUECUBU.

AKANCHOB: Mayan, Yucatan. Husband of goddess of birth Akna.

AKEN – see MAHAF.

AKER: Egyptian. An Earth god who faced both ways, like the Roman JANUS. Represented as the foreparts of two lions, joined together, each with a human head. He presided over the point where the eastern and western horizons of the Underworld met. He opened the gate to the Underworld, neutralized any snake or fly venom in those who passed him, and imprisoned the coils of the serpent APEP after Isis had cut him to pieces. His back supported RA's boat as it travelled from west to east during the night.

AKERBELTZ: ('Black He-Goat') Basque goat god. Invoked by Basque witches at their sabbats, which were known as Akelarre ('field of the he-goat').

AKSELLOAK: Eskimo. The spirit of rocking stones, considered benevolent.

AKSHOBHYA: Buddhist. One of the five DYANI-BUDDHAS. Coloured blue, riding an elephant and carrying a thunderbolt. Rules the East.

AKUPERA: Hindu. In Vedic myth, the tortoise whose back supports the Earth.

ALBERICH – see ANDVARI.

ALEION BAAL, ALEYIN, ALEYN: Phoenician. Son of Baal, or sometimes another name for him. God of spring, clouds, wind and rain. He gave water to crops and vegetation. With seven companions, he led a pack of wild animals, including eight wild boars.

ALEXIARES – see ANICERUS.

ALIGNAK, ANINGAN: Eskimo Moon god. He and his sister were originally human but were banished from the Earth for incest; he became the Moon and she the Sun.

ALLAH: Islamic. The supreme god of Moslem monotheism. Corresponds to YAHWEH: Mohammed regarded the Jewish and Christian god as being Allah, and Jesus as being a prophet of Allah, born of the Virgin Mary by Allah's will. He denied that Jesus was, or ever claimed to be, a god – or that Mary was, or that Jesus claimed her to be, a goddess. (See the Koran, Surahs 3:45-59 and 5:110-120). Jews and Christians, though erring, Mohammed called 'Children of the Scripture'.

ALL-FATHER: A title (in various languages) given to many gods – e.g. BAHLOO, ODIN.

ALPHAEUS: Greek. A Peloponnesan river god, who fell in love with the nymph Arethusa. Artemis turned her into a fountain to help her escape, but Alphaeus followed her underground to Sicily, where their waters mingled. One of the two rivers (the other being the PENEUS) which HERAKLES diverted to clean out the Augean Stables.

AMALIVACA: Venezuelan. Culture hero of the Orinoco River Indians, who taught them farming and the arts of life.

AMA-NO-MINAKANUSHI-NO-KAMI: ('Divine Lord of the Middle Heavens') Japanese. The supreme Heavenly deity.

AMATHAON: Welsh. A magician, son of the goddess Dôn, who taught his craft to his brother GWYDION. His theft of a dog and a roebuck from Annwn, the Otherworld, caused the Battle of the Trees between Gwydion and ARAWN, ruler of Annwn. 'Said to take his name from the Welsh word *amaeth*, a ploughman, but it may be the other way about: that ploughmen were under the patronage of the god Amathaon' (Graves, *The White Goddess*, p. 51).

AMATSU-MIKABOSHI ('August Star of Heaven'), AMA-NO-KAGASEO ('Brilliant Male'): Japanese god of evil.

AMBISAGRUS: Continental Celtic, equated by the Romans with JUPITER.

AMENHOTEP-SON-OF-HAPU: Egyptian. Like IMHOTEP, an historical character later deified for his wisdom. Chief scribe and architect to Amenhotep III (Eighteenth Dynasty, c. 1400 BC).

AME-NO-OSHIDO-MIMI: Japanese. Son of the Sun goddess Amaterasu, who wanted to send him to Earth to rule over it, but he took one look at its disturbed state and refused to go.

AME-NO-WAKAHIKO: Japanese. Renowned for his courage. Sent to Earth by the gods, he married a mortal woman, Shitateru-Hime, and ruled over the land. He was later killed by the anger of the god Taka-Mi-Musubi.

AMERETAT – see AMESHAS SPENTAS.

AMERGIN: Irish. The bard and spokesman of the Milesian (Gael) invaders of Ireland in the mythological cycle, and one of their leaders against the then occupiers, the Tuatha Dé Danann. Traditional author of the poem 'I am a stag of seven tines' (see p. 100). It was he who granted the wish of the three Tuatha queens, Éire, Fodhla and Banbha, daughters of the DAGDA, that Ireland be named after them. He is said to be buried under Millmount hill in Drogheda.

AMESHAS SPENTAS, AMESHASPENDS, THE: Persian, Zoroastrian. The Benign Immortals, powers of good under the command of ORMAZD, each with his special responsibility. They were Vohu-mano (Bahman), the Spirit of Good, presiding over useful animals; Asha-Vahishta (Arbidihist), Supreme Righteousness, governing fire; Khshthra-Vairya (Shahriiver), Ideal Dominion, making the Sun and heavens move and ruling metals; Spenta-Aramaiti (Sipendarmith), Benign Piety, presiding over the Earth; Haurvatat (Khordadh), Perfection, ruling the waters; and Ameretat (Mourdad) Immortality, ruling plant life.

AM-HEH: ('Devourer of Millions') Egyptian. A menacing Underworld god who dwelt in a lake of fire. Represented with the head of a hunting dog.

AMIDA: Japanese Buddhist version of AMITABHA.

AMITABHA. ('Infinite Light') or AMITAYUS ('Infinite Duration'): Buddhist. One of the five DHYANI-BUDDHAS. Coloured red, holding a lotus and escorted by a peacock. He reigns over the West and the wonderful paradise of Sukhavati and is the deity of happy rebirth prior to final deliverance. Called Amida in Japan.

AMOGHASIDDHI: Buddhist. One of the five DHYANI-BUDDHAS. Coloured green, carrying a double thunderbolt and riding an eagle. He presides over the North.

AMOR (1), CUPID: Roman. God of love, son of Venus. Equivalent of the Greek EROS.

AMOR (2), MARTU: Amorite. Chief god of that people of the mountain regions West of the Jordan. His wife was Ashirat, a Sun or Evening Star goddess.

AMUN-RA: Egyptian Sun god. See Chapter XXVII. 777: Tarot: Twos, Fours, Kings or Knights, Wheel of Fortune; gems: star ruby, turquoise, amethyst, sapphire, emerald; plants: amaranth, olive, shamrock, aloe; animals: man, unicorn, elephant; mineral: phosphorus; perfume: musk, cedar, saffron, all generous odours; magical weapons: Lingam, Inner Robe of Glory, Wand, Sceptre or Crook.

AMURRU: Phoenician god of the West.

AN: The Sumerian sky god, equivalent of the Assyro-Babylonian ANU.

ANANGA – see KAMA.

ANANSE: African, Ashanti. The spider who provided the material with which NYAME brought the first human beings to life, and who married Nyame's daughter. He acted as intermediary for mankind's complaints to Nyame and taught them farming.

ANATINA, ANATIWA: Brazilian, Karaya and Ges Indians. A malevolent being who caused the Flood, from which the ancestors of the Karayas escaped with the help of Saracura, the water hen.

ANDVARI, ALBERICH: Scandinavian. A dwarf, guardian of the treasures of the gods, including the Tarnkappe, garment of invisibility. He had the power to change himself into a fish; LOKI netted him and forced him to give up Draupnir, the magic ring of the AESIR, but Andvari put a curse on it first. His totem animal was the pike.

ANGRA MAINYU – see AHRIMAN.

ANGUS – see AENGUS.

ANHERT, ANHUR – see ONURIS.

ANINGAN – see ALIGNAK.

ANPU – see ANUBIS.

ANRA MAINYU – see AHRIMAN.

ANSA – see ADITYAS.

ANSAR, ANSHAR, ASSORUS: ('Host of Heaven') Babylonian sky god. His sister and wife was the Earth goddess Kishar. Their parents were LAKHAMU and Lakhmu. Kishar bore him the great gods ANU, EA (then called Nudimmud) and many others – the IGIGI and the ANUNNAKI. Ansar was later identified with the Assyrian ASSUR.

ANTAEUS: Greek. A giant, son of POSEIDON and Gaia. He forced strangers to wrestle with him and could not be beaten while touching the Earth. HERAKLES lifted him off the ground and strangled him.

ANU, ANUM: ('Sky') Assyro-Babylonian. Sky and supreme god, son of ANSAR and Kishar. Commanded the fight to control Tiamat, but from the sky, which he never left. With his companion the goddess Antu, he presided over the universe. Arbiter of the gods and goddesses, who addressed him as 'father'. Creator of the stars, who punished the wicked on his behalf. Also a Hittite sky god and equivalent of the Sumerian AN. Father by Anata of ENLIL (BEL) and in some versions of GIBIL and

NUSKU. (Do not confuse with Celtic goddess Anu.)

ANUBIS, ANPU, ANUP, WIP: Egyptian. Jackal-headed god presiding over embalming, the conducting of souls to the Underworld and the weighing of their hearts. Local god of Abydos. Son of OSIRIS (or, in another version, of SET) and Nephthys, he was adopted by Isis and became her guardian. He helped her restore the body of OSIRIS to life, after he had been murdered by SET. 777: Tarot: Eights, Moon, (Cups) Queens; gems: opal (especially fire opal), pearl; plants: moly, anhalonium lewinii, unicellular organisms, opium poppy; animals: jackal, hermaphrodite, fish, dolphin; mineral: mercury; perfumes: storax, ambergris; magical weapons: Names and Versicles and Apron, Twilight of the Place, Magic Mirror.

ANUNAKI, THE: Babylonian. Earth and Underworld gods, born of ANSAR and Kishar, or created by MARDUK at the same time as the Heavenly gods the IGIGI. They made up the assembly of gods over which ANU and ENLIL presided and decided the destiny of mankind. See also INIGI, THE.

ANZU – see ZU.

AO CH'IN, AO JUN, AO KUANG and AO SHUN – see DRAGON KINGS, THE.

APEDEMAK: Sudanese, Meroitic culture. Lion-headed war god. He had an important temple at Musawwarat, north of the Sixth Nile Cataract from about 300 BC to AD 500. Token animal the elephant. See also SEBIUMEKER.

APEP, APEPI, APOPHIS: Egyptian serpent god. See p.135. 777: Tarot: Death; gem: snakestone; plant: cactus; animals: scorpion, beetle, lobster or crayfish, wolf; perfume: Siamese benzoin, opoponax; magical weapon: Pain of the Obligation.

APIS: Egyptian. The sacred bull of the Serapeum at Saqqara, near Memphis – a succession of living bulls each in turn regarded as an incarnation of OSIRIS (or sometimes of PTAH). His actions were considered prophetic. Each new one was sought out as a calf by certain criteria, and his discovery occasioned public rejoicing; children born on that day were often named 'Apis-is-found'. Sixty-four mummified bulls were discovered at Saqqara in 1851.

APISIHARTS: Amerindian, Blackfoot. Morning Star (Venus) god.

APLU: Etruscan forerunner of APOLLO, surviving in Etruscan witchcraft.

APO: Persian. One of the YAZATAS, personifying water.

APOCATEQUIL: Inca. A lightning god and chief priest of the Moon god. Son of GUAMANSURI, first mortal to descend to Earth, and twin brother of PIGUERAO. He brought his mother to life again after she had been murdered by her brothers.

APOLLO: Greek and Roman. Son of ZEUS and Leto, and twin brother of Artemis, though a day younger. Born on the island of Delos. A god of the Sun, fertility, light and truth, medicine, music, poetry, fine arts and eloquence. With the advance of patriarchy, he absorbed several formerly goddess functions; for example, having slain the Python of Mount Parnassus, he took over the neighbouring shrine of Delphi (originally

Gaia's property), whose oracular priestesses, known as Pythonesses, became administered by male priests. He also took control of the nine Muses (originally three, a Triple Goddess of Inspiration). Father of ASCLEPIUS by Coronis, of ARISTAEUS by Cyrene and of ORPHEUS by Calliope. His attributes were the lyre and bow, and the laurel tree was sacred to him. 777: Tarot: Sixes, Emperors or Princes, Temperance, Sun; gems: topaz, yellow diamond, jacinth, crysoleth; plants: acacia, bay, laurel, vine, rush, sunflower, heliotrope; animals: phoenix, lion, child, centaur, horse, hippogriff, dog, lion, sparrowhawk; perfumes: olibanum, lign-aloes, cinnamom, all glorious odours; magical weapons: Lamen or Rosy Cross, Arrow, Lamen or Bow and Arrow. (As Charioteer) Tarot: Chariot; gem: amber; plant: lotus; animals: crab, turtle, sphinx; perfume: onycha; magical weapon: Furnace. (As Diviner) Tarot: Lovers; gems: alexandrite, tourmaline, Iceland spar; plants: hybrids, orchids; animals: magpie, hybrids; perfume: wormwood; magical weapon: Tripod.

APOPHIS – see APEP.

APSU: Assyro-Babylonian sweet-water god who, with his mate Tiamat, the sea-water goddess, begat the original chaotic world. In the fight against Apsu and Tiamat, the god of wisdom and water EA gained control of Apsu. Originally a goddess, identical with Tiamat.

AQAS-XENA-XENAS: Amerindian, Chinook. Boy hero who climbed a chain shot by an arrow, reached the Evening Star and married her daughter the Moon. He then took part in a war between these two and the Morning Star and its daughter the Sun.

AQUILO: Roman. God of the North Wind, equivalent of the Greek BOREAS.

ARALLU, THE – see UTUKKU, THE.

ARAWN: Welsh. King of Annwn, the Otherworld. He fought the Battle of the Trees against AMATHAON and GWYDION, sons of the goddess Dôn. He rode a pale horse, leading a pack of white hounds with red ears in pursuit of a stag. ARTHUR stole a magic cauldron from him.

ARCAS: Greek. Son of ZEUS and Callisto, who gave his name to Arcadia. Zeus raised him to Heaven as the star Arcturus, and his mother as the Great Bear constellation, to escape Hera's anger.

ARCHER, THE EXCELLENT: Chinese. Also called I. Possessed the drink of immortality. His wife Ch'ang-o stole it from him and fled to the Moon to escape his anger.

ARCHONS: Manichaean. The Sons of the Dark who swallowed up the bright elements of primal man.

ARDHANARISVARA: Hindu. A strange representation of SHIVA as half god, half woman; nevertheless regarded solely as an aspect of Shiva, with his essential energy manifesting in a feminine mode.

ARES: Greek god of war and violence. See Chapter VI. 777 Tarot: Fives, Death, Tower; gems: ruby, snakestone, any red stone; plants: oak, nux vomica, nettle, cactus, absinthe, rue; animals: basilisk, scorpion, beetle, lobster or crayfish, wolf, horse, bear; minerals: iron, sulphur; perfumes: tobacco, Siamese benzoin, opoponax, pepper, dragon's blood, all hot pungent odours; magical weapons: Sword, Spear, Scourge or Chain, Pain of the Obligation.

ARIKUTE – see TAWENDUARE.

ARISTAEUS: ('The Very Good') Greek. Son of APOLLO and the nymph Cyrene, or of URANUS and Gaia. Originally an important PAN-type god of Thessaly. Like Apollo, was brought up by the centaur CHIRON, who taught him medicine and soothsaying. Protector of flocks and agriculture, especially of the vine and olive. Said to have invented bee-keeping.

ARJUNA: Hindu. Friend of INDRA from boyhood. His debate with Indra on the morality of war (which Arjuna questioned) is the theme of the *Bhagavad Gita*.

ARTHUR: Greatest of the British Celtic legendary heroes; based on the almost certainly historical Artorius, a *Dux Bellorum* ('Leader of Battles', commander-in-chief) who led the Britons against the Saxon invaders after the withdrawal of the Roman legions. More archetypal legends have attached themselves to him than to any other historical British figure. (He may, for example, have absorbed many which earlier belonged to GWYDION.) Most of the Arthurian stories familiar today are medieval Christianizations of much older Celtic myths. The legendary Arthur was the son of King Uther Pendragon and Igraine, Duchess of Cornwall, adulterously conceived when MERLIN'S magic enabled Arthur to take the visible form of the Duke. Merlin raised him, and he claimed the throne at the age of fifteen on Uther's death by being the only one able to draw the sword Excalibur from its stone. His wife was Gwynhwyfar (Guinevere) who can be seen to embody an earlier Triple Goddess concept. He was mortally wounded in battle with the rebellious Mordred, his son by his sorceress sister Morgan le Fay, and was carried dying to Avalon (Glastonbury) – again, significantly, by three mysterious women. A typical saviour figure, as 'the once and future king', who will return at the hour of his country's need.

ASAR-HAP – see SERAPIS.

ASCLEPIUS: Greek god of healing and medicine. Known to the Romans as Aesculapius. Son of APOLLO and Coronis. He was brought up by the centaur CHIRON, who taught him the arts of healing; he became a skilled physician, even bringing the dead to life. This was leaving the Underworld underpopulated, so ZEUS killed him with a thunderbolt. In due time he became a god. Father of Hygeia, goddess of health. His symbol was the snake. His sanctuaries were places both of worship and of medical treatment.

ASGAYA-GIGAGEI: Amerindian, Cherokee. Bisexual thunder god, known as the Red Man or Red Woman.

ASH: Egyptian god of the Western Desert, including its fertile oases. Normally human-headed, sometimes hawk-headed, sometimes three-headed – lion, snake and vulture. Apparently the original god of Ombos (Nebut) in Upper Egypt (near the modern Qena) before SET took over that role.

ASHA, ASHA-VAHISHTA – see AMESHAS SPENTAS.

ASHI-NADZUCHI: Japanese Earth god. His wife was the Earth goddess Tenazuchi-no-Kami.

ASIA-BUSSU – see NYAMIA.

ASK, ASKR: ('Ash') The Scandinavian Adam. His Eve was Embla ('Vine'). After the Flood, the gods ODIN, HOENIR and LODUR made them out of lifeless tree-trunks, in his case from an ash tree.

ASMODEUS: Hebrew. Possibly from Aesmadaeva, 'Furry demon'. In the Talmud, king of the Shedin demons. His story in the Book of Tobit comes from a Median, and ultimately from a Persian, one – see AESMA.

ASOPUS: Greek. A river god of Boeotia, also found in Thessaly and the Peloponnese. His wife was Merope. Their daughter Aegina was ravished by ZEUS.

ASSORUS – see ANSAR.

ASSUR, ASSHUR: Assyrian supreme god, taking the place of MARDUK and identifying with the Babylonian ANSHAR. Primarily a war but also a fertility god. Originally a war and Moon god of the city of the same name. In later versions his wife was the Chaldaean and Sumerian grain goddess Ninlil; also named as a husband of Ishtar. Usually portrayed as a winged disc, but sometimes in human form riding a bull. His emblem, a god in a horned cap using a bow and arrow, was the Assyrian battle standard, and he was the patron of soldiers. As a fertility god, his emblem was a female goat.

ASTRAEUS: Greek. Titan, son of Crius and Eurybia, and first husband of the dawn goddess Eos, who bore him the four winds BOREAS (North), ZEPHYRUS (West), EURUS (East) and NOTUS (South), and, according to some versions, Astraea, goddess of justice and purity. Also said to be the father of the stars.

ASURAS, THE: Hindu. Powerful negative beings, in contrast to the positive DEVAS. See p.103)

ASVINS, THE – see NASATYAS, THE.

ATAKSAK: Eskimo god of joy. He lives in Heaven and looks like a sphere, wearing shining cords.

ATAOKOLOINONA – see NORIANANAHARY.

ATAR (1): Persian. In Zoroastrian myth, son of AHURA MAZDA, and one of the YAZATAS. Genius of fire, protector of the Earth against evil, and bringer of gifts to mankind. The ninth month and the ninth day of each month were named after him.

ATAR (2): Phoenician. Son of EL and Asherah, chosen to rule the world for a time after BAAL had been killed by MOT. Known as 'the Terrible', Overlaps with ATTER.

ATATARHO: Amerindian, Iroquois. A culture hero who always wore a garment of living snakes to symbolize his powers as a warrior and a magician.

ATEN, ATON: Egyptian. A name given to the Sun's disc; see p.134).

ATHAR: Southern Arabian. Masculinization of Ishtar on the upsurge of patriarchy.

ATHTAR: Phoenician. Originally god of the star Venus, also associated with vegetation. Appealed to by the goddess Anat after the death of BAAL.

ATIUS-TIRAWA – see TIRAWA.

ATLAS: Phoenician and Greek. Son of URANUS and Gaia; in other versions, of IAPETUS by Clymene or Asia. After the war with the Titans, in which Atlas sided with the rebels, ZEUS punished him by ordering him to stand at the western end of the world and support the sky on his shoulders. In Phoenician tradition, brother of Astarte, BAITULOS, DAGON, EL, PONTUS and ZEUS DEMAROS, and in Greek tradition of PROMETHEUS and EPIMETHEUS. Father, by Pleione or Aethra, of the Pleiades, the Hyades and the Hesperides, and of Maia (mother by Zeus of HERMES), DARDANUS, Electra and Taygete; and, in one version, of the nymph-sorceress Calypso.

ATLI: ('Grandfather') Scandinavian. The name of Attila, King of the Huns, in Scandinavian legend. In the Volsung Saga, he is Brynhild's brother and Gudrun's second husband. He fought and killed Gudrun's brothers for the treasures of Nibelungen, and she killed him in revenge. Sometimes also a name for THOR. Called Etzel in the Niberlungenlied.

ATMU – see ATUM

ATON – see ATEN

ATRI: Hindu. Son of Brahma, noted for his wisdom.

ATTER: Northern Semitic. Male war god. His female counterpart was Attar. Both were associated with the planet Venus.

ATTILA – see ATLI.

ATTIS, ATYS: Anatolian vegetation god, lover of the Earth, mountain and wild beast goddess Cybele. When he planned to marry a king's daughter, Cybele turned him insane, and he castrated himself, gave her his genitals and died, being later restored to life. (Cybele's priests, the Corybantes, often worked themselves into a frenzy and castrated themselves in her honour.) The rituals of Cybele and Attis, mourning his death and then celebrating his resurrection, reflect the archetypal Earth-goddess and sacrificed vegetation god theme (see Chapter V), paralleling those of Ishtar/Astarte/Aphrodite and DUMUZI/TAMMUZ/ADONIS, though in a more savage and frenetic manner than they. The Cybele/Attis cult spread into Greece, though mainly among Phrygian slaves, and to some extent into the Roman Empire, where it survived until Christianity became officially imposed. 777: Tarot: Hermit; gem: peridot; plants: snowdrop, lily, narcissus; animals: virgin, anchorite, any solitary animal or person; perfume: narcissus; magical weapons: Lamp and Wand, Bread.

ATUM, ATMU, TEM: Egyptian. Predynastic Sun god of Heliopolis, with two wives, Nebhet Hotep and Iusas. Later identified with RA, especially as the setting Sun (Atum-Ra). See also ATEN.

ATYS – see ATTIS

AUAHI-TUROA: Australian Aborigine. Culture hero who brought fire to mankind.

AUGUST PERSONAGE OF JADE – see JADE.

AULANERK: Eskimo. He lives naked in the sea and struggles, causing the waves. Regarded as beneficent.

AUMANIL: Eskimo. Lives on land and guides whales.

AUSTER: Roman. God of the South Wind, corresponding to the Greek NOTUS.

AVAGDU: Welsh. Son of Cerridwen and TEGID. He was the ugliest boy in the world, and his sister Creirwy was the most beautiful girl.

AVALOKITESVARA, PADMAPANI: Indian Buddhist. A DHYANI-BODHISATTVA. Gifted with complete Enlightenment, he remained in this world for the salvation of mankind and animals. No sufferer appeals to him in vain. Portrayed holding a pink lotus and with an image of AMITABHA bound in his hair.

AVANC – see ADDANC.

AWHIOWHIO: Australian Aborigine god of whirlwinds.

AWONAWILONA: Amerindian, Pueblo and Zunni. He created the Earth and the sky from a green scum on the waters of the Deluge, by causing the Sun to shine on it.

AWUN: Formosan. God of destruction.

AZAZIL: Islamic devil who refused to prostrate himself before Allah after the creation of Adam. Condemned to death, but the sentence postponed to the Day of Judgement. May have been a pre-Hebrew and pre-Islamic goat god.

AZIDAHAKA: Persian, Zoroastrian. Serpent demon who cut YIMA, the first mortal, in two.

AZRAEL: Islamic angel of death. (But see also reference to him on p.59.)

BAAL: ('Lord') Phoenician fertility, vegetation and storm god. See Chapter V. Baal was also a general name for a god, as Baalat (Belet, Belit, Beltis), 'Lady', was for a goddess.

BAAL-HAMMON: Carthaginian. His consort was Tanit, and their names suggest a common source with the Irish BALOR and Dana and the Welsh BELI and Dôn.

BABBAR: Sumerian. An early Sun god of Larsa.

BABI: Egyptian. A fierce baboon god, dangerous but also representing the warlike aspirations of the Pharaoh, and virility; his phallus is the bolt on the door of Heaven, and also the mast of the Underworld ferryboat. Spells were needed against him, as he lived on human entrails, but he could also be invoked against snakes and rough waters.

BACABS, THE: Mayan deities of the four cardinal points, supporting the four corners of the Earth, and of agriculture, rain and fertility. They were Mulac (North, white), Kan (East, yellow), Cauac (South, red) and Ix (West, black). Similarities to HORUS, FOUR SONS OF.

BACCHUS: Roman god of wine. Greek equivalent DIONYSUS. 777: Tarot: Devil; gem: black diamond; plants: Indian hemp, orchis root, thistle; animals: goat, ass; perfumes: musk, civet; magical weapons: Secret Force, Lamp.

BACKLUM-CHAAM: Mayan equivalent of PRIAPUS.

BADÉ, BADESSY: Haitian voodoo, African (Benin) origin. Sky and wind god. Associated with DAMBALLAH. Son of the twins MAWU-LISA and brother of SOBO.

BADUH: Semitic. Patron of messages, ensuring their speedy transmission. Invoked by writing the numerals 8, 6, 4, 2, representing his name in Arabic. This custom still common in Egypt and Iran within living memory.

BAHLOO: Australian Aborigine. All-Father, created by Yhi, the Sun and Mother goddess. Together they created animals and mankind.

BAIAME, B-IAME: Australian Aborigine. Moon god, mischievous but unmalicious. Usually represented as the lover of Yhi, the Sun goddess, and enemy of DARAWIGAL, the force of evil.

BALARAMA: Hindu. An avatar of VISHNU as the fair-haired twin brother of KRISHNA. See also SHESHA.

BALDUR: Scandinavian Sun god of goodness and wisdom. Son of ODIN and Freya, and husband of Nanna, who bore him FORSETI. Loved by all except LOKI, who brought about his death (see p.117). Nanna committed suicide on his funeral pyre. Associated with the zodiacal sign Gemini.

BALOR: Irish. The Old God who appears in legend as king of the Fomors. Husband of Dana or Ceithlenn, father of Eithne and thus grandfather of LUGH, the bright Young God who supplanted him. Had a poisoned eye which could slay with its glance; it took four men to raise his eyelid in battle. At the Second Battle of Magh Tuireadh (Moytura), Lugh killed him by hurling a slingstone into his great eye. Welsh equivalent BELI.

BANEBDJEDET, BANADED, BINDED: Egyptian. Ram god of the North-East Delta. Worshipped with his consort, the fish goddess Hatmehyt (originally more important than he).

BANNIK: Slavonic. Domestic spirit of the washhouse, who had to be propitiated but who could be questioned about the future.

BARON CIMITIÈRE: Haitian voodoo god of cemeteries.

BARON PIQUANT: Haitian voodoo. Similar to BARON CIMITIÈRE; master of magic.

BARON SAMEDI, GHEDI: Haitian voodoo. God of death, eroticism and resurrection.

BASSO-JAUN: Basque. A woodland god living in the deepest forests or in caves.

BA-TAU – see HEY-TAU.

BEGOCHIDDY: Amerindian. The great god of the Navajos.

BEL: ('Lord') Assyro-Babylonian, originally Sumerian. Identified with ENLIL and with MARDUK. His wife was Beltis/Belit ('Lady'), or in some versions the Chaldaean Earth and war goddess Esharra.

BELI: Welsh Father god, husband of Dôn, father of Arianrhod and grandfather of LLEU LLAW GYFFES. Irish equivalent BALOR.

BELIAL, BELIY YA'AL: ('Worthlessness') Hebrew name for the Devil or the Underworld.

BES: Egyptian. Protector of women in pregnancy and childbirth, associated with the goddess Tuaret. Of dwarfish and grotesque appearance but benevolent, especially to married couples and their children. A popular god throughout the eastern Mediterranean, fond of merrymaking and music and with erotic overtones. Seems to have been Babylonian in origin, coming to Egypt in the Eighteenth Dynasty (c.1400-1300 BC).

BHAGA: Hindu. One of the ADITYAS. In the dispute between SHIVA and DAKSHA, Bhaga was blinded by the monster Virabhadra which Shiva had created.

BHRIGUS, THE: ('Shining Ones') Hindu. Aerial storm gods, intermediate between Earth and Heaven.

B-IAME – see BAIAME.

BIELBOG – see BYELBOG.

BILE: Alternative name for BELI, in his capacity as ruler of the Underworld.

BIMBO-GAMI: Japanese god of poverty.

BIRAL – see BUNJIL.

BISHAMON, TAMON: Japanese god of war and good luck. Guardian of the North. One of the SHICHI FUKUJIN and of the SHI TENNO.

BITH: In Irish legend, son of Noah and father of Cesara, the first occupier of Ireland. His wife was Birren.

BLOOD-CLOT: Amerindian.

BN-YM – see KHOSER-ET-HASIS.

BO: Benin, Ewe peoples. Protector of those engaged in war. His priests carried axes bound round with sticks, symbols of thunder and lightning, very like the *fasces* borne by Roman lictors.

BOCHICA: Colombian. Civilizing hero and solar god who taught the Chibchas building, agriculture and the arts and gave them laws and a calendar with solar festivals. He banished his beautiful but mischievous wife Chia to the sky, where she became the Moon goddess. He defeated the demon Chibchacum and sentenced him to bear the Earth on his shoulders; earthquakes are Chibchacum shifting his burden. Bochica's civilizing mission completed, he handed over power to two chiefs, spent another 2,000 years on Earth as an ascetic, then ascended to Heaven as a dawn or Morning Star god.

BOG: A general Slavonic word for a god, from the Persian *bagi* and the Sanskrit *bhaga*, indicating richness and power; e.g. BYELBOG, CHERNOBOG.

BOLTHORN: Scandinavian giant, grandfather of ODIN.

BONUS EVENTUS: ('Good Outcome') Roman. An ancient god of agriculture and good luck.

BOR: Scandinavian. Son of BUR, and father by Bestla (daughter of BOLTHORN) of ODIN, Vili and Ve.

BOREAS: Greek god of the North Wind. Son, with the other three Winds (see EURUS, NOTUS, ZEPHYRUS), of the Titan ASTRAEUS and the dawn goddess Eos. His wife was Orithyia.

BORMANUS: An early Continental Celtic god.

BORVO: ('To boil') Continental Celtic god of hot springs, in which role he replaced Sirona (Dirona), said to be his mother. Equated by Romans with APOLLO. May be the same as Borve in the LLYR legend.

BOSSU: Haitian voodoo. A family of spirits, most of them malevolent.

BRAGI: Scandinavian. God of wisdom and poetry, son of ODIN and Freya, and husband of Iduna, goddess of Spring and youth.

BRAHMA: Hindu. In Bengal he is seen as the son of Kali and brother of SHIVA and VISHNU. In other versions, son of Prakriti, the world womb from which all springs. Or born from Narayana, a golden egg floating upon the waters. He was said to have divided himself into a male half, called Purusha or Skambha, and a female half, called Satarupa. His wife, born of his body, is Sarasvati, goddess of speech, music, wisdom, knowledge of the arts. Another named wife is Teeree, who gave birth by him to an egg, one half of which formed the celestial beings, the other mankind and all Earth creatures. Usually portrayed with four faces and four arms, seated on a lotus throne. One of the Trimuri. Brahma is the latecomer to Vedic religion and has remained a theological concept rather than a popular diety. See p.102. 777: Tarot: Fours, Wheel of Fortune; gems: amethyst, sapphire, lapis lazuli; plants: olive, shamrock, hyssop, oak, poplar, fig; animals: unicorn, eagle; perfumes: cedar, saffron, all generous odours; magical weapons: Wand, Sceptre or Crook.

BRAMBRAMBULT: Australian Aborigine. A pair of heroic brothers who went to Heaven as Alpha and Beta Centauri, while their mother, Dok, became Alpha of the Southern Cross.

BRAN: Manx/Welsh. Son of LLYR and Iweridd and brother of Branwen, who was ill-treated by her husband, Matholwch, King of Ireland. Bran set out with an army of the men of Britain to avenge her; they defeated the Irish but Bran was mortally wounded. Branwen and his friends took his head to Harlech for seven years, where it continued to talk with them, then for eighty years to Gwales (Grassholm?) in Penvro (Pembrokeshire?) and finally to London, to bury it on the White Hill (either Tower Hill or where St Paul's now stands). He is known as Bendigeidfran, 'Bran the Blessed'.

BRES: Irish. Son of a Fomorian father and a Tuatha Dé Danann mother, he was married to Brighid (Bríd), daughter of the DAGDA, in a dynastic alliance. He became king of the Tuatha but lacked the necessary qualities of generosity and lost his title when he was satirized by the bard Cairbre and boils appeared on his face. This led to renewed war between the Fomorians and the Tuatha and to the latter's victory at the Second Battle of Magh Tuireadh (Moytura). (See also BALOR.)

BRIAN – see IUCHAR.

BRIHASPATI: Hindu. Teacher of the gods. Identified with the planet Jupiter. His wife is the star goddess Tara.

BRIMOS: Greek. Known from the cry in the Eleusinian rituals: 'The noble goddess has born a sacred child: Brimo has borne Brimos.'

BROUERIUS – see HECATONCHEIRES.

BUDDHA, THE: Indian. Human founder of the Buddhist religion, virtually deified in later popular Buddhism but not by its serious thinkers, who know this is incompatible with his message. He was born about 560 BC to a princely family of the Sakyas, who ruled parts of Nepal and Oudh. His legend says that his mother, Queen Maya, conceived him miraculously, experiencing a vision of him entering her womb as a tiny snow-white elephant; at this moment the Earth showed its joy by such miracles as musical instruments playing themselves and trees being suddenly covered in blossom. Maya gave birth to him from her right side, without pain, standing in a garden, and seven days later died of joy. Siddhartha, as the young prince was called, was brought up by Maya's devoted sister, Mahaprajapati. He married the princess Yasodhara and at first was content with the joys of life at his father's Court. But realization of what life was like to the unprivileged inspired a desire for asceticism. At the age of twenty-nine he left his wife and their little son Rahula and became a wandering monk under the new name of Gautama. Six years later, sitting in contemplation under the Bodhi Tree, he received enlightenment and became the Buddha, 'Enlightened One'. For forty-five years, until his death, he taught his Noble Eightfold Path, often called the Middle Path because it avoids both bodily indulgence and asceticism. He taught that a soul must reincarnate repeatedly till it is perfect enough for Nirvana, reabsorption into the divine essence. Hinduism named the Buddha as the ninth avatar of VISHNU, as a compromise between the two faiths. 777: Tarot: Sixes, Emperors or Princes; gems: topaz, yellow diamond; plants: acacia, bay, laurel, vine; animals: phoenix, lion, child; perfume: olibanum; magical weapon: Lamen or Rosy Cross.

BUDHA: Hindu, considered the founder of the lunar dynasties. Said to be radiant with power and beauty. Son of the star goddess Tara through her abduction by the Moon god SOMA; BRAHMA compelled him to release her, but she was already pregnant with Budha.

BUMBA: Congo, Bushongo tribe. He created the universe by vomiting forth the Sun, Moon and stars, and eight species of animal from which all others are descended. He also gave laws to mankind.

BUNJIL: Australian Aborigine, Kulin and Wotjobaluk tribes. He gave life to the twin Eves Kunnawarra ('Black Swan') and Kuururuk ('Native Companion'). 'You are to live with men,' he told them. 'Man is not complete without you, nor will you be complete without him.' Another version is that he formed the first two men from clay, and his brother or son found the first two women at the bottom of a lake. He taught mankind farming and hunting and established tribal rituals. Known as Biral in the Northern Territory, Nurrundere on the Murray River, Pun-Gel in Victoria.

BUR, BURI: Scandinavian first man, father of BOR and grandfather of ODIN.

BURIASH: Kassite storm god, similar to HADAD and TESHUB.

BUSSUMARUS: ('Large-lipped') Continental Celtic, identified by the Romans with Jupiter.

BYELBOG, BIELBOG: ('White God') Slavonic god of light, day and good fortune. Guardian of forest travellers. His opposite was CHERNOBOG ('Black God').

CABEIRI, THE: Greek minor underground smith gods, said to be sons of HEPHAESTUS. Originally underground spirits of Phrygia.

CADMUS: Greek. Son of Agenor (son of POSEIDON) and Telephassa, and brother of Europa. Builder and first king of Thebes. Said to have given the Greeks their alphabet. He was allowed to marry ZEUS's daughter Harmonia. She brought him a divine dowry, including a necklace made by HEPHAESTUS containing irresistible love-charms. They eventually left Thebes and became king and queen of Illyria, turning into great serpents – i.e. they were identified with Illyrian snake-deities.

CAGN – see KAGGEN.

CAIPRE – see OGHMA.

CAMAXTLI, XIPE: Aztec, a war god of Tlaxcala. Overlaps with MIXCOATL.

CAMAZOTZ: Guatemalan, Quiche Indians. A bat god, defeated in battle with HUN-APUT. Same as Mayan ZOTZILAHA CHIMALMAN.

CAMULOS: Irish. A king of the Tuatha Dé Danann, fused with some earlier god; he may have been Cumhal, warrior king father of FIONN, and original of King Cole of the nursery rhyme.

CARADOC, CARADAWG (1): Welsh. Son of LLYR. Known as 'Strong Arm'. According to the *Mabinogion*, first cousin and chief adviser of ARTHUR.

CARADOC, CARADAWG (2): Welsh. Son of BRAN. May perhaps be identified with the historical Caratacus (Caractacus), chief of the Silures, who spent some time as a captive in Rome.

CARREFOUR – see MAIT' CARREFOUR.

CASTOR and POLLUX: Greek and Roman (though the Romans called Pollux Polydeuces). Castor was the son of Tyndareus, King of Sparta, and his wife Leda, who also bore him Clytemnestra; these two were mortal. But ZEUS, in the form of a swan, seduced Leda, fathering Pollux and Helen (cause of the Trojan War), who were immortal. Nevertheless, Castor and Pollux became known as Dioscuri, 'Sons of Zeus'. They sailed with the Argonauts. When Castor was killed, Zeus enabled the brothers to be united as the constellation Gemini. Another version had them spending alternate days in the Underworld and on Earth. 777: Tarot: Lovers; gems: alexandrite, tourmaline, Iceland spar; plants: hybrids, orchids; animals: magpie, hybrids; perfume: wormwood; magical weapon: Tripod.

CASWALLAWN: Welsh. In legend, son of BELI; he usurped the kingdom of Britain and dispossessed the sons of LLYR. Historically, leader of the Catuvelauni who opposed Julius Caesar in 54 BC, better known as Cassivelaunus.

CATEQUIL: Incan god of lightning and thunder, to whom children were sacrificed.

CAUAC – see BACABS, THE.

CENN CRUAICH – see CROM CRUAICH.

CENTAURS: ('Those Who Round Up Bulls') Greek. Originally portrayed as hairy giants, they became creatures with the body of a horse and the torso, arms and head of a man. Their ancestor was IXION of Thessaly, son of ARES, who had the temerity to desire Hera. Zeus tricked him by forming a cloud in Hera's likeness, with which Ixion mated to produce Centaurus, who in turn mated with the mares of Pelion to found the race of Centaurs. Probably a memory of the pre-Dorian Greeks' first traumatic sight of horse-riding invaders. The most famous Centaur was the wise CHIRON.

CENTIMANES – see HECATONCHEIRES.

CENTZON HUITZNAUA: ('400 Southerners') Aztec star gods of the South.

CENTZON MIMIXCOA: ('400 Northerners') Aztec star gods of the North.

CERBERUS: Greek. The three-headed dog who guarded the entrance to the Underworld to keep out the living. Son of TYPHON and the snake-woman Echidna. Among the few who succeeded in tricking him were AENEAS, ORPHEUS, ODYSSEUS and HERAKLES.

CERNUNNOS: The only known name of the Celtic Horned God. The name appears only on the altar of Nautes, now in the Cluny Museum in Paris, but many other representations (such as on the Gundestrup Cauldron) are clearly of the same god. See Chapter XXI.

CHAC, CHAC-MOOL: Mayan. A rain and thunder god who became a personification of the four BACABS. Equivalent to the Aztec TLALOC.

CHALCHIUHTOTOLIN: ('Jewelled Fowl') Aztec. Variant of TEZCATLIPOCA.

CHANDRA: ('Moon') Hindu. One of the VASUS. Produced at the Churning of the Ocean. Probably a pre-Vedic Moon god. Husband of the cow-goddess Rohini. 777: Tarot: High Priestess; gems: moonstone, pearl, crystal; plants: almond, mugwort, hazel, moonwort, ranunculus; animal: dog; perfumes: menstrual blood, camphor, aloes, all sweet virginal odours; magical weapons: Bow and Arrow.

CHAOS: Greek. Personification of the limitless void out of which the universe emerged. Husband of Nyx ('Night') and father of EREBUS, though other versions have these two as brother and sister.

CHAQUEN: Colombian. Chibcha Indian god of boundaries.

CHARON: Greek. Son of EREBUS and his sister (? – see CHAOS above) Nyx ('Night'). Ferryman of the dead across the River Styx into the Underworld.

CHARUN – see VANTH.

CHEIRON – see CHIRON.

CHEMOSH: Moabite war god, the SHAMASH of the Babylonians.

CHENG-HUANG: Chinese. Protective god of walls and ditches; each locality has its own Cheng-huang.

CHERNOBOG, CZARNOBOG: ('Black God') Slavonic god of darkness and evil, counterpart of BYELOBOG ('White God').

CHERUBIM: Hebrew. An order of angels usually below the SERAPHIM. Formidable winged beings quite unlike the 'cherubs' of European art. Described in Ezekiel i and x. Cherubim of beaten gold protected the Mercy Seat (Exodus xxv:18-20). Equivalent of the Assyrian Kherubu.

CHESED, GEDULAH: ('Mercy') The Kindly Ruler, fourth Sephira of the Cabalistic Tree of Life. The JUPITER sphere. Takes the forms manifested by Binah (see under CHOKMAH) and administers for and governs them. The anabolic process, compared with the katabolic process of GEBURAH. Cabalistic symbols: Solid Figure, Tetrahedon, Pyramid, Equal-armed Cross, Orb, Wand, Sceptre, Crook. Tarot: Fours. Magical image: a mighty crowned and throned king.

CHIBCHCACUM – see BOCHICA.

CHIMATA-NO-KAMI: Japanese god of crossroads.

CHIMINIGAGUA: South American, Chibcha. Creator god who set the light free from within himself to banish the primordial darkness and created blackbirds to carry it over the Earth.

CHIN. Yucatan Mayan god of vice.

CHINIGCHINICH: Amerindian, California, Acagchemem tribe. A god, portrayed as a coyote, to whom a bird was sacrificed annually, to bring back to life a woman, Chinigchinich, once turned into a bird.

CH'IN SHU-PAO – see YU CH'IH CHING-TE.

CHIQUINAU: Nicaraguan god of air and the nine winds.

CHIRON, CHEIRON: Greek. The wise CENTAUR, son of CRONUS and Philyra.

CHOKMAH: ('Wisdom') The Supernal Father, second Sephira of the Cabalistic Tree of Life. Raw directionless energy, the first manifestation of KETHER, the first Sephira, which is pure existence. The fertilizing energy of Chokmah is taken by Binah, the Supernal Mother (Third Sephira) and given form and boundaries. The Yod of the TETRAGRAMMATON, in polarity with the first Heh, Binah. He represents the male potency of the cosmos, as Binah represents the female. Cabalistic symbols: Lingam, Phallus, Inner Robe of Glory, Standing Stone, Tower, Uplifted Rod of Power, Straight Line. Tarot: Twos. Magical image: a bearded male figure.

CHONCHONYL: Chilean, Araucanian Indian. Human-headed, with wings for ears. Kills sick people and sucks their blood.

CHRIST: ('Anointed One') Christian. Deified form of Jesus (Yeshue), a great Hebrew teacher and healer of the First century AD. Jesus himself would certainly have regarded such deification as blasphemous; see p.52. The story of his Virgin Birth was added later (in two Gospels only) to tally with other divine-impregnation births; whatever one's views of his Crucifixion and Resurrection, they do reflect the archetypal Sacrificed God theme – see Chapter X. In the Christian concept of a divine Trinity, Christ is the Son element. The fact that Christ is based on a historical human (like so many other god-forms) does not necessarily invalidate the effectiveness of the god-form itself.

CHUN – see VIRACOCHA.

CIAGA: Nicaraguan. A little water god who took part in creation.

CIAN: Irish. Son of DIANCHECHT, and father by Eithne of LUGH. May be equated with MacKINELY.

CILENS: Etruscan. Guardian of gates. Roman equivalent SUMMANUS.

CINTEOTL, XOCHIPILI: Aztec maize god. Son of love and fertility goddess Tlazolteotl, who was also called Teteoinian, 'Mother of God'. Lord of the fourth hour of the night. May originally have been a maize goddess.

COCIDIUS – see SEGOMO.

COEM: Brazilian, Tupi-Guarani tribes. He and his brothers Hermitten and Krimen escaped the Deluge by climbing trees or hiding in caves.

COEUS, COEIUS: Greek. Titan, father by Phoebe of the orgiastic goddess Leto, and grandfather of APOLLO and Artemis.

COLO-COLO: ('Basilisk') Chilean, Araucanian Indian. Born from a cock's egg. Causes fever and death by sucking the victim's saliva.

CONSUS: Roman. Earth god of grain and harvest. His festival, the Consualia, was celebrated twice yearly, after the sowing and after the harvest.

COTI – see KAGGEN.

COTTUS – see HECATONCHEIRES.

COXCOXTLI: The Aztec Noah. His wife was Xochiquetzal, and their 'Mount Ararat' was Colhuacan. Elements of the Babel story too: till the Flood, there was only one language, but afterwards there were many, mutually incomprehensible.

COXINGA: A seventeenth-century Chinese, born of a Japanese mother, and later deified by both cultures. A mixture of ruthless pirate and brilliant administrator, he ruled the China Seas during the Manchu take-over and held Formosa (where he is still deeply respected) for the losing Ming dynasty. Called Coxinga by the Dutch but known properly in China as Cheng Cheng-Kung, and in Japan as Tei Seiko.

COYOTE: Amerindian. A trickster figure common to many North American tribes; but in general his tricks were more creative than those of (for example) the Scandinavian LOKI; they tended to represent the natural phenomena that helped mankind.

CREDNE: Irish. Bronze-worker hero of the Tuatha Dé Danann who, together with the smith Goibniu and the woodworker Luchtaine, made the weapons with which the Tuatha defeated the Fomors.

CRIMINELLE: Haitian voodoo. A manifestation of GHEDE, who possesses humans and causes them to bite their own arms. Friends of the victim must prize his jaws away before he tears the flesh.

CROM CRUAICH: ('The Bowed One of the Mound') Irish. Also known as Cenn Cruaich, 'the Lord of the Mound', and Crom Dubh, 'the Black Bowed One'. An ancient sacrificial god particularly associated with the festival of Lughnasadh. The last Sunday in July is still called *Domhnach Chrom Dubh* ('Crom Dubh's Sunday') even though it has been Christianized as the day of the spectacular pilgrimage up St Patrick's mountain, the 2,410-foot Croagh Patrick in Co. Mayo.

CRONUS: Greek and Phoenician. Son of URANUS and Gaia. Father by Rhea of ZEUS, HADES, POSEIDON, Hestia, Hera and Demeter. See Chapter XXV. Also married his sister Dione and gave her the city of Byblos. In Phoenician mythology, Dione bore him Persephone: he also married his sister Ashtart. Equated by the Romans with SATURN.

CUCHAVIRA: Colombian, Chibcha. Air and rainbow god who healed the sick and protected women in childbirth.

CUCHULAIN: The greatest warrior-hero of Irish legend, with the possible exception of FIONN MAC CUMHAL. Probably of earlier, more universal Celtic origin; he may correspond to the Continental ESUS, and his actual name, Setanta, was also that of a British Celtic tribe, the Setantii. Took the sobriquet Cuchulian ('Hound of Culain') when he offered to replace the hound of the smith Culain which he had killed. Son of LUGH (or of Sualtim) by Dechtire, and husband of Emer. There are many stories of his prowess from his youth onwards, but the most famous in his defence of Ulster against Queen Medhbh of Connacht as told in the *Táin Bó Cuailgne* (see Bibliography under Kinsella). While the men of Ulster lay in an enchanted sleep, he held off Medhbh's armies day by day single-handed. In the end he was so weakened that he tied himself to a post to keep upright and died still fighting. A famous statue in the GPO in Dublin portrays his death.

CUKULCAN: ('Bird-snake') Yucatan Mayan law-giving god.

CULHWCH: Welsh. Son of Kilydd and the sow-goddess Goleuddydd. Suitor of Olwyn, daughter of Ysbadadden, King of the Giants, who knew he must die if Culhwch married her, but failed to prevent it. An archetypal legend of the Young Hero supplanting the Old King as consort of the Goddess-Queen of Sovereignty.

CUPID: Roman god of love. Son of Venus and MERCURY or MARS. See p.128).

CYCLOPES: Greek. One-eyed giants, children of Gaia by her son URANUS. Lived in Sicily and helped HEPHAESTUS forge ZEUS's thunderbolts and the arms of the heroes. APOLLO finally slew them in anger when one of Zeus's thunderbolts struck down his son ASCELPIUS.

CZARNOBOG: – see CHERNOBOG.

DA-BOG, DAJDBOG, DAZHBOG: ('God Who Gives') Slavonic Sun god, also god of fire, and hearth and the home. Son of sky god SVAROG. His statues, of wood with silver head and golden moustache, stood in the castle of Kiev. In Serbia, demoted to a demon. See also SVAROZHICH.

DAGAN – see DAGON (3).

DAGANOWEDA – see HIAWATHA.

DAGDA, THE: ('The Good God') Irish, principal older god of the Tuatha Dé Danann. (See Chapter XXIII.)

DAGON (1): Phoenician. Son of URANUS and Gaia. Described in one version as a corn god – perhaps through confusion with Dagon (3), but seems to have become a sea god.

DAGON (2): Ben Dagon, son of Dagon (1); fought on the side of BAAL against EL.

DAGON (3): Babylonian god of agriculture, usually known as Dagan.

DAI-ITOKU-MYDO: Japanese Buddhist. Terrible manifestation of AMIDA, depicted with six heads, six arms and six legs, and surrounded by flames. Lives in the West and combats evils and poisons. He defeated EMMA-O, ruler of Hell.

DAIKOKU: Japanese god of wealth and luck. One of the SHICHI FUKUJIN. Pre-Buddhist. Depicted with a magical hammer and manifests as a rat. Father of EBISU.

DAINICHI: Japanese Buddhist god of purity and wisdom, sometimes regarded as a goddess.

DAINICHI NYORAI, MAHA-VAIROCANA-TATHAGATA: Japanese Buddhist divinity of the Tendai, Shingon and Kegon sects.

DAITYAS: Hindu Titans who fought against the gods. Children of KASYAPA and Diti, a form of the ultimate cosmic mother.

DAJDBOG – see DA-BOG.

DAKSHA: An early Hindu god. Son of BRAHMA, whose thumb gave birth to him. Father of goddess Diti (see DAITYAS) and Sati (also known as Uma) who married SHIVA, and also of the twenty-seven goddesses of the lunar stations, wives of SOMA. He quarrelled with Shiva, who cut off his head; after their reconciliation, Daksha was given a goat's head.

DALHAN: Islamic. A cannibalistic demon who lives on desert islands and eats shipwrecked sailors.

DAMBALLAH: Haitian voodoo. The venerable and benevolent father god, treated with great respect; the origin of all life and wisdom, himself unchanging; in a sense remote, yet ubiquitous and reassuring. Envisaged as a serpent, so St Patrick's picture is sometimes used to represent him.

DANAUS: Greek. King of Argos, who commanded his fifty daughters (the Danaids, worshipped in Argos as spring and river nymphs) to kill their husbands on their wedding night. Only Hypermnestra disobeyed him, and her husband Lyncaus eventually succeeded Danaus. The legend concerns an attempt to circumvent matrilinear succession, and its failure.

DANH: Benin. Snake god.

DAN-PETRO – see PETRO.

DARAMULUM: Australian Aborigine. An ancient culture hero whom medicine men invoke for power.

DARAWIGAL: Australian Aborigine. The force of evil, opposed to BAIAME.

DARDANUS: Greek. Founder of the Trojan race. Son of Electra from her seduction by ZEUS, and brother of Harmonia (see CADMUS).

DASAN – see MAKILA.

DAZH-BOG – see DA-BOG.

DEDWEN, DEDUN: Egyptian (Nubian). Presided over the natural resources of Nubia, in particular incense, and respected as such by the Pharaohs.

DEIMOS – see PHOBOS.

DEIVOS – see DJEVS.

DELBAETH: Irish. Son of OGHMA GRAINAINEACH. Father of the supreme mother goddess, Dana, and of the triple goddesses Badbh, Macha and the Morrigan. According to one account, also father of Boann, goddess of the River Boyne. All this is doubtless a late patriarchalization.

DEMOPHOON: Greek. Son of King Celeus of Eleusis and his wife Metaneira; Demeter, incognito, was his nurse. In later versions, identified with his elder brother Triptolemus, to whom Demeter gave the first grain of corn and whom she taught the art of ploughing and harvesting, which he toured Greece to pass on. Triptolemus may be cognate with with *tripolos*, 'thrice-ploughed furrow', and recall a fertility rite in which Demeter mated with her lover IASION.

DEUCALION: The Greek Noah. Son of PROMETHEUS, who warned him of the coming Flood so that he built an ark. After nine days the Flood subsided, and on the tenth he and his wife Pyrrha landed on Mount Othrys or Mount Parnassus. They repopulated the Earth by throwing over their shoulders 'the bones of their mother' (i.e. stones from the Earth). Those which he threw became men, while hers became women. Their son Hellen, who succeeded Deucalion as king of Thessaly, gave the name 'Hellenes' to the Greeks.

DEUS FIDIUS: Roman, Sabine origin. God of hospitality.

DHANVANTARI: Hindu. Physician of the gods; possibly inventor of *amrita*, the ambrosia of the gods.

DHARMA: Hindu. Husband of Sradda ('Confidence'), goddess of faith, or of Samnati (Sannati), or of Medha ('Understanding'), and also cohabited with Pritha (Kunti).

DHARME: Hindu. Sun god of the Oraons of Bengal, who annually celebrate his mating with the Earth Mother.

DHRTARASTRA – see MO-LI, THE.

DHYANI-BUDDHAS, THE: The five Buddhas of Meditation: Vairocana, solar, colour white; Ratnasambhava, ruling the South, yellow;

AMITABHA (Infinite Light) or AMITAYUS (Infinite Duration), ruling the West and its paradise Sukhavati, offers happy rebirth, red; Amoghsiddhi, ruling the North, green; and Akshobhya, ruling the East, blue.

DIANCECHT: Irish. Healer god of the Tuatha Dé Danann. His son MIACH and daughter Airmid made the silver hand which replaced the one lost by NUADA at the First Battle of Maigh Tuireadh (Moytura).

DIANUS: Early Roman oak god, from whom JANUS evolved.

DIARMAID, DIARMUID: Irish. Hero of the archetypal love story of Diarmaid and Gráinne. Gráinne, daughter of the King of Ireland, was betrothed to FIONN MAC CUMHAL but at a feast in her father's house fell in love with Diarmaid O'Duibne and pursuaded him to run away with her. Fionn pursued them for seven years (or, in other versions, a year and a day), finally pretending to make peace with them but trapping Diarmaid into being killed by a boar. The pursuit is commemorated by many dolmens in Ireland being known as 'Diarmaid and Gráinne's Bed'. The dead Diarmaid was taken to Brugh na Boinne (Newgrange) by the love god AENGUS MAC ÓG, who 'breathed aerial life' into him.

DIONYSUS: Greek, originally Thracian. God of vegetation, fertility and wine. Son of ZEUS and Semele, daughter of King Cadmus of Thebes. Jealous Hera destroyed Semele with divine fire while she was carrying him, but Zeus rescued the foetus and embedded it in his own thigh till it was ready for birth; hence Dionysus's title Dithyrambos, 'Twice-born'. Educated by SILENUS. He married Ariadne, whom he found on Naxos, where THESEUS had abandoned her. His legends include many travels, to all parts of Greece and to Asia Minor; even to the Underworld to rescue his mother, Semele, whom he renamed Thyone and brought to immortality on Olympus. He brought civilization and viniculture to many countries. Widely worshipped, often with ecstatic rituals; his female followers the Maenads (also called Bacchantes) sang and danced in orgiastic frenzy, in early times involving human sacrifice and later mere flagellation. His retinue also included SATYRS. He had many festivals, varying from place to place, including the Lenaea in December, when he was offered the new wine, the Anthesteria at the end of February, when the last year's vintage was tasted, and the Greater (or Urban) Dionysia at the beginning of March. Dionysys absorbed many other regional deities, including the Phrygian SABAZIUS, the Lydian BASSAREUS and the Cretan ZAGREUS (in which identification he was the son of Zeus and Demeter or Persephone). In Orphic philosophy, his bucolic nature was underplayed and he became the god of immortality, 'who is destroyed, who disappears, who relinquishes life and then is born again' (Plutarch).

DIOSCURI, THE – see CASTOR AND POLLUX.

DIS: Roman Underworld god, identified with ORCUS and with the Greek PLUTO and HADES. According to Julius Caesar, the Gauls claimed descent from him.

DJEVS, DEIVOS: The probable original Indo-European name of the Sky Father god, from which such forms as ZEUS, JOVIS and DYAUS derive.

DOGODA: Slavonic god of the West Wind, gentle and caressing.

DOMOVOI: Slavonic house-god, generally ape-like, but could take many forms, including human. Helpful and protective and could warn of coming trouble but had to be propitiated and treated kindly. His counterparts in the yard were the Dvorovoi, who detested animals with white fur and had to be placated with small offerings; in the bathhouse, the Bannik; and in the barn, the Ovinnik.

DONAR: Teutonic thunder god. Inferior to ODIN, a god of peasants rather than warriors – though in Scandinavia he became much more important as THOR. Known as THUNAR to the Anglo-Saxons; Thursday is 'Thunar's day'. A fertilizing god, because of the rain he brings. His tree was the oak.

DONN: Irish lord of the dead.

DUA: ('Today') Egyptian personification of 'today', together with his brother the lion god SEF ('yesterday').

DUAMUTEF – see HORUS, FOUR SONS OF.

DUMUZI: Sumerian vegetation god, equivalent of ADONI/ADONIS/ TAMMUZ. See Chapter XIX.

DWYVAN: The Welsh Noah, who with his wife Dwyfach built their ark Nefyed Nav Nevion, filled it with animals and survived the flood caused by ADDANC. A Celtic myth distorted by Christian additions.

DYAUS, DYAUS-PITAR: Hindu sky or Sun god. Husband of Earth and creator goddess Prithvi, and father of INDRA, AGNI, BHAGA, VARUNA, the dawn goddess Ushas and the night goddess Ratri. A primitive Aryan sky-father god who had already receded by the time the Vedas were written. May originally have been a Sun-mother goddess.

DYLAN: Welsh sea god. Son of Arianrhod by her brother GWYDION, and brother to LLEU LLAW GYFFES. According to the *Mabinogion*, as a baby, 'he immediately made for the sea, and when he came to the sea he took on its nature and swam as well as the best fish ... no wave ever broke beneath him.' Known as Dylan Eil Ton, 'Son of the Wave'. He married the Lady of the Lake, who bore him Vivienne (or Nimue), mistress of MERLIN. Cf. DYONAS.

DYONAS: Breton. Named in the courtly romance *Vivienne and Merlin* as 'god-son of Diana, goddess of the woods', and father of Vivienne, the mistress who enchanted MERLIN in the Forest of Broceliande – where there is still a Lake of Diana. Cf. DYLAN.

EA: Chaldaean and Assyro-Babylonian god of water, wisdom and magic. First known as Nudimmud or Nidim. Played a part in Ishtar's rescue of TAMMUZ from the Underworld, and in the Babylonian Flood story (see UTNAPISHTIM). Son of Bau, primeval goddess of the Dark Waters of the Deep, or of the Earth goddess Kishar. His wife was the Earth goddess Damkina (Ninki); the sea goddess Gasmu ('The Wise') is also mentioned as his wife or daughter in Chaldaean myth. God of wisdom and divination, and patron of smiths and carpenters. His many children included the storm god MARDUK; the Queen of Heaven, Inanna; the goddess of springs and canals, and interpreter of dreams, Nanshe; and Nina, oracular goddess of Nineveh. Ea and Marduk took part in the subduing of APSU and Tiamat, deities of the primordial Chaos. See also ENKI, who overlaps with him.

EAR – see TYR.

EBISU: Japanese god of labour. One of the SHICHI FUJUKIN. Son of

DAIKOKU. Portrayed with a fishing-rod and fish; may originally have been a God of fishermen.

EBO: Benin, Ouidah. War spirit.

ECALCHOT: Nicaraguan wind god.

ECHUA: Yucatan god of travellers.

EDA MALE: African, Yoruba. Male and female twins involved in the Ogoboni tribe's initiation rites.

EDIMMU, THE – see UTUKKU, THE.

EEYEEKALDUK: Eskimo healing spirit. Lives in a stone on land and looks like a tiny black-faced man. It is dangerous to look in his eyes.

EGIL – see ORVANDILL.

EHECATL: Aztec wind god, sometimes confused with QUETZALCOATL.

EITE, ADE: Etruscan Underworld ruler, with his consort Persipnei; originals of the Roman HADES and Persephone.

EKCHCUCAH, EKCHUAH: Mayan. God of travellers and of cacao planters. Black skinned.

EL: ('God') The original Semitic god. In the Phoenician pantheon, he was the Old King, Father of Years, god of rivers and streams and the fertility they bring. He dwelt by the sources or mouths of rivers. His wife was Elat ('Goddess'), otherwise called Asheratian, Ashera-of-the-Sea, after whom the Hebrew tribe of Asher was named. (Elat in fact seems to have been thousands of years older than he, the original mother-goddess of the Semites.) In one version, he was the son of URANUS and rebelled against him together with his brothers and sisters. His children included Persephone, Athene, EROS and (by Damkina) MARDUK. The solar goddess Sapas, Torch of the Gods, was also his daughter, and the Morning Star Sahar and the Evening Star Salem were his sons. As the Moon husband of the Sun goddess, his name was Eterah, TERAH, Jarah or Jerah – all meaning 'Moon'. (Though Terah sometimes appears as a separate god in conflict with El – see KERET.)

ELIUN: ('The All-Highest') Phoenician primordial father god. His wife was the mother goddess Beruth (after whom Beirut is named). In one version, they were the parents of URANUS (see EL) and Ge (Gaia).

EL-KHADIR: Islamic. The Old Man of the Sea of Moslem legend, and of the Arabian Nights. Still venerated by the Alaouites of Syria.

EMMA-O, EMMA-HOO, YAMA-RAJA: Japanese Buddhist. Lord of Yomi (Jigoku), the Otherworld, and judge of the dead. He judges only men, leaving women to his sister.

EMRYS – see MERLIN.

ENOIL: British Celtic sea god, possibly the same as DYLAN. His name persists as St Endellion, patron of a north Cornish parish.

ENDYMION (1): Greek. Loved by the Moon goddess Selene, who asked ZEUS to make him immortal. Zeus did so, on condition that he remained eternally asleep; so Selene went each night to gaze on her sleeping lover.

ENDYMION (2): Greek. A king of Elis to whom Selene bore fifty daughters, representing the fifty lunar cycles between the Olympic Games. May be a different version of (1).

ENIGORIO and ENIGOHATGEA: Amerindian, Iroquois. Twin brothers in the Iroquois Creation legend; Enigorio created rivers and fertile vegetation, while Enigohatgea opposed him by creating deserts, harmful plants and natural disasters.

ENKI: ('Lord of the Earth') Chaldaean, Sumerian and Assyro-Babylonian water and wisdom god; overlaps with EA. Like him, said to be son of the primeval goddess Bau and father of the Queen of the Gods Inanna/Ishtar. Agriculture came from his mating with the Earth goddess Ninhursag, but he was unfaithful to her with their daughter Ninsar, Ninsar's daughter Ninkurra, and Ninkurra's daughter Uttu. Ninhursag cursed him (underlining the harmful effects of uncontrolled water) but the other gods persuaded her to mitigate the curse (recognizing the beneficial effects of controlled water).

ENKIDU: Sumerian. Hero in the GILGAMESH legend, created by the goddess Aru (Arurua, Nintu) who pinched clay in the image of the god ANU and cast it onto the Earth. Lived with and befriended animals, till a courtesan lured him away from them and took him to Uruk, where Gilgamesh was king; the two became firm friends. Some identify Enkidu with ENKI.

ENLIL: Sumerian air, storm and mountain god. Son of the sky god ANU and the Earth goddess Ki, whom he separated to form the present world. He created the cattle god LAHAR and the goddess of grain and cultivation Ashnan. His wife was Ninlil, also a grain goddess; one version says he raped her and was banished to the Underworld, but she followed him and gave birth to SIN and NINURTA.

ENMESHARRA: Babylonian god of the Underworld Aralu or Meslam.

ENURTA: Babylonian war god. Son of ENLIL. His wife Gula brought both illness and good health.

ENZU – see NANNAR.

EPIMETHEUS – see PROMETHEUS.

EPUNAMUN: Of Inca origin, war god of the Araucanian Indians. Similarities with PUNCHAU.

EREBUS: ('Darkness') Greek. Born of CHAOS. Father by his sister Nyx of Nemesis, goddess of fate, Hemera ('Day'), EROS and CHARON. Also a name for the first part of the Underworld to be met by dead souls.

ERICHTHONIUS: A son of HEPHAESTUS and Gaia. Reared by Athena, he became king of Athens and instituted her worship there.

EROS: Greek god of love and the principle of relatedness. See Chapter XXVI

ESAUGETUH EMISSEE: ('Lord of Wind') Amerindian, chief god of the Creek Indians. A wind and creator god. He made the ancestors of the tribe out of wet clay as the Flood receded.

ESHMUN, ESMUN: ('He Whom We Invoke') Phoenician. The Baal (patron god) of Sidon. A god of health and healing.

ESSUS, ESUS: Early Continental Celtic agriculture god, worshipped by the Essuvi. His consort may have been the bear-goddess Artio.

ETERAH – see EL.

EURUS: Greek god of the East Wind. Son, with the other three Winds (see BOREAS, NOTUS, ZEPHYRUS), of the Titan ASTRAEUS and the dawn goddess Eos.

EVANDER: Roman. Son of HERMES and Carmenta, goddess of childbirth and prophecy. He and his mother came from Arcadia to Italy where he founded a town, Pallanteum, on the Tiber. Later he called it Rome after his daughter Roma, who became patron goddess of the city. He was said to have brought the Greek alphabet and Greek deities to Italy. Carmenta adapted the Greek letters to invent the Roman alphabet.

EVENOR: Greek/Atlantean. According to Plato's account of Solon's interview with the Egyptian priest, he was 'one of the Earth-born primeval men' of Atlantis. POSEIDON fell in love with his wife Leucippe ('White Mare'), fathering on her five pairs of male twins, between whom he divided the five areas of Atlantis.

EVUA: Guinea. Sun god of the Agni and Indene and Sanwi.

EXCELLENT ARCHER, THE – see ARCHER.

FA: Benin. God of destiny, considered as fixed only within certain limits, and consulting Fa may help one to modify it.

FAMIEN: Guinea, Agni tribe. Cares for sick, combats evil and makes women fertile. Attached to individuals; his 'owner' keeps a fetish knife which represents him.

FARBAUTI: The Scandinavian MERLIN, 'he who striking gave birth to fire'. Husband of Laufey, 'the wooded isle', who provided fuel for the fire. Father of LOKI, HELBLINDI and Byleifstr.

FATI, FADU: Polynesian, Society Islands. Moon god, son of ROUA by Taonoui, mother of the stars.

FAUNUS: One of Rome's most ancient nature gods. Son of SATURN's son Picus, and father or husband of Fauna, goddess of Earth and fields. Protected woods, fields and shepherds. Worshipped in sacred groves, where he gave oracles, chiefly during sleep. Said to have been one of the first kings of Latium, and a lawgiver; also inventor of the rustic pipes. Also called Lupercus; the Lupercalia (15 February) were among Rome's most important festivals.

FAVONIUS: Rome personification of the West Wind, equivalent of the Greek ZEPHYRUS.

FEBRUUS: Roman god of February, 'the cleansing month' and month of the dead. Probably Etruscan.

FENRIS-WOLF, THE, FENRIR: Scandinavian devourer, son of LOKI and the giantess Angurboda, Hag of the Iron Wood. Brother of Hel, goddess of the kingdom of the dead, and of the Midgard Serpent of the ocean surrounding the Earth.

FERGUS: Irish. Name of several legendary characters, but this particular one's virility was such that, when his wife, the woodland goddess and ruler of beasts, Flidais, was away, he needed seven ordinary women to satisfy him.

FERGUS MAC ROI: Irish. King of Ulster who loved Nessa, mother of CONCHOBAR; he suffered exile for her sake, and Conchobar inherited his throne. Later became tutor to CUCHULAIN, Conchobar's nephew; but he took Queen Medhbh's side in her war with Ulster.

FETKET: Egyptian. Butler of RA, who supplied him with drinks.

FIDES: ('Faith') Roman, Sabine origin. Personification of good faith, especially in verbal contracts.

FINTAAN: Irish. Husband of Noah's granddaughter Cesara (Cessair), first occupier of Ireland in the mythological cycle. They left for 'the western edge of the world' forty days before the Flood, with Cesara in charge of the expedition. Cesara appears to have been a pre-Celtic matriarchal goddess, with Fintaan as her less-important consort.

FIONN MAC CUMHAL (FINN MAC COOL): Irish. Son of Cumhal, King of the Tuatha Dé Danann. As a child, he burned his finger on the Salmon of Knowledge, sucked it and thus acquired all knowledge. Became leader of the Fianna, a famous mobile group of warriors and hunters. Said to have lived 200 years. See also DIARMAID.

FISHER KING: Celtic. A central figure in the Grail legend. See Chapter XVI.

FOMAGATA, THOMAGATA: Colombian, Chibcha Indians. A terrifying storm god, portrayed with one eye, four ears and a long tail.

FORSETI: Scandinavian. A god of justice and peace, one of the AESIR. Son of BALDUR and Nanna. Originally Frisian; Heligoland was earlier called Forsetisland. Teutonic name Vorsitzer ('President, Chairman').

FRAVAK: Persian. He and his sister Fravakian were the children of MASHIA and Mashiane (the Persian Adam and Eve), and progenitors of the fifteen races of mankind. See also GAYOMART.

FRAVASHIS, THE: Zoroastrian ancestor spirits. Not part of the orthodox teaching, but a popular relic of ancestor worship.

FREY, FREYR: Scandinavian god of fertility. Son of NJORD and the giantess Skadi, and brother of the fertility and Moon goddess Freya. He won his wife Gerda, daughter of the giant Gymir, after a desperate battle with the giants and after threatening to turn her from a beautiful young woman into an old one. His chariot was drawn by two boars, Gullibursti and Slidrurgtanni; he was probably originally chief of a boar clan of the VANIR before they merged with the AESIR. His ship, *Skidbladnir*, could hold all the Aesir but could be folded up. In Sweden every year, his image travelled the country accompanied by a beautiful girl called 'Frey's Wife', who also acted as priestess of his great temple at Uppsala.

FUDO-MYOO: Japanese Buddhist god of wisdom, identifiable with Dianichi. With his sword of wisdom and mercy, he battles against avarice, anger and folly. Portrayed surrounded by flame.

FUFLUNS: Etruscan equivalent of BACCHUS or DIONYSUS.

FUGEN BOSATSU: Japanese Buddhist. One of the most important Bodhisattvas, representing wisdom, intelligence and a deep understanding of human motives. Sits at the end of the Path of Extinction of Errors and has the power to prolong life.

FU-HSI: Chinese. Sage said to have lived 5,000 years, brother or husband of the creator goddess Nu-Kua who fashioned the first humans out of yellow earth.

FU-HSING: Chinese god of happiness. Originally a mortal, deified after death. His symbol is the bat.

FUKU-KENSAKU KANNON: Japanese Buddhist. A god of the Taizokai, world of forms.

FUKUROKUJU: Japanese god of wisdom and longevity, one of the SHICHI FUKUJIN. Portrayed long-headed, attended by a crane, deer or tortoise.

FUTSUNUSHI: Japanese fire and lightning god. Son of Ihatsusu-nowo and Ihatsusu-nome (both meaning 'hollow pipe').

GAD: ('Goat'?) Chaldaean. With his wife Gadda ('She-goat'?), deities of fortune.

GADEL: Irish. Said to have been an ancestor of the Milesians (Goidels, Gaels) and to have divided the Gaelic language into five dialects – for soldiers, poets, historians, physicians and the common people. Perhaps originally an Achaean deity of the River Gadylum on the southern shore of the Black Sea.

GAHONGAS, THE: Amerindian, Iroquois. Dwarf spirits living in water and rocks.

GANDAYAKS, THE: Amerindian, Iroquois. Dwarf spirits responsible for making vegetation flourish and caring for fish in rivers.

GANDHARVAS, THE: Hindu. Musicians and choristers of Swarga, the Heaven of INDRA. Associated with the Apsaras, the celestial nymphs. Very fond of women; a love-marriage without nuptial rites is described as Gandharva.

GANESA: Hindu elephant-headed god of good fortune, wisdom and literature. Son of Parvati, who created him out of dust mixed with the mist of her body. Leader of the armed forces of SHIVA. Depicted four-armed, riding a rat. Fat, jolly and popular. His two wives are Buddhi (representing intellect and intuition) and Siddhi (achievement). Known as Shoden in Japan. 777: Tarot: Nines; gem: quartz; plants: banyan, mandrake, damiana; animal: elephant; mineral: lead; perfumes: jasmine, ginseng, all odiferous roots; magical weapons: Perfume and Sandals.

GANYMEDE: Greek. Cup-bearer to ZEUS. Son of Tros (after whom Troy was named) and Callirhoe. 777: Tarot: Star; gem: artificial glass; plants: olive, coconut; animals: man or eagle, peacock; perfume: galibanum; magical weapon: Censer or Aspergillus.

GAOH: Amerindian, Iroquois. Wind god.

GAVIDA: Irish. A smith god, brother of MAC KINELY. Equivalent of GOBNIU and GOVANNON.

GAYOMART: Persian. He and the bull Gosh were the original creatures who produced all life – a human-animal pair reflecting the idea that all creation stems from ritual sacrifice. He was killed by AHRIMAN, but his posthumous twin children MASHIA and Mashiane (born from his seed buried in the earth for forty years) became the Persian Adam and Eve. (See also FRAVAK.)

GEB, KEBU, SEB, SIBU, SIVU: Egyptian Earth god. Son of the air god SHU by his twin sister Tefnut, and brother and lover of the sky goddess Nut – see p.81. Geb (or, in other versions, Thoth) presided over the trial of the dispute between Horus and Set. Earth deities are almost universally female but to the Egyptians the equivalent of the Earth Mother was the Nile valley – the Earth as a whole being mainly the surrounding desert.

GEBANN: Irish. Druid of the Tuatha Dé Danann. Father of the South Munster goddess Cliona of the Fair Hair, renowned for her great beauty, and connected with the O'Keefe family.

GEBURAH: ('Strength') The fifth Sephira of the Cabalistic Tree of Life, the MARS sphere; necessary destruction of the outworn or negative; the katabolic process, compared with the anabolic process of CHESED. Cabalistic symbols: Pentagon, Five-petalled Tudor Rose, Sword, Spear, Scourge, Chain. Tarot: Fives. Magical image: a mighty warrior in his chariot.

GEDULAH – see CHESED.

GENERAL, THE SNIFFING and GENERAL, THE PUFFING: Chinese. The two Buddhist temple door gods. The Puffing General always has his mouth open, and the Sniffing General has his mouth shut.

GENGEN WER: ('The Great Honker') Egyptian. The primeval goose who carried the cosmic egg from which all hatched. Also called Negeg ('Cackler'). AMUN as a creator god sometimes appears in this form.

GENOS: ('Race') The Phoenician Adam; his Eve was Genea. Children of Protogonos ('First-Born') and Aion ('Life'). They were the first to worship the Sun. Their children were Light, Fire and Flame.

GHANAN: Mayan god of agriculture.

GHANSYAM DEO: Hindu. A harvest god of the Gonds. At his festival he is said to descend upon one of his worshippers and possess him for a couple of days, as a scapegoat for the community's sins.

GHEDE: Haitian voodoo. God of death, and also of resurrection; symbols in his places of worship include the phallus as well as grave-diggers' tools. Supremely wise, protector of children, and a powerful healer.

GIBIL, GIRAU, GIRRU: Babylonian. Fire and light god, son of ANU and husband of Ninkasi. Arbiter of law and order. Patron of metal workers.

GILGAMESH: Sumerian hero of *The Epic of Gilgamesh*. Said to have been the fifth divine king of Erech (Uruk) after the Flood (the fourth having been TAMMUZ). Son of the third king, Lugulbanda, by a high priestess of the goddess Ninsun. He and his friend ENKIDU (representing the natural man) underwent many adventures and conflicts in which the gods SHAMASH and ENLIL took sides for and against them. Gilgamesh was desired by the goddess Ishtar, but he spurned her; in revenge she conjured up the Bull of Heaven which brought a seven-year drought. The Bull was finally killed, but one of the friends had to die, and the lot fell on Enkidu. Gilgamesh then underwent further adventures alone. He was probably either an actual king of the fourth millennium BC or earlier, or a Hyksos invader of Babylonia in the eighteenth century BC (or elements of both), to whom many archetypal myths became attached (as with ARTHUR).

GIRAU, GIRRU – see GIBIL.

GLAUCUS: Greek. Granted the gift of prophecy by APOLLO, he became deified as a sea god, appearing to sailors to predict danger. Thin-bodied and covered with seaweed. Every woman he wooed repulsed him, except Syme, who returned his love.

GLOOSKAP, GLUSKAP: Amerindian, Algonquin. Creator god who made the solar system and mankind out of the body of his dead mother, while his brother Maslum created things hurtful to humans. Glooskap means 'Liar', because he was more crafty than his malignant brother, and finally defeated him.

GNABIA: Australian Aborigine, Northern Territory. The women of the Anula tribe believe the sound of the bull-roarer at boys' initiations is Gnabia's voice; he swallows the boys and then disgorges them as initiated men.

GOG: British. Gog and Magog were said by Geoffrey of Monmouth to be giants who were the sole survivors after Brut destroyed all the other giants of Britain in the Battle of Totnes, and Brut installed them as gatekeepers of London. But they seem originally to have been a god and his mother or wife goddess, deities of a horse cult. (Robert Graves gives a different interpretation – *The White Goddess*, pp. 237-8.) The Wandlebury Hill figures discovered by Cambridge archaeologist T.C. Lethbridge (see Bibliography) he believed represented these two. Wandlebury adjoins the Gog-Magog Hills.

GOIBNIU: Irish. Smith of the Tuatha Dé Danann, who with CREDNE and LUCHTAIN made the weapons with which the Tuatha defeated the Fomors. Uncle of LUGH. Equivalent to GAVIDA and GOVANNON.

GOU: Benin. Moon god, son of Lissa, the chameleon mother-goddess, and brother of the Sun god MAOU.

GOVANNON: Welsh. Smith of the gods, British equivalent of GAVIDA and GOBNIU. Son of BELI and Don. Slayer of DYLAN.

GOZANZE-MOO: Japanese Buddhist. The terrible aspect of Ashuku. His four faces each have three eyes. He lives in the East.

GRANNOS: Early Continental Celtic god of mineral springs. An inscription to him was also found at Musselburgh, near Edinburgh.

GREAT SPIRIT, THE: Amerindian. The common term, in many tribal languages, for the supreme father-god; often symbolized by the Sun.

GRONW: Welsh, Lord of Penllyn, lover of LLEU LLAW GYFFES' wife Blodeuwydd. He and Lleu fought and both were killed, but Lleu was magically revived. A type of the OAK KING/HOLLY KING rivalry.

GUARACY: Brazilian, Tupi-Guarani tribes. Sun god, creator of all animals. (See also JACY and PERUDA.)

GUCUMATZ: Mayan and Guatemalan, Quiche Indian. God of farming and domestic life, able to assume many animal shapes, but generally portrayed as a feathered serpent. Corresponds to Aztec QUETZALCOATL.

GUECUBU: ('The Wanderer Without') Chilean, Araucanian Indian. Malicious god, evil twin of AKA-KANET: responsible for all mankind's troubles.

GUKHIN-BANDA: Assyro-Babylonian, patron of goldsmiths.

GUNDARI-MOO: Japanese Buddhist. The terrible manifestation of HOSHO, with three eyes, fanged mouth, eight arms, snakes round wrists and ankles, and a skull on his head.

GUNNAR, GUNTHER: See SIEGFRIED.

GUNPUTTY: Hindu. An elephant-headed god believed to be incarnated in each generation of a family at Chinchbad near Poona, beginning with a Brahmin of Poona in 1640, Moorab Gosseyn, and continuing to the present day.

GURUHI: Guinea, Agni tribe. A terrible god who exacts sacrifices and has the ability to poison and torture suspected sorcerers but who gives great power to his followers. Symbolized by a stool supporting an iron ball. May not be looked upon by women, children or non-initiates.

GWALU: Nigerian. Rain god of Yoruba tribe.

GWION: Welsh. Ordered by Cerridwen to stir her magical cauldron, he accidentally splashed three drops onto his fingers, which he sucked and thus acquired all knowledge. Cerridwen pursued him, both shape-changing – as a greyhound chasing a hare, an otter chasing a fish, a hawk chasing a bird and finally a hen pecking a grain of corn. She swallowed the grain and as a result gave birth to TALIESIN, the great bard. The chase may relate to the initiation ritual of a Druid or bard.

GWYDION AP DÔN: Welsh. Son of BELI and Dôn. Brother of Arianrhod, and father by her of LLEU LLAU GYFFES and DYLAN. Bard and magician, king of the British Celts; many of his legends later absorbed by ARTHUR. See LLEU LLAW GYFFES for his story.

GWYN: ('The White One') Welsh. Son of LLYR or LLUDD. An early Underworld god, ruler of the souls of slain warriors. Also leader of the Wild Hunt, like HERNE. There was a Gwyn cult in pre-Christian Glastonbury.

GYGES – see HECATONCHEIRES.

GYMIR – see FREY.

HA: Egyptian. God of the desert, and also defender against invaders from the desert such as Libyan tribes.

HADAD, ADAD, ADDU: Babylonian, Phoenician, Syrian and Hittite. Babylonian storm and thunder god, later equated with RAMMON (RIMMON). Also brought fertilizing rain. His wife was Shala the Compassionate. In his Phoenician form, a storm and cloud god, also known as Martu ('the Amorite') and Kurgal ('the Great Mountain'); probably the BAAL of Mount Lebanon. His mother was Asherat-of-the-Sea (after whom the tribe of Asher was named) and his wife was also called Asherat. In Syria, a god of virility. In his Hittite and Kassite form, a storm god similar to TESHUB, and brother to Ishtar in her Hittite form.

HADES: Greek god of the Underworld, and also a name for the Underworld itself. Son of CRONUS and his sister Rhea, and brother to ZEUS, POSEIDON, Demeter, Hera and Hestia. He abducted Persephone (Kore), daughter of Zeus and the corn-goddess Demeter, from Earth. (See p.44 and also *The Witches' Goddess*, Chapter XIII.) Zeus arranged a compromise whereby Persephone spent half the year in the Underworld with Hades, and half on Earth – thus personifying the vegetation cycle. Hades was also known as Pluto ('Wealth') in his role as guardian of the treasures of the Earth, including the winter-sleeping vegetation. (Pluto was also the name of his Roman equivalent.) By Olympian standards, he was remarkably faithful to Persephone – his only lapses were with the nymph Minthe, whom Persephone trod into the ground to become the plant mint, and with Leuce, daughter of Poseidon, who died a natural death and became the white poplar, tree of the Elysian Fields. 777: Tarot: Fives, Judgement, Wands (Kings or Knights); gems: ruby, fire opal; plants: oak, nux vomica, nettle, red poppy, hibiscus; minerals: iron, sulphur, nitrates; perfumes: tobacco, olibanum, all fiery odours; magical weapons: Sword, Spear, Scourge or Chain, Wand or Lamp, Pyramid of Fire.

HALIRRHOTHIUS: Greek. Son of POSEIDON, he was killed by ARES for having raped his daughter Alcippe. Poseidon summoned Ares before the Twelve Olympians on a hill near the Acropolis in Athens; Ares was acquitted. The hill became known as the Areopagus, and the Athenians judged criminal cases there.

HANUMAN: Hindu. Monkey god, noted for his learning. Son of the wind god VAYU or of KASARI and Angana (Anjana), an Apsara (celestial nymph) who herself sometimes takes monkey form. One of the monkey generals of the Ramayana. 777: Tarot: Eights, Magician; gems: opal (especially fire opal), agate; plants: moly, anhalonium lewinii, vervain, herb mercury, marjolane, palm; animals: hermaphrodite, jackal, swallow, ibis, ape; mineral: mercury; perfumes: storax, mastic, white sandal, mace, all fugitive odours; magical weapons: Names and Versicles and Apron, Wand or Caduceaus.

HAOKAH: Amerindian, Sioux. Thunder god who uses the wind as a stick to beat the thunder drum. Also a hunter god, depicted with horns. Cries when he is happy, laughs when he is sad, and feels heat as cold and cold as heat.

HAP – see SERAPIS.

HAPI, HAPY – see HORUS, FOUR SONS OF. Also god of the annual Nile flood, on which fertility depended. He lived in a cavern on the Isle of Bigeh near the First Cataract. Represented as male but with one pendulous breast and a prominent belly.

HAPIKERN: Mayan. Yucatan. An evil god, enemy of mankind, at constant war with NOHOCHACYUM.

HARAKHTE – see RA-HARAKHTE.

HAR HOU – see HOU.

HARI-HARA: Hindu. The dual personality formed by the combination of SHIVA and VISHNU. The name Hari alone is sometimes applied to Shiva or Vishnu, in the aspect which carries off souls to save them.

HARINAGAMESI: ('Man with the Antelope Head') Indian, Janaist. General of the heavenly infantry.

HARMAKHIS – see HOR-M-AKHET.

HAROERIS – see HORUS THE ELDER.

HARPAKHRAD, HARPOCRATES – see HORUS THE YOUNGER.

HARUT – see MARUT.

HASAMMELIS: Hittite. Protector of travellers.

HASHYE-ALTYE: Amerindian, Navajo. The talking god.

HASTSEHOGAN: Amerindian, Navajo. God of the home.

HATIF: Arabic. A pre-Islamic jinn, heard but not seen, who gave advice, directions and warnings.

HAURUN: Canaanite. Identified in Egypt with the Greek Sphinx at Giza, possibly originally from a settlement of Canaanite workers nearby. A 'House of Haurun' was built in front of the Sphinx. In Egypt, regarded as a protector against wild animals and as a healer; but in Canaanite tradition he seems to have been a portender of death.

HAURVATAT – see AMESHAS SPENTA.

HAYAMA-TSU-MI: Japanese god of the lower mountain slopes.

HAY-JI, HAYA-TSU-MUJI-NO-KAMI: Japanese whirlwind god.

HEAVENLY FATHER: Hebrew, Essene. His six angels were of Eternal Life, Creative Work, Peace, Power, Love and Wisdom. His complement was the Earthly Mother, with her six angels of Earth, Life, Joy, the Sun, Water and Air. Mankind stood at the intersection between these two polarized groups of forces and must attune itself to both. Jesus's statement 'I and the Father are one' would seem to derive from the Essene's Friday night ritual statement 'The Heavenly Father and I are one' – and it is interesting that their Saturday morning ritual began with 'I and the Earthly Mother are one'.

HEAVENLY MASTER OF THE FIRST ORIGIN, HEAVENLY MASTER OF THE DAWN OF JADE OF THE GOLDEN DOOR – see JADE, AUGUST PERSONAGE OF.

HECATONCHEIRES, CENTIMANES, THE: ('Hundred-Handed') Greek. With the CYCLOPES and TITANS, represented the raw forces of Nature. They were three: Cottus the Furious, Briareus the Vigorous and Gyges the Big-Limbed.

HEH – see NEHE.

HEIMDAHL: Scandinavian. Guardian of Bifrost, the rainbow bridge from Earth to Asgard. Son of nine virgins (i.e. of a group of priestesses). Tall and handsome, with teeth of pure gold. His horse was called Culltoppr, his sword Hoefu and his horn Gjallar. He fought LOKI to regain Freya's necklace which Loki had stolen. Said to have repopulated the world after some disaster.

HEITSI-EIBIB: African, Hottentot. Willing to aid mortals, he can assume the form of any animal. He did not create the animals but gave them their characteristics. Born either of a cow or of a virgin who ate a certain herb. A dying and resurrecting god. His ritual 'graves' are in mountain defiles; people passing one throw a stone on it for luck, praying 'Give us more cattle.'

HELBLINDI: Scandinavian. Son of FARBAUTI and brother of LOKI. Also a name given to ODIN, which suggests he was a memory of an earlier god.

HELIOGABALUS: A Syrian Sun god, symbolized by a conical stone.

HELIOS: Greek Sun god. Son of HYPERION and the Titaness Theia, and brother to Moon goddess Selene and dawn goddess Eos (Aurora). Eos orginally accompanied him through the sky during the day, but this role was later taken over by Hemera. His many wives included Clymene (who bore him the female heliades and PHAETON, and Pasiphaë, who married King Minos of Crete); the nymph Rhodos (daughter of Aphrodite by POSEIDON, after whom the island of Rhodes is named and who bore him the male heliads); and the oceanid Perse (whose children included the sorceress Circe). (Another version gives Rhodos as daughter of Poseidon and Amphitrite, and mother of seven children by Helios.) 777: Tarot: Sun; gem: crysoleth; plants: sunflower, laurel, heliotrope; animals: lion, sparrowhawk; perfumes: olibanum, cinnammon, all glorious odours; magical weapns: Lamen or Bow and Arrow.

HENGIST: Saxon. Supposed leader, with Horsa, of the Anglo-Saxon invasion of Britain in the fifth century AD – but see *The Witches' Goddess* p.141.

HENO – see HINO.

HEPHAESTUS: Greek smith and craftsman god. See Chapter VII.

HERAKLES: Greek. Son of Alcmene by ZEUS. Roman name Hercules. In Tyre, linked with Astarte; a cult of Astarte and Tyrian Herakles, served by priestesses, existed in London, Carlisle and Corbridge, Northumberland, in Roman times, probably due to the presence of Eastern traders. His Earthly wife was Deineira, daughter of DIONYSUS and Althaea; he wrestled with a bull-headed snake (the River Achelous personified) to win her, and tore off one of its horns, which became the Cornucopia. At the wedding he 'accidentally' killed a cup-bearer, but the victim must originally have been the bride's father. Then he fought and killed the CENTAUR Nessus, who had tried to rape her. Before he died, Nessus gave Deineira some of his blood as a charm to keep Herakles' love, to put on his shirt. But it poisoned Herakles by burning him. The details of his death are typical of the Dying King who marries the Goddess-Queen to ensure the fertility of the land but who knows he is ultimately doomed. The Twelve Labours of Herakles were imposed on him by the Delphic Oracle after he had killed his children in a fit of madness sent by the jealous Hera. When he was admitted to Olympus as a god, Zeus gave him his and Hera's daughter Hebe ('Youth', 'Puberty') as wife; they had two children, Alexiares and Anicerus.

HERES: Canaanite name for SHAMASH.

HERMAKHIS: Egyptian. The rising or setting Sun; a name given to HORUS or RA.

HERMAPHRODITE: Greek. Son of HERMES and Aphrodite, he united with the nymph Salmacis to become one bisexual body.

HERMES: Greek. Messenger of the gods, the god of intellect, communication, commerce and travel; on occasion also a trickster, bringing good luck to thieves. Originally, like PAN, who was then said to be his son, Hermes was Arcadian and in that form seems also to have been horned and goat-footed (see p.76). He was the Psychopompos, conducting dead souls to the afterlife. Son of ZEUS and the Pleiad Maia. His many reputed lovers included Aphrodite, Hecate and Persephone. His symbols were the caducaeus, the winged cap and winged sandals. Roman equivalent MERCURY. 777: Tarot: Eights, Magician; gems: opal (especially fire opal), agate; plants: moly, anhalonium lewisii, vervane, herb mercury, marjolane, palm; animals: hermaphrodite, jackal, swallow, ibis, ape; mineral: mercury; perfumes: storax, mastic, white sandal, mace, all fugitive odours; magical weapons: Names and Versicles and Apron, Wand or Caducaeus.

HERMOD: Scandinavian. Son of ODIN who went to Hel to try to bring back his brother BALDUR.

HERNE: British Celtic horned god. See Chapter XXI.

HESPER, HESPERUS: Greek. The Evening Star (Venus). Son of ATLAS and the dawn goddess Eos. Called Vesper by the Romans. His Morning Star brother was PHOSPHORUS.

HESUS: Gaulish. A war god similar to TEUTATES.

HEY-TAU. Phoenician. God of the Byblos region, known from about 3000

BC. A god of trees, of great economic importance locally. Known to the Egyptians as Ba-Tau.

HIISI: Finnish. One of the triad of evil spirits, the others being Lempo and Paha.

HIMAVAT: Hindu. God of the Himalayas, and father of Parvati, wife of SHIVA.

HINE-NUI-TE-PO – see ROHE.

HINO, HINU, HINUN, HENO: Amerindian, Iroquois. Thunder god, brother of the West Wind; together they defeated the Stone Giants, aboriginal inhabitants of the land.

HINOKAGU: Japanese. Fire god, son of IZANAGI and his sister/wife Izanami-No-Kami.

HIPPOMENES – see MELANION.

HIRANYAKSHA, HIRANYAKASIPU: Hindu. The first incarnation of RAVANA. A demon who dethroned INDRA to become ruler of the universe and expel the gods from Heaven. he was destroyed by VARAHA, the boar avatar of VISHNU, during the Deluge.

HIRIBI: ('The Summer's King') Hittite. The Moon god YERA gave him 10,000 gold shekels for the hand of his daughter Nikkal, goddess of the fruits of the Earth. 'Daughter of the Summer's King' may mean the bride of the new Moon after the harvest, still a favourite time for weddings in the area.

HIRUKU: Japanese. A solar god, grandson of the supreme Sun goddess Amaterasu. Probably an early Sun god overshadowed by her as a result of the conquest by the Yamato tribe.

HMIN: Burmese. A demon of ague, afflicting travellers.

HOCHIGAN: African, Bushman. A being of the time of creation, who hated animals. Originally animals could talk, but one day Hochigan disappeared and the animals' power of speech vanished with him.

HOD: ('Glory') The eighth Sephira of the Cabalistic Tree of Life. The HERMES Sephira, personifying intellect and concept-forms – balanced by his counterpart the seventh Sephira, Netzach, the Aphrodite Sephira, personifying Nature and the instincts and emotions. Cabalistic symbols: Names and Versicles and Apron. Tarot: Eights, magical image: a hermaphrodite.

HODER, HODUR: Scandinavian. One of the AESIR. God of the night, a blind son of ODIN. Tricked by LOKI into causing the death of his brother BALDUR (See p.117).

HOENI, HOENIR: Scandinavian. One of the AESIR, brother of ODIN. Involved in Creation legend, giving ASK and Embla, the first humans, mobility and intelligence. May originally have been WE or WILI. Described as tall, fair and fleet of foot.

HOLDER: Scandinavian. Seducer of his rival BALDUR's wife, Nanna.

HOLLY KING: Celtic God of the Waning Year. See Chapter IX.

HO-MASUBI, KAGO-ZUCHI: Japanese fire god. Son of IZANAGI and Izanami, who died giving birth to him.

HOOKE: Hittite war god. He defeated the dragon Illuyankas with the help of the goddess Inaras.

HOR-M-AKEHT: Egyptian. A name of HORUS THE ELDER, meaning 'Horus on the Horizon' – i.e. as the rising Sun, symbol of resurrection. Greek rendering Harmakhis.

HORUS THE ELDER, HAROERIS: Egyptian. A falcon-headed sky god, pre-dynastic in origin. Son of GEB and Nut, and brother of OSIRIS, Isis, SET and Nephthys. He had two eyes, the Sun and the Moon. A story of his first fight with Set, in which Set stole his Sun-eye and parts of his Moon-eye, and THOTH helped recover them, is an early variant of the conflict between Osiris, Set and HORUS THE YOUNGER. Both represent the struggle between the powers of light and fertility on the one hand, and darkness and death on the other. *777*: Tarot: Fives, Tower; gem: ruby, any red stone; plants: oak, nux vomica, nettle, absinthe, rue; animals: basilisk, horse, bear, wolf; minerals: iron, sulphur; perfumes: tobacco, pepper, dragon's blood, all hot, pungent odours; magical weapons: Sword, Spear, Scourge or Chain.

HORUS THE YOUNGER, HARPAKHRAD: Egyptian. Son of OSIRIS and Isis. See Chapter XVIII. Portrayed both as a child (often being suckled by Isis in paintings and statues barely distinguishable from the later Christian Madonna and Child) and as an adult. Greek name Harpokrates. *777*: Horus the Younger, under the name Harpocrates, is one of the very few deities whom Crowley allocates to the Veils beyond Kether (Ain, Ain Soph and Ain Soph Aur).

HORUS, FOUR SONS OF: Egyptian. Said to have been born to HORUS THE YOUNGER by his mother, Isis. The Four were portrayed on the canopic jars which contained the organs removed from bodies about to be mummified. They were associated with the elements, the four cardinal points and their guardian goddesses. The Four were as follows: Duamutef ('He Who Praises His Mother') jackal-headed guardian of the stomach, associated with Fire, the East and the goddess Neith. Hapi, dog- or ape-headed guardian of the lungs, associated with Earth, the North and the goddess Nephthys. (See also separate entry under HAPI.) Imset (Mestha, Mesti), human-headed guardian of the liver, associated with Water, the South and the goddess Isis. Qebesenuf ('He Who Cools His Brother'), falcon-headed guardian of the intestines, associated with Air, the West and the goddess Selkhet.

HOTEI: ('Linen Bag') Japanese god of laughter and happiness. One of the SHICHI FUKUJIN. Portrayed as very fat and carrying on his back the bag which gives him his name,

HOU, HAR HOU: Guernsey. An oak god, probably the same as HU GADARN.

HOU-CHI: Chinese culture hero linked with Chou dynasty, said to have been born of a virgin. Deified for having taught the Chinese agriculture.

HOW-TOO: Chinese. An Earth monster god manifesting as trees and rivers. Domestic animals were sacrificed to him.

HSUAN-T'IEN SHANG-TI: ('Supreme Lord of the Dark Heaven') Chinese. Enemy of demons and evil spirits. Also Regent of Water. Portrayed as tall, loose-haired, barefoot, standing on a turtle surrounded by a snake.

HU: Egyptian. God personifying the authority of a word of command, specifically the Pharaoh's. He was born from a drop of blood from RA's phallus.

HUAHUANTLI – see TEOYAOMIQUI.

HUAILLEPENYI: Chilean, Araucanian. God of fog. Believed responsible for deformed birth of children. Portrayed with the body of a ewe, head of a calf, and tail of a seal.

HUEHUETEOTL – see XIUHTECUHTLI.

HU GADARN, HU THE MIGHTY: Welsh culture hero, ancestor of the Cymry, whom tradition says he brought to Wales from the East (variously identified as Constantinople or Ceylon). Said to have taught them to plough and to use song as an aid to memory. In the Welsh Deluge story, he dragged the dragon Addanc, who caused the Flood, from its lair by the lake of Llyn Llion with his team of oxen.

HUITZILOPOCHTLI, UITZILOPOTCHLI: ('Humming Bird of the South') Aztec war, storm and Sun god, and protector of travellers. Humans were sacrificed to him. Son of the star god MIXCOATL and Moon and Earth goddess Coatlicue ('Serpent Skirt'). He was born fully armed.

HUNAB-KU, KINEBAHAN: ('The One God') Supreme god of the Mayas. His wife was the goddess of weaving, Ixasaluoh.

HUN-AHPU-VUCH: ('Grandfather') Guatemalan Sun god; husband of the Moon goddess Hun-Ahpu-Myte ('Grandmother'). Both represented in human form but with the face of the tapir, a sacred animal.

HUNTIN: African, Kaffir. A tree spirit to whom fowls were sacrificed.

HUN-TUN: Chinese god of the chaos which preceded the active forces YANG and Yin.

HURAKAN: Guatemalan, Quiche Indian. A wind god known as 'The Heart of Heaven'. When the gods were angry with the first humans, he caused the Deluge which destroyed them.

HURUING WUHTI: Amerindian, Hopi. Two deities with the same name, who created the animals, and then the first man and woman out of clay.

HVARE-KHSAETA: Persian pre-Zoroastrian Sun god.

HYMEN: Greek god of marriage and wedding feasts. Attendant on Aphrodite, whose son he was by DIONYSUS.

HYMIR: Scandinavian. A sea giant, father of TYR, and owner of a magic cauldron.

HYPERION: Greek. An early Sun god, son of URANUS and Gaia. Father by the Titaness Theia of Sun god HELIOS, Moon goddess Selene and dawn goddess Eos.

HYPNOS: Greek god of sleep. Son of the night goddess Nyx. Dwelt in the Underworld with his son Morpheus ('Dreams') and his twin brother Thanatos ('Death'). Roman name Somnus.

HYPOSOURANIOS – see OUSOOS.

I – see ARCHER.

IACCHUS: Greek. A title of DIONYSUS: in fact, a combination of the Cretan Dionysus and the Canaanite BEL. 777: Tarot: Aces, Sixes, Emperors or Princes, all twenty-two Trumps; gems: diamond, topaz, yellow diamond; plants: almond in flower, acacia, bay, laurel, vine; animals: god, phoenix, lion, child, sphinx (if sworded and crowned); minerals: aur. pot., carbon; perfumes: ambergris, olibanum; magical weapons: Swastika or Fylfat Cross, Crown, Lamen or Rosy Cross.

IAH – see AH.

IAHU, IAHU-BEL – see YAHWEH and BEL.

IAO – see YAHWEH.

IAPETUS: Greek. A Titan, son of URANUS and Gaia, and father by Asia (or in other versions of the Titaness Themis or the oceanid Clymene) of ATLAS and PROMETHEUS. Robert Graves equates him with the biblical Japheth.

IASION: Greek. In one story, lover of Demeter in a crop-fertility rite in a 'thrice-ploughed furrow'.

IBLIS: Islamic name for Devil. Sometimes appears as an individual, sometimes synonymous with SHAITAN, and applied to AZAZIL.

ICTINIKE. Amerindian, Sioux. Son of the Sun god. Expelled from Heaven for deceitfulness. Known as 'the Father of Lies'.

IDA-TEN, WEI-T'O: Japanese and Chinese Buddhist. Known as Ida-Ten in Japan and Wei-t'o in China. Guardian of the law, and watcher over the conduct of monasteries.

IDRIS THE GIANT: Welsh. Said to have such knowledge of the stars that he could foretell everything 'up to the day of doom'. His mountain is Cader Idris ('Chair of Idris') near Dolgellau; whoever spends the night on it will be either inspired or mad by the morning.

IGIGI, THE: Babylonian spirits of Heaven, in contrast to the ANUNAKI. Children of ANSAR and Kishak, and led by Ishtar.

IHO-IHO – see IO.

IHY, IHI, AHI: ('Sistrum-player') Egyptian god of the sistrum, an instrument especially sacred to his mother, Hathor. His father is given as HORUS or RA.

I KAGGEN: Western Bushmen creator god, envisaged as a preying mantis. His wife is Hyrax.

IKTO. Amerindian, Sioux. The inventor of human speech.

ILAH: Southern Semitic Moon god, similar to ILMAQAH.

ILMA: Finno-Ugric air god. Father of the creator goddess Luonnotar ('Daughter of Nature') or Ilmatar ('Mother of the Waters').

ILMAQAH: Semitic Moon god, more ancient than ALLAH in his pre-Islamic lunar role.

ILMARINEN: Finno-Ugric. The magical smith of the Kalevala epic, who forged the talisman Sampo with 'the point of a swan's feathers, the milk of a sterile cow, a small grain of barley, and the fine wool of a fecund ewe'.

IMHOTEP: Egyptian. In fact, a deified historical human, the first named non-royal person in Egyptian history. Architect to the Pharaoh Zoser (c.2780 BC), he built the Step Pyramid (first of the pyramids) at Saqqara, and the temple beside it (model for the later temple architecture). Credited with being the inventor of cut-stone building. In due course his memory became deified, replacing NEFERTUM as Sekhmet's husband and considered the son to PTAH and Nut. (Cf. AMENHOTEP-SON-OF-HAPU.)

IMSET – see HORUS, FOUR SONS OF.

IN: Japanese equivalent of YANG – The Japanese Yin being Yo.

INACHUS: Pre-Greek river god, who turned in Classical times into a legendary king of Argos. Son of OCEANUS and Tethys, and father of Io, who was turned into a heifer to escape ZEUS's attentions; Io was also pre-Greek, a Moon-cow and barley goddess of Argos.

INARI: Japanese god of agriculture (especially rice) and prosperity. One of the most popular deities in Japan. Patron of tradesmen and in old Japan of sword-forging smiths. Portrayed as an old man, with two foxes as his messengers; by popular confusion, the fox is often worshipped as the God of Rice. Sometimes regarded as a goddess; he absorbed the attributes of an earlier mother goddess, Ukemochi.

INCUBI: Christian. Demons who seduced women while they sleep. The female equivalents who seduce men are Succubi.

INDRA (1): Hindu. God of battles and of rain; his weapon was the thunderbolt. Son of DYAUS and Prithvi. May have been a deified actual king. Important in Vedic myth, in which he played a somewhat swashbuckling role, he was much demoted by the Brahmins in favour of VISHNU. Portrayed riding an elephant. He lived in Swarga, halfway between Heaven and Earth on a mountain beyond the Himalayas. His wife is the voluptuous Indrani (Aindri), or Saki ('Skill') who may correspond to her. 777: Tarot: Fours, Wheel of Fortune; gems: amethyst, sapphire, lapis lazuli; plants: olive, shamrock, aloe; animals: unicorn, eagle; perfumes: cedar, saffron, all generous odours; magical weapons: Wand, Sceptre or Crook.

INDRA (2): Persian. An early evil spirit.

INFONIWU: Formosan creator god.

INGUNARFREY: A Swedish name for FREY.

IN-SHUSHINAK: Assyro-Babylonian. Principal god of Elam and Susa, where he was regarded as creator of the world and ruler of gods and mankind. Similar to ADAD and NINURTA.

INTI, APU-PUNCHAU: Inca. Sun god and supreme deity of the Inca pantheon. Apu-Punchau means 'The Head of Day'. Portrayed as a man with a golden Sun-disc for head. His sister and wife was the Moon goddess Mama Quilla. Ancestor of all the Incas; only they were allowed to speak his name. Children and animals were sacrificed at his annual festival.

IO: Maori and Polynesian. An early supreme god who has diminished in importance. In Tahiti known as Iho-Iho or Io-i-te-vaki-naro. (Do not confuse with the Greek priestess Io, loved by ZEUS.)

IOSKEHA: Amerindian, Huron. He and his twin brother Tawiskara were sons of MASTER OF WINDS and Breath of Winds. Ioskeha created mankind after defeating the Great Frog who had swallowed the waters of the Earth. Iosheka represented good and taught mankind many skills. Tawiskara stood for evil; all his creation were monstrous.

ISHWARA: Hindu, Rajputana. Fertility god. Earthen images of him and his wife Isani (Gouri) – hers being the larger – are placed together, and a small trench is sown with barley. When it sprouts, women dance round it and give their husbands the young shoots to wear in their turbans.

ITALAPAS, ITALPAS – see COYOTE.

ITUM – see NEFERTUM.

ITZAMNA, ZAMNA, KABUL: Mayan Moon god, father of gods and mankind, and god of the West. He taught mankind writing and the use of maize and rubber. Squirrels were sacrificed to him.

ITZLACOLLUHQUI: Aztec god of the curved obsidian knife. Equatable with TEZCATLIPOCA.

ITZLI: Aztec god of the stone knife and of the second hour of the night. Equatable with TEZCATLIPOCA.

IUCHAR: Irish. Iuchar, Iucharba and Brian were three sons of the goddess Anu and grandsons of BALOR. Said to have married Éire, Fodhla and Banbha, the three goddesses after whom Ireland was named. (But see also MAC CECHT, MAC CUILL and MAC GREINE.) One account makes them the joint fathers of LUGH by Clothru, a ring of red circles on his neck and belly showing which part each had fathered. Another version makes them murderers of Lugh's father CIAN, for which crime they had to gather the Treasures of the Tuatha Dé Danann.

IUCHARBA – see IUCHAR.

IX – see BACABS, THE.

IXION: Greek. Son of ARES and ancestor of the CENTAURS. Of pre-Olympian origin.

IXTLILTON: Aztec god of medicine and health. Known as 'Little Black Face'. His priests were physicians or shamans and specialized in the healing of children.

IZANAGI: ('He Who Invites') Japanese creator god. Father (either by himself alone or by intercourse with his sister/wife Izanami, 'She Who Invites') of Amaterasu, the Sun goddess, and the Moon god TSUKIYOMI. Izanagi and Izanami were the first beings to come to Earth and gave birth to the island of Japan and to many other deities.

JACY: Brazilian, Tupi-Guarani tribes. Moon god, creator of plant life. See also GUARACY and PERUDA.

JADE, AUGUST PERSONAGE OF (YU-TI): Chinese. Lord of the sky and chief god of Heaven. Also known as the Jade Emperor (Tung Wang Kung), the August Supreme Emperor of Jade (Yu-huang-shang-ti) or Father-Heaven (Lao-tien-yeh). He created mankind out of clay. His wife is Wang-mu Yiang-yiang ('Queen Mother Wang'), who rules the K'un-lun Mountain, dwelling-place of the immortals at the centre of the Earth. Their daughter Chih-ni ('Heavenly Weaver-Girl') weaves his robes. He lives in a palace which exactly corresponds to that of the Emperor of China. In northern China, at least, he is believed to have created human beings. He is the second member of the supreme triad, the first being the Heavenly Master of the First Origin (who preceded him) and the Heavenly Master of the Dawn of Jade of the Golden Door, who will one day succeed him.

JAGANNATHA, JUGGERNAUT: ('Lord of the World' – the name Juggernaut is an English corruption.) Hindu. A god worshipped in the town of the same name in Orissaa. His temple was built by a rajah after a vision of VISHNU. The goddess Kesora is also worshipped there. The famous Car of Juggernaut is a huge sixteen-wheeled wooden structure dragged annually by fifty men to the temple and said to contain a bride for the god. Devotees used to commit suicide under its wheels, believing this would give them eternal life.

JAH-ACEB: ('The Heel God') Canaanite. Seems to have been worshipped at Beth-Hoglah ('The Shrine of the Hobbler') near Jericho. The reference is to the sacred king whose heel must not touch the ground (see Graves, *The White Goddess*, pp. 324-7). Probably the real name of the biblical Jacob.

JALANDHARA: Hindu. Born of Ocean and the Ganges. He fought and defeated the gods, took over Heaven and tried to abduct SHIVA'S wife Parvati. But Shiva united the gods and goddesses to win their home back.

JAMBAVAN: Hindu king of the Bears. Jambavati, wife of Krishna, is of his family.

JAMBHALA: Buddhist Hindu. God of wealth, comically fat, holding a lemon and a mangosteen.

JANICOT: Basque. An oak god, much referred to by Pierre de Lancre in his early seventeenth-century campaign against witchcraft in the Pays de Labonde. May have links with the Roman JANUS. Dealt with in depth in Doreen Valiente's *ABC of Witchcraft*, pp. 208-11.

JANUS: Roman god of doorways and of the turn of the year, who gave his name to January. In his morning aspect, known as Matutinus. His wife and partner was Jana. A very early couple, he was originally the oak god DIANUS, and she was the woodland and Moon goddess Diana/Dione, Janus's mother. 777: Tarot: Twos, Kings, Knights; gems: star ruby, turquoise; plant: amaranth; animals: man; mineral: phosphorus; perfume: musk; magical weapons: Lingam, Inner Robe of Glory.

JARAH, JERAH, TERAH: Semitic New Moon god – originally masculine, later becoming feminine as Bride of the Sun.

JEHOVAH – see YAHWEH.

JEN HUANG: Chinese Buddhist and Taoist. The first rulers of Earth, nine sons of Tou Mou, a goddess living on the Pole Star and having power over life and death. Probably of Hindu origin.

JERAH – see JARAH.

JERAHMEEL: ('Beloved of the Moon') Judaean, Hebron valley. The Israelities took the Garden of Eden story from the Jerahmeelites, and the original garden seems to have been in the Hebron valley.

JESSIS: Early Semitic father god.

JESUS – see CHRIST.

JIKOKU: Japanese. Guardian of the East. One of the SHI TENNO.

JIMMU TENNO – see WAKA-MI-KE-NO-MIKITO.

JIZO BOSATSU: Japanese and Chinese Buddhist. Appears in many apects, all helpful to suffering mankind: protector of children, averter of fires, redeemer of sinful souls, helper in childbirth etc. Perhaps a pre-Buddhist sea god.

JOCA-HUVA: Haitian, Taino tribe. A sky god, son of the goddess Atabel; unlike other Taino deities, these two were never portrayed in images.

JOROJIN: Japanese god of longevity and good luck, similar to FUKURO-KUJU. One of the SHICHI FUKUJIN. Portrayed with a tortoise or crane.

JO-UK, JUOK, JUCK: Sudanese, Shilluk tribe. Creator god who made mankind (both white and brown), giving them 'long legs like flamingos' so that they could run and walk, two arms for hoeing and weeding, and so on, feature by feature. The title Jo-Uk, is given to Shilluk kings.

JOVE – see JUPITER.

JUCK – see JO-UK.

JUGGERNAUT – see JAGANNATHA.

JUMALA: Finno-Ugric supreme god, probably originally a sky god. His symbol was the oak tree. A somewhat abstract deity, he was later replaced by UKKO.

JUOK – see JO-UK.

JUPITER, JOVE: Roman Supreme god. Developed from the Etruscan thunderbolt god TINIA. The Roman Jupiter was at first mainly a god of weather – of light, rain, wind and storm, all important to a farming people. Later his city and state functions superseded his agricultural ones. He became Jupiter Optimus Maximus, 'Best and Greatest'. Like most Roman deities, he absorbed much of the mythology of his Greek counterpart, ZEUS, and portrayals of him were practically all derived from Greek art. His sister/wife was Juno, important throughout Italy from very ancient times, which importance survived the effects of patriarchy much more than that of the Greek Hera. 777: Tarot: Aces, Fours, Magician, Wheel of Fortune; plants: almond in flower, olive, shamrock, aspen, red poppy, hibiscus, nettle; animals: god, unicorn, eagle, man; minerals; aur. pot.; perfumes; ambergris, cedar, galbanum, saffron, all generous odours; magical weapons; Swastika or Fylfat Cross, Crown, Wand, Sceptre, or Crook, Dagger or Fan.

JURUPARI: Brazilian, Tupi-Guarani tribes. Principal god of the Uapes tribe. A man's god; women who saw his ritual symbols were put to death.

KABOI – see KAMU.

KABUL – see ITZAMNA.

KAGGEN, CAGN – see I KAGGEN.

KAGO-ZUCHI, KAGU-ZUCHI: – see HO-MASUBI.

KAKE-GUIA: Guinean, Agni tribe. Bull-headed god who conducts souls to the supreme god NYAMIA.

KALKI: ('Time') Hindu. In Vedic myth the tenth and last avatar of VISHNU, when he will appear as a white horse in the sky.

KAMA, KAMADEVA: Hindu god of love, son of VISHNU and Lakshmi. Portrayed, like EROS, as a winged child with a bow and arrow. His wife is the erotic Rati ('Pleasure'), known as 'the Fair-Limbed'.

KAME amd KERI: Caribbean, Bakairi tribe. Twin brothers who populated the world with animals and fixed the Sun and Moon (which had been carried aimlessly by two birds) in their present courses.

KAMI-NARI: Japanese. God of Rolling Thunder, much venerated and with many shrines. Trees struck by lightning are sacred and must not be cut down.

KAMU-NAHOBI: Japanese. The god who puts right what has gone wrong – particularly after calamities caused by the malignant god YASO-MAGA-TSU-BI.

KAN – see BACABS, THE.

KANATI THE HUNTER: Amerindian, Cherokee. His wife is the corn goddess Sheu ('Maize').

KANA-YAMA-HIKO: Japanese god of mountain minerals, with female counterpart Kana-Yama-Hime.

KANE – see TANE.

KANNON BOSATU: Japanese Buddhist. One of the most venerated Bodhisattvas, worshipped by all Buddhist sects from the earliest times, in seven principal forms. Of infinite compassion, he comes to the help of all mankind. One of the two companions of AMIDA.

KAPPA: Japanese dwarf river god, who causes drowning. To avoid him, one bows to him; he then bows back, and all the water pours out through a hole in his skull, making him harmless.

KARLIKI, THE: Slavonic. Russian dwarfs of the Underworld. They and the Lychie (see LESHY) wood spirits were said to have fallen from Heaven with SATAN – a Christian belittling of old gods.

KARORA: Australian Aborigine, Northern Aranda. Creator god of the bandicoot totem tribe, himself a bandicoot. Dreaming in the primeval darkness, he caused the Sun to appear, and gave birth to bandicoots and finally to the first man.

KARTTIKEYA, KUMARA, SKANDA: Hindu. In late Vedic myth, a war god who led the forces of good to defeat the demon Tarika.

KARU: Brazilian, Mundruku tribe. A culture hero who created the mountains by blowing feathers about.

KASHIWA-NO-KAMI: Japanese. Protector god of oak trees.

KATCOCHILA: Amerindian, Wintun. He set fire to the Earth in revenge for the theft of his magic flute, but the fire was put out by a flood.

KATHAR-WA-HASIS: Phoenician. A craftsman god. He was said to live in Egypt, suggesting that it was from there that technical skills had spread.

KAWA-NO-KAMI: Japanese collective name for a river god; each river has its own.

KEELUT: Eskimo. An evil Earth spirit, looking like a hairless dog.

KEKUI: Egyptian. A god created, together with the goddess Kekuit, by THOTH with the aid of PTAH and KHNUM, in the Hermopolis creation story.

KELPIE: Scottish. A god of lakes and rivers, often in the form of a horse, who made travellers drown.

KEMOSH: Referred to in II Kings 23:13 as a god of the Moabites.

KEREMET: Slavonic, Wotyak people. A mischievous god who was placated by rituals mating him to Mukylcin, the Earth Mother.

KERET: Phoenician. Son of EL, and soldier of El's daughter the goddess Sapas. He was king of Sidon and fought on El's orders against an invasion by the Moon god TERAH.

KETHER: ('Crown') The first Sephira of the Cabalistic Tree of Life. Pure being, the First Manifest, which 'may be for us at our stage of development the Great Unknown, but it is not the Great Unknowable' (Dion Fortune, *The Mystical Qabalah*, p. 110). Though Kether's magical image of traditionally 'an ancient bearded king seen in profile', Kether is not strictly speaking a 'male god', because the polarity of gender does not manifest till the second and third Sephiroth, Chokmah and Binah. Kether contains the potentiality of creative polarization; it is the ultimate essence of being from which polarization springs, expressing itself in the other nine Sephiroth. Cabalistic symbols: the Point, the Crown, the Swastika. Tarot: the four Aces, roots of the powers of the four elements.

KHASM – see AESMA.

KHEBIESO, SO: Benin, Ewe peoples. Lightning god, associated with BO.

KHENSU – see KHONSU.

KHENTI-AMENTIU: ('First of the Westerners') Egyptian. One of the named husbands of the vulture-goddess Nekhbet, protector of Upper Egypt (the other being HAPI). A title of Abydos of WEPWAWET. Sometimes a title of OSIRIS.

KHEPHRA, KHEPHERA, KHOPRI: ('He Who is Coming into Being') Egyptian. The scarab-beetle god of the dawn Sun; a self-created creator. Both aspects are symbolized by the ball of dung which the scarab beetle rolls and which hatches into a new scarab beetle. He is described as raising his beauty into the body of the sky goddess Nut, and his spittle as forming the Earth. 777: Tarot: Chariot, Death, Moon; plants: lotus, cactus, unicellular organisms, opium poppy; animals: crab, turtle, sphinx, scorpion, beetle, lobster or crayfish, wolf, fish, dolphin; perfumes: onycha, Siamese benzoin, opoponax, ambergris; magical weapons: Furnace, Pain of the Obligation, Twilight of the Place and Magic Mirror.

KHEREBU: Assyrian. Heavenly spirits, origin of the biblical CHERUBIM.

KHERTY: ('Lower One') Egyptian. A ram-headed god personifying both danger and protection from danger.

KHNUM, KHNEMU: Egyptian creator god, envisaged with a potter's wheel. His first wife (sometimes also mentioned as his daughter) was Sati, goddess of the Cataracts, and his second was Anuket, 'the Clasper', confining the Nile between rocks at Philae and Syene. They were worshipped at Elephantine. Other wives named in some versions were Haket, goddess of childbirth, giving life to the men and women he shaped on his potter's wheel, and the primordial creator goddess Neith.

KHONS, KHONSU, KHENSU: ('Wanderer') Egyptian. A Moon god, son of AMUN-RA and Mut in the Theban triad. Mostly portrayed human-headed with the side-lock of youth, sometimes hawk-headed, but in both cases crowned with the lunar disc and crescent. Sacred animal: the baboon. In the Pyramid Age, his character is completely different from his Theban image: he is a bloodthirsty god, appealed to by the Pharaoh as a source of strength in defeating malevolent deities.

KHOPRI – see KHEPHRA.

KHORS: Slavonic. A health and hunting god, portrayed as a stallion.

KHOSER-ET-HASIS, BN-YM: Phoenician. An early sea god, who fought against BAAL by raising the sea and river levels. The LEVIATHAN was one of his creatures.

KHSHATHRA: Persian, Zoroastrian. Personification of dominion, and genius of metals. One of the six Immortal Holy Ones attendant on AHURA MAZDA.

KHUMBAM: Assyro-Babylonian. God of Elam, a mountainous region east of Babylon. His wife was Kiririsha, supreme goddess of Elam. He may be identified with MARDUK.

KIHO TUMU: Polynesian. Supreme god of the Tuamotu archipelago.

KI'I – see TI'I.

KINGMINGOARKULLUK: Eskimo. A benevolent land-dwelling spirit who sings joyously when you see him.

KINGU: Assyro-Babylonian. God of the powers of darkness. Son/lover of Tiamat, the primordial sea mother goddess, who put him in command of monsters in her conflict with the gods led by EA.

KINICH-AHAU: ('Lord of the Face of the Sun') Mayan Sun god, and god of medicine. His wife was Ixalvoh, goddess of weaving.

KINTU: The Mozambique Adam. He married the Daughter of Heaven.

KISIN – see USUKUN.

KITCHE MANITOU: Amerindian, Muskwari. Destroyed the world twice, first by fire and then by a flood.

KITCKI MANITOU: Amerindian, Algonquin name for the GREAT SPIRIT.

KMUKAMTCH: Amerindian, Klamath. A demon who tried unsuccessfully to destroy the world by fire.

KODOYANPE: Amerindian, Maidu. Survivor with COYOTE of the Deluge. Together they created mankind out of wooden images; then they quarrelled, and Kodoyanpe had to flee to the East.

KOLPIA: Phoenician wind god. Father by Baau, the personified promordial substance, of Aion ('Life') and Protogonos ('Firstborn').

KOMOKU: Japanese. Guardian of the South cardinal point. One of the SHI TENNO.

KOMPIRA: Japanese Buddhist. A popular god, patron of sailors. Portrayed as a plump man sitting cross-legged and holding a purse.

KOODJANUK: Eskimo. Important god who gives help and healing. Envisaged as a very large white-bodied, black-headed bird, with a hooked beak.

KOZAH: Persian storm god.

KREMARA: Slavonic, Polish. Protector of pigs. Beer was offered to him in the hearth. Piglets were weaned from the sows by Priparchis.

KRIMEN – see COEM.

KRISHNA: Hindu. The eighth avatar of VISHNU, and the most human and charming. Son of Devaki, sister of King Kamsa of Mathura, who killed her children at birth because of the prophecy that one of them would assassinate him. But Devaki and her husband managed secretly to hide him and his brother Balarama with a cowherd's family. He grew up strong and often mischievous, even challenging the rain god INDRA, who was so impressed by his impudence that he and his wife Indrani made him a friend of their son ARJUNA. Many stories are told of his relations with shepherdesses and cowherds' wives. When they all wanted to dance with him at once, he reduplicated himself so that there were enough Krishnas to go round. His character was generous and kindly as well as erotic. When he was fully grown, he returned to Mathura and killed Kamsa.

Later he became involved in war. Finally he died accidentally from a hunter's arrow and rose to Heaven.

KSHITIGARBHA: Indian, Central Asian and Chinese Buddhist. A Bodhisattva controlling the six paths taken by souls after they have been judged. In China, where he is known as Ksitigarbha or Ti-tsang Wang-p'u-sa, he is always invoked when someone dies, because of his great compassion and determination to save souls.

KU – see TU.

KUAN-TI: Chinese. A war god who, untypically, concentrated on the averting of war. Also a judge god, popular hearer of complaints.

KUBERA, KUVERA: Hindu. A god of wealth, living with his treasures deep in the Earth, listening to music. In Buddhist tradition, god of dark spirits; one of the LOKAPALAS. His wife, Hariti, who suckled 500 demons, was said to have been converted to Buddhism by BUDDHA himself.

K'UEI-HSING: Chinese god of examinations, assistant to (but more popular than) the god of literature WEN CH'ANG.

KUKAILIMOKU: Polynesian, Hawaii. War god.

KUKULCAN: ('The Feathered Snake whose Path is the Waters') Mayan. An early great god, inventor of the calendar and patron of craftsman. Later merged with QUETZALCOATL and equivalent to GUCUMATZ.

KUKU-NO-CHI: Japanese god of tree-trunks.

KUKSU: Amerindian, Pomo and Maidu. To the Pomos, a creator god, with his brother MARUMDA. Their mother goddess, Ragno, had to rescue them when their mistakes got out of hand. To the Maidu, the first man.

KUMARA – see KARTIKEYA.

KUMARBIS: Hittite sky god. His messenger goddess was Imbaluris.

KUNADO: Japanese. A road god, 'of the places not to be visited'.

KUPALA, KUPALO: Slavonic. A god of joy, but also a sacrificed god. Particularly associated with bathing in rivers and in night-gathered dew at his Midsummer festivals, at the end of which an image of him was passed through fire and then thrown into a river. See also YARILO.

KURGAL: Canaanite name for the Babylonian ADAD.

KURKIL: Siberian. A Mongol creator god, envisaged as a raven who flew to create the Earth and mankind and to teach the arts of civilization.

KURMA: Hindu. The second, tortoise, avatar of VISHNU or BRAHMA. As a tortoise, he went to the bottom of the ocean to recover the treasures of the Vedic tribes lost during the Flood.

KURUPIRA: Brazilian. Protector of forest animals but hostile to mankind. Gnome-like, with backward-pointing feet. Sacrifices were made to propitiate him.

KURWAICHIN: Slavonic, Polish. Protector of lambs.

KUVERA – see KUBERA.

LADON: Greek. A river god of Arcadia.

LAHAR: Sumerian and Chaldaean cattle god, created by ENLIL at the same time as Ashnan, goddess of grain and cultivated fields.

LAKHMU: Babylonian. Born of Mommu or Tiamat, the primordial ocean. He and Lakhamu were monstrous serpents who gave birth to Anshar, the male principle, and Kishar, the female principle. Lakhmu was used by Tiamat in her fight with MARDUK.

LAMASSU – see UTUKKU, THE.

LAO TIEN-YEH: ('Father-Heaven') Japanese. A title of the AUGUST PERSONAGE OF JADE (see under JADE).

LARES: Roman family and public gods of crossroads and fields, regarded as protective of the locality for which they were responsible. Public Lares were two in number, but a family Lar was always single. The corresponding indoor gods were the PENATES.

LATPON: Phoenician. Son of EL, who 'shared the gift of wisdom' with the goddess Asherat-of-the-Sea.

LAULATI: Melanesian, Lifu Island. Creator god.

LEGBA. Haitian voodoo creator Sun god. Closely associated with Loco, the first priest, 'chief of Legba's escort', and Ayizan, the first priestess. Ayizan is sometimes called Legba's wife and sometimes Loco's.

LEI-KUNG: Chinese thunder god. Portrayed as ugly, loinclothed, with a blue body, winged and clawed, and carrying drums, a hammer and chisel.

LEMPO – see HIISI.

LEODEGRANCE: ('Pilot') Welsh. A title of BRAN.

LESHY: Slavonic forest (*les*) god. He and his wife Leshachikha were parents of the Leshonki or Leshies. He had a blueish face, green eyes, which often popped out, and a long green beard. The Leshies, who threw no shadow, died in October and revived in Spring (when they were most dangerous). They were jealous of their territory, leading travellers astray but usually releasing them in the end. The spell against them was to take your clothes off under a tree and put them on again backwards. See also KARLIKI, THE.

LEUCETIOS: Continental Celtic. A thunder god.

LEVIATHAN: Phoenician. A seven-headed monster vanquished by BAAL with the help of MOT. The story is the source of the biblical one.

LIBANZA: Congo. Supreme god of the Upoto tribe. He gave immortality to the Moon but denied it to mankind.

LIBER PATER: Roman. An early Latin fertility god; his wife was Libera. Later a god of the vine, by confusion with DIONYSUS. His festival, the Liberalia on 17 March, was the date on which boys became men and put on the *toga virilis*.

LINGLESSOU: Haitian voodoo. An aspect of Loco (see LEGBA). Said to eat glass.

LINGODBHAVA: Hindu. SHIVA in his lingam (phallic) aspect.

LIR – see LLYR.

LITAVIS: Early Celtic. Possibly Breton in origin; Llydaw is the Welsh name for Brittany.

LJESCHI, THE – see LESHY.

LLAWEREINT – see LLUD.

LLEU LLAW GYFFES:('Lleu Strong-Hand') Welsh. Son of Arianrhod and her brother GWYDION. For his story, see the *Mabinogion*, or Chapter XVI of *The Witches' Goddess*. Also worshipped in Gaul. Carlisle (Luguvalium), Lyon (Lugdunum), Leyden in the Netherlands and

Legnica in Poland were all named after him or his Irish equivalent LUGH; both were clearly originally the same – the principal Celtic Young God.

LLYR, LIR: Welsh, Irish, Manx. The original of Shakespeare's King Lear. His daughter Creiddylad, Welsh form of the maiden over whom two rivals must battle 'every first of May until Doomsday', corresponds to Cordelia – the only one who will not bow to her father's will and who marries the man of her own choice. In Welsh myth, husband first of Penardun and then of Iweridd, the daughter of Dôn. For the story of Llyr's other daughter, Branwen, see BRAN. His sons were Bran and MANANNÁN MAC LIR. In Irish myth he was a king of the Tuatha Dé Danann; his first wife was Aebh, by whom he had a daughter, Fionuala, and three sons, Hugh, Fiacha and Conn; Aebh then died. His second wife was Aoife, who turned the four children into swans out of jealousy. The Children of Lir flew around Ireland as swans for 900 years, till the hermit Mochavog baptized them and they changed to aged human shape and died; doubtless a Christian tidying-up of a much older myth.

LOA (1): Haitian voodoo. General name for a deity.

LOA (2): Micronesian, Marshall Islands, Ralik group. Creator god.

LOCO – see LEGBA.

LODEHUR, LODUR: Scandinavian. Associated with HOENI and ODIN in the creation of the first humans. Odin gave them breath, Hoeni a soul and reason, and Lodehur warmth and colouring. May be a variant of LOKI.

LOKI: Scandinavian trickster god. See Chapter XXIV. 777: Tarot: Eights; gem: opal, especially fire opal; plants: moly, anahalonium lewinii; animals: hermaphrodite, jackal; mineral: mercury; perfume: storax; magical weapons: Names and Versicles and Apron.

LOKAPALAS, THE: Hindu. In Vedic myth, guardians of the eight quarters of the world. They were INDRA, East; AGNI, South-East; YAMA, South; SURYA, South-West; VARUNA, West; VAYU, North-West; KUBERA, North; and SOMA, North-East.

LONO: Polynesian fertility god. He fell in love with Kaikilani, a beautiful Hawaiian. She became a goddess, and they lived happily, surf-bathing in Kealakekua Bay, till he killed her in a jealous rage when he doubted her fidelity. Mad with remorse, he stormed about the island and finally left, promising to return on a floating island of plenty. Hawaiian fertility rituals at the start of the fertile season dramatize his story. When Captain Cook reached Hawaii in 1778, the islanders believed he was Lono and welcomed him but a later incident convinced them otherwise, and he was killed.

LOZ: Babylonian. Co-ruler of Meslam, the Underworld, with NERGAL and his consort, Ninmug (Ereshkigal).

LUCHTAIN – see CREDNE.

LUCIFER: ('Light-bearer'). On the Christian use of the name, see p.55. In Tuscan witch legend, Diana, the first of all creation, divided herself in two; the darkness was herself, and the light was her brother Lucifer. She desired him, but he fled from her as she pursued him round the heavens. Finally, by shape-changing into a cat, she got into his bed. He woke to find his sister beside him. From their union was born Aradia, the witches' teacher-goddess.

LUDD, LLUD, NUDA, NUDD: British Celtic river god after whom Ludgate Hill in London is named. He seems to have replaced TAMESIS as the god of the River Thames. Like NUAD, whom he overlaps, he had an artificial hand and he was sometimes called Llawereint, 'Silver-Handed'. Confused with NODENS and may originally have been the same.

LUGH: Irish. Son of CIAN of the Tuatha Dé Danann and Eithne, daughter of BALOR, King of the Fomors. Commanded the Tuatha forces in the victorious Second Battle of Mag Tuireadh (Moytura) against the Fomors, in which he killed his grandfather, Balor. The outstanding Irish Young God figure, supplanting the Old God (Balor); much associated with skills; known as Lugh Samhioldanach ('of many arts') and Lugh Lámhfhada ('of the long hand'). Root of the Gaelic name for August, Lughnasadh ('Festival of Lugh'). Corresponds to the Welsh LLEW LLAW GYFFES.

LUGULBANDA: Sumerian. Third Divine King of Erech, and father by the High Priestess of Ninsun of the hero GILGAMESH.

LUGUS: Continental form of LUGH or LLEW LLAW GYFFES.

LU-HSING: Chinese god of salaries. A historical person deified.

LUKHMU: Chaldaean. He and his sister Lakhamu, children of the primordial sea mother Tiamat, personified the primeval sediment. They were invoked on the completion of a building.

LUSIOS: ('He Who Frees from Guilt') Greek. A title of DIONYSUS.

LYCHIE, THE – see LESHY.

MAAHES: Egyptian lion-headed god, son of Bast by RA. Of Nubian origin. Sometimes identified with NEFERTUM.

MABON: ('Great Son') Welsh. A great hunter with a swift horse and a wonderful hound. May have been a mythologized actual ruler. Stolen from his mother, Modron ('Great Mother'), when he was three nights old, but eventually rescued by King ARTHUR. In this sense, the masculine counterpart of Persephone – the male fertilizing principle seasonally withdrawn. Modron thus corresponds to Demeter. He appears as Maponus in Romano-British inscriptions.

MACACHERA: Brazilian. The spirit of roads. Regarded as helpful by the Potiguara Indians but as malevolent by the Tupinambas.

MAC CECHT: Irish, Tuatha Dé Danann. Son of the Plough (or 'whose god was the plough'). Husband of Fodhla, the Mother aspect of the Triple Goddess symbolizing Ireland – he, appropriately, representing the Earth element. See also MAC CUILL and MAC GREINE.

MAC CUILL: Irish, Tuatha Dé Danann. Son of the Hazel (or 'whose God was the Hazel' or 'whose God was the sea'). Husband of Banbha, the Crone aspect of the Triple Goddess symbolizing Ireland – he representing the primordial Water element. See also MAC CECHT and MAC GREINE.

MAC GREINE: Irish, Tuatha Dé Danann. Son of the Sun (or 'whose God was the Sun'). Husband of Éire, the Maid aspect of the Triple Goddess symbolizing Ireland – he representing the Fire element. See also MAC CECHT and MAC CUILL.

MACKINELY: Irish. Son of BALOR and Danu or Ceithlenn, and father by Eithne of LUGH. He may be equated with CIAN.

MACUILXOCHITL – see XOCHIPILLI.

MADER-ATCHA: Lapp. Creator of the human soul; his wife, Mader-Akka, created the body.

MAEANDER: Greek. God of the river of the same name in Phrygia.

MAGNI: ('Might') Scandinavian. Son of THOR by his first wife, the Giantess Jarnsaxa. At Ragnarok, the Twilight of the Gods, he and his brother Modi ('Courage') took possession of Mjolnir, their father's hammer. The brothers survived Ragnarok.

MAGOG – see GOG.

MAH: Persian. Moon god and ruler of time.

MAHAF: Egyptian. The ferryman of the boat which navigated the waters of the Underworld. Custodian of the boat itself was Aken, who had to be awakened by Mahaf every time it was needed.

MAHAVIRA: ('Great Man') Hindu, Janaist. He decided to leave Heaven and be incarnated on Earth to save mankind. He first chose to enter the womb of Devananda, wife of the Brahman Rishabhadatta, but later transferred to that of Trisala, wife of Siddhartha. When he was born, the gods and goddesses came down from Heaven to show their joy.

MAHIUKI: Polynesian. King of the land of the dead.

MAHOU – see MAO.

MAHRKUSHA: Persian, Zoroastrian. A demon who destroyed all living creatures by a flood, except YIMA, whom AHURA MAZDA saved.

MAIRE-MONAN: ('Transformer') Brazilian, Tupi tribe. Had the power to transform men and women into other shapes in punishment for their sins. Angered by this, humans arranged a festival in which he had to leap bonfires. He was burned to death (giving birth to thunder and lightning) and was then carried up to Heaven, where he became a star. Often confused with his predecessor, MONAN.

MAIT' CARREFOUR: Haitian voodoo Moon god.

MAKILA: Amerindian, Pomo. Culture hero of a bird-totem clan. He and his son Dasan came from the waters and brought civilization with them.

MAKONAIMA – see SIGU.

MALLANA DEVA: Hindu, Keljhar, Muhl. He and his wife Mallana Devi are represented by a pair of dolmens at each of fifteen villages; the shepherds offer wooden figures to them to avert death from the sick.

MAMERS – see MARS.

MAMMON: Because of Jesus's statement 'Ye cannot serve God and mammon' (Matthew vi:24, Luke xvi:13), often thought to have been a pagan god. In fact, simply an Aramaic word meaning 'gain' or 'wealth'.

MAMURIUS: Roman. An erotic shepherd god, early form of MARS.

MANABOZHO, MICHABO, WINABOJO: Amerindian, Algonquin. Culture hero, grandson of Nokomis ('Grandmother'), the Earth Mother who nourishes all living things. Regarded as the inventor of written signs and as the source of arts and crafts. Inventor of the fishing-net. He took refuge from a flood which submerged the world, and sent out first a raven, then an otter, then a muskrat. The first two did not return, but the muskrat came back to say the flood had subsided. He married the muskrat and became ancestor of the Algonquins. Known as 'the Great Hare', though the root meaning of his name was 'Dawn'. Probably originally a Sun god; he lives where the Sun rises. Model for Longfellow's Hiawatha.

MANANNÁN MAC LIR: Irish and Manx god of the sea, after whom the Isle of Man is named. Son of LIR. He had a self-propelled ship called *Wave-Sweeper* and a horse called 'Splendid Mane'. He deserted his first wife, Fand, goddess of healing and pleasure, but returned to her later. He had a magic cauldron which was stolen from him by CUCHULAINN. Welsh equivalent MANAWYDDAN.

MANAWYDDAN: Welsh: Son of LLYR and Penardun, brother of BRAN and Branwen, and second husband of the fertility and Otherworld goddess Rhiannon. Irish equivalent MANANNÁN MAC LIR.

MANCO CAPAC, MANCOCOAPAC: Inca. He and his sister/wife Mama Occlo (Mama Oullo Huaca) were instructed by the Sun and the Moon and descended to Earth at Tiahuanaco to found the Inca capital of Cuzco and become the first rulers of the Inca empire, teaching the people the arts of civilization. From then on, brother-sister marriages became the rule for Inca royalty.

MANDULIS, MERWEL: Nubian. Sun god of Lower Nubia. Egyptian name Merwel. He had a temple at Philae, where he was regarded as a close companion of Isis.

MANEROS: Egyptian name for HERAKLES.

MANI: Nordic Moon god. He seized Hjuki and Bil when they were fetching water from the well, and they have followed him in the sky ever since, visible from Earth (may recall a pair of asteroids which have since disappeared). Seems to be the origin of the 'Jack and Jill' nursery rhyme.

MANITOU: Amerindian, Algonquin and others. A spirit inherent in all natural phenomena, and controlling them. Iroquois equivalent ORENDA.

MANNUS – see TUISTO.

MANTUS: Etruscan. Ruler of the Underworld, with his wife, Mania.

MANU: Hindu. Name given to the ruler of the world during a Manvantara, which equals 857,139,000 divine years (a divine year being 360 human years). The present Manu is Vaivasvata.

MAO, MAHOU, MAOU: Benin. Sun and creator god. Son of the mother goddess Lissa and brother of the Moon god GOU. He seems to have replaced Lissa as the creator of all things.

MAPONUS – see MABON.

MARA: Hindu Buddhist. A major demon who tried to defeat the Bodhisattva SIDDHARTHA, first by sending his daughters to seduce him and then by direct attack, but failed.

MARCO, PRINCE: Slavonic. A Serbian legendary hero, son of a dryad, who sleeps mounted on his horse in a cave. His sword slowly rises from its sheath, and when it is fully out, he will ride forth to save his country from its enemies.

MARDUK: Assyro-Babylonian god of the Spring Sun; originally a vegetation god. First son of EA by the antediluvian Earth goddess Damkina (Ninella, Damku). One of the named consorts of Ishtar, though he also appears as the husband of the fertility goddess Zarpanitu (Zerpanitum) ('She Who Produces Seed'). In Sumerian myth, he and the goddess Aru (Aruru, Ninti) together created 'the seed of mankind'; in later patriarchal times, he created mankind by himself. He gradually took over the aspects of other gods, becoming chief god of the Babylonian pantheon. He is the Bel of the Old Testament.

MAREREWANA: Guinean, Arawak tribe. The Arawak Noah, who escaped the Deluge in a canoe with his followers.

MARIS: Etruscan name for MARS:

MARISHI-TEN: Japanese, of Chinese origin. Protector of soldiers and averter of fires.

MARMOO: Australian Aborigine. The Spirit of Evil who devastated the world with swarms of poisonous and devouring insects. The Mother-Spirit Nungeena and the Father-Spirit BAIAME had to restore it by creating birds to eat up the insects.

MARNAS: The god of Gaza, who in Christian times became the personal enemy of the hermit-abbot St Hilarion.

MARS. Roman god of war. See Chapter VI. 777: Tarot: Fives, Emperor, Death, Tower; gems: ruby, jacinth, any red stone; plants: oak, nux vomica, nettle, tiger lily, geranium, cactus, absinthe, rue; animals: basilisk, ram, owl, scorpion, beetle, lobster or crayfish, wolf, horse, bear; minerals: iron, sulphur; perfumes: tobacco, dragon's blood, Siamese benzoin, opoponax, pepper, all hot pungent odours; magical weapons: Sword, Spear, Scourge, or Chain, Horns, Energy, Burin, Pain of the Obligation.

MARSABA: Melanesian, Rooke Island. The Devil.

MARUMDA: – see KUKSU.

MARUTS, THE: Hindu. Storm and wind spirits. In Vedic myth, the eleven sons of RUDRA and Prisni (in another version, their mother was Diti, daughter of DAKSHA) who became the companions of INDRA. Also called the RUDRAS. 777: Tarot: Fool, (Swords) Emperors or Princes; gems: topaz, chalcedony; plant: aspen; animals: eagle, man; perfume: galbanum; magical weapon: Dagger or Fan.

MASHIA, MASHYA: The Persian Adam; his Eve was Mashyoi (Mashiane). They were born from the body (or seed) of GAYOMART after it had lain in the Earth for forty years. They gave birth to seven couples. Like the Biblical Adam and Eve, they first recognized that all was created by the principle of good (ORMAZD), and called it God, but were later led astray by his evil counterpart (AHRIMAN, ANGRA MAINYU).

MASLUM – see GLOOSLAP.

MASSIM-BIAMBE: Congo, Mundang tribe. The omnipotent, immaterial, sexless creator, forming a triad with the male god PHEBELE and the goddess Mebeli. Phebele and Mebeli had a son, Man, and Massim-Biambe gave him a soul and the breath of life.

MASTER OF WINDS: Amerindian, Iroquois and Huron. His wife, Breath of Wind, gave birth to twins who fought in her womb; Master of Winds set them in the sky as Sun and Moon.

MATARISVAN: The Hindu PROMETHEUS, who captured the thunderbolt and gave mankind the secret of the fire element.

MATH AP MATHONWY: Welsh. King Math of Gwynedd, son of

Mathonwy and brother of Dôn, a central figure in the *Mabinogion* story of the birth of LLEU LLAW GYFFES. A great magician, he taught his craft to his nephew GWYDION.

MATOWELIA: Amerindian. Chief god of the Mojave tribe of Colorado. He lived 'above the Sun' and guided travellers on their journeys. The souls of the cremated dead went to him; the uncremated became night owls.

MATSYA: Hindu. The first avatar of VISHNU, as a great horned fish.

MAUI (1) Polynesian Sun god. His sister was the Moon goddess Sina (Ina).

MAUI (2) Polynesian and Maori culture hero. Brought up by the gods, he raised the sky to its present position, created many islands by fishing for them and gave fire to mankind. He tried to make men immortal by penetrating the body of Underworld goddess Hine-Nui-Te-Po ('Great Goddess of Darkness'), but she crushed him to death, since when all humans must die.

MAWU-LISA: Haitian voodoo, African Benin origin. Twin children of NANAN-BOUCLOU, they engendered all the gods, including BADÉ and SOBO.

MAYON: Tamil equivalent of KRISHNA.

MAZDA – see AHURA MAZDA.

MEHEN: Egyptian. Serpent god coiled protectively around the kiosk on the deck of the boat on which RA travelled through the Underworld at night.

MEKE MEKE: Polynesian, Easter Island (Rapa-Nui). Creator god, probably equivalent of TANGAROA. Envisaged as a bird man; eggs were offered to him at his annual festival.

MELANION (also called HIPPOMENES): Greek. Successful suitor of Nature and hunting goddess Atalanta, who would only marry the man who could beat her in a race. He won by dropping the three golden apples which Aphrodite had given him; by pausing to pick them up, she lost the race and married him. The couple were later turned into lions for profaning a temple of ZEUS; a patriarchal demotion?

MELEAGER: Greek hero, son of birth goddess Althaea ('She Who Makes Grow') and Oenus, the first man to plant a vineyard in Greece. Atalanta (see MELANION) brought about his death in circumstances suggesting the sacrificed god theme. In one account, Atalanta bore him a son, Parthenopaeus ('Son of a Virgin' – not in the celibate sense; cf. AENGUS MAC ÓG).

MELKART, MELQART, MELICERTES: ('God of the City') Phoenician. An early Sun god, later a sea god. Tutelary god of Tyre. Said to be son of ZEUS DEMAROS. As Melicertes, also worshipped at Corinth.

MEMNON: Greek. Son of dawn goddess Eos by one of her human lovers, Tithonus. He became king of Ethiopia. He helped his uncle Priam at the siege of Troy and was slain by ACHILLES; he was then made immortal. Dewdrops were said to be Eos's tears, weeping for her son's death.

MENDES, RAM OF: Egyptian. A form of OSIRIS. Herodotus wrongly called it 'the Goat of Mendes'.

MEN-SHEN, THE: Chinese door gods, having various names.

MENTHU – see MONT.

MENU: Lithuanian Moon god, who may be the same as MANI.

MERCURY: Roman. God of communication and travel, messenger of the gods, and patron of merchants. Greek equivalent HERMES. 777: Tarot: Eights, Magician, Chariot; gems: opal (especially fire opal), agate, amber; plants: moly, anhalonium lewinii, vervain, herb mercury, marjolane, palm, lotus; animals: hermaphrodite, jackal, swallow, ibis, ape, crab, turtle, sphinx; mineral: mercury; perfumes: Names and Versicals and Apron, Wand or Caducaeus, Furnace.

MERLIN, MYRDDIN: Welsh and British Celtic. Sometimes known as Emrys. An early legendary bard, magician and seer, only later associated with ARTHUR. (The spelling 'Merlin' seems to have been invented by Geoffrey of Monmouth; he was writing for Norman-French readers, and 'Myrddin' was too like 'Merde', French for 'shit'.

MERODACH: Assyro-Babylonian creator god. Son of EA, and husband of Ishtar.

MERUL and MERUIL. African. Twin gods of Nubia.

MESHLAMTNEA – see NERGAL.

MESTHA, MESTI – see HORUS, FOUR SONS OF.

METSIK: Estonian. A wood spirit, patron of cattle.

METZLI: Aztec Moon god, sometimes identified with TEZCATLIPOCA.

MEULER: Chilean, Araucanian. God of winds, represented as a lizard.

MIACH: Irish. Son of DIANCECHT, the father of medicine, and himself a physician. With his sister Airmid, made King NUAD's silver hand, for which Diancecht killed him. Healing grasses grew on his grave.

MICHABO – see MANABOZHO.

MICTLA, MICTLANTECUHTLI: Aztec. Co-ruler with his sister/wife Mictlancihautl of the Underworld, which was known as Mictlan. Usually represented as raven-headed, with a rapacious beak.

MIDER, MIDIR: Irish. King of the Gaelic Underworld. Son of the DAGDA and Boann, goddess of the River Boyne. His wife was the outstandingly beautiful Étain Echraidhe ('horse-riding'), personifcation of reincarnation. He had a magic cauldron which his daughter Blathnat helped CUCHU-LAINN to steal.

MII-NO-KAMI: Japanese. God of wells.

MILCOM: Referred to in 2 Kings xxiii:13 as a god of the Ammonites.

MILETUS: Greek. A son of APOLLO who migrated from Crete to Caria, founded the city of Miletus and was the ancestor of the Milesians (the 'Sons of Mil' of Irish tradition).

MIMIR: Scandinavian. Uncle of ODIN, and guardian of Otherir, the meadow of poets. God of prophecy and wisdom and also of inland waters, ponds and springs. He would drink from the spring flowing from the root of Yggdrasil, the ash tree that overshadows the world. Odin asked him for a drink of the magic water, but Mimir demanded one of his eyes in return. Odin agreed, and Mimir used his eye as a drinking-cup.

MIN: Egyptian. God of sexual potency, always portrayed ithyphallic. Mostly human-headed, occasionally lion-headed. Protector of the mining regions of the desert East of the Nile, and of desert travellers. Bouquets of flowers were offered to him to promote fertility of the Nile valley; particularly sacred to Min was the long lettuce (*lactuca sativa*), which is phallic in shape and has a sap like semen.

MINATO-NO-KAMI: Japanese. God of river mouths.

MINEPA: Mozambican. An evil genius opposed to the supreme god MULUKU.

MINOS: Greek. Son of ZEUS and Europa. The most famous legendary king of Crete. He married Pasiphaë, daughter of HELIOS, the Sun god, who bore him Ariadne. POSEIDON caused Pasiphaë to fall in love with the white bull of Minos, and she gave birth to the Minotaur. Pasiphaë and Ariadne were probably the Mother and Maid aspects of the same Moon goddess, Minos the god or high priest of the Cretan bull cult, and the Minotaur that totem turned into a monster by Athenian patriarchy. After his death, Minos became a judge in the Underworld, deciding which souls should go to the Elysian Fields and which to punishment in Tartarus. 777: Tarot: Justice; gem: emerald; plant: aloe; animal: elephant; perfume: galbanum; magical weapon: Cross of Equilibrium.

MINOTAUR, THE – see MINOS.

MIROKU BOSATSU: Japanese Buddhist. The future BUDDHA, dwelling in the Tushita heaven. He will come to Earth 5,670 million years after the entry of Buddha into Nirvana.

MISCA: Nicaraguan. God of traders.

MISHARU: Assyro-Babylonian god of law and order. Son of the Sun god SHAMASH and the dawn goddess Aya. His brother was Kittu, god of justice.

MITHRA, MITHRAS: Persian. God of light and moral purity, and later a Sun god and god of victory in war. His central legend involved his killing of a bull as a fertility rite, the bull's blood causing vegetation to flourish; animals were sacrificed to him. One of the most important of the pre-Zoroastrian pantheon. His cult spread widely in the Roman Empire, particularly among soldiers; there are the remains of a temple of Mithras to be seen in the City of London. Some consider it was a near thing whether Christianity or Mithraism became the official Imperial religion. His origin is the Hindu MITRA; much Zoroastrian mythology has Indian roots.

MITRA: Hindu. One form of the Sun god. Son of the primordial Mother Aditi, and brother of VARUNA and of the ADITYAS. Origin of the Persian MITHRA.

MIXCOATL: Aztec hunting (later a stellar) god. Son of childbirth goddess Cihuatcoatl. Father by the Moon and Earth goddess Coatlicue ('Serpent Skirt') of the war and storm god HUITZILOPOCHTLI, and by the flower and craftsmanship goddess Xochiquetzal ('Flower Feather') of the wisdom and priestcraft god QUETZALCOATL.

MNEVIS: Egyptian. Sacred bull of the Sun god of Heliopolis, an incarnation of RA. Originally an autonomous bull god.

MOCCOS, MOCCUS: Continental Celtic pig god, or god of a pig-totem clan. Identified under Roman influence with MERCURY.

MODI – see MAGNI.

MO-LI, THE: Chinese Buddhist. Four brothers, believed to have been deified human generals famous for their victories. Their statues guard the entrances to Buddhist temples. See GENERAL, THE SNIFFING and GENERAL, THE PUFFING.

MOLOCH: Hebrew deliberate misvocalization of m-l-k (malek, melek), 'king', as a derogatory title for a 'heathen' god – in particular probably BAAL-HAMMON of Carthage.

MOMUS: Greek god of mockery and spiteful criticism.

MONAN: ('Ancient') Brazilian, creator god of the Tupis. Angry with mankind for their ingratitude, he sent down a fire which consumed everything but one survivor, Irin Mage ('He Who Sees'). Monan took him up to heaven, but Iran Mage persuaded him to reprieve the Earth by sending a flood to put the fire out. Often confused with his successor, MAIRE-MONAN.

MONJU BOSATSU: Japanese Buddhist. A Bodhisattva personifying intelligence, compassion and contemplation.

MONT, MONTU, MENTHU: Egyptian. Theban war god, from about 2000 BC onwards. Adopted for a time by AMUN and Mut and called their son. Portrayed as falcon-headed or bull-headed. His wives were a solar goddess, Rat-Taui, and a local goddess, Tjenenyet. Identified with APOLLO by the Greeks. 777: Tarot: Emperor, Tower; gems: ruby, any red stone; plants; tiger lily, geranium, absinthe, rue; animals: ram, owl, horse, bear, wolf; perfumes: dragon's blood, pepper, all hot pungent odours; magical weapons: Horns, Energy, Burin, Sword.

MO-ROGROG: Polynesian. A name for LONO.

MORPHEUS: Greek god of dreams. He dwelt in the Underworld alongside his father, Thanatos (Death), and his uncle, Hypnos (Sleep).

MOT: Canaanite god of death and sterility. See Chapter V.

MOUTH: Phoenician. A god of death, son of CRONUS and Rhea, who died and was deified.

MUARI, MWARI: Rhodesian. God of the Mtawara tribe. His chief wife was Mashongavudzi; the reigning chief's first wife still takes this name.

MUKASA: African. God of Lake Victoria, propitiated by the Baganda tribe before long journeys. Virgins were provided for him as wives.

MU KING: Chinese. Born of the primeval mist, he was the first living creature and became ruler of the immortals.

MUKUNDA: ('Liberator') Hindu. A title of VISHNU.

MULAC – see BACABS, THE.

MULCIBER: Roman. A title of VULCAN.

MULLO: Continental Celtic. Patron of muleteers. Sometimes identified with MARS. Probably originally an ass totem divinity.

MULUKU: Mozambican. Supreme god. He created a man and a woman, but when they ignored his advice and failed to support themselves, he created two monkeys, gave the monkeys' tails to the human couple and told the monkeys to become humans and the humans monkeys. His evil opponent is MILEPA.

MUNGAN-NGANA: Australian Aborigine. Culture hero of the Kundei tribe, who taught them to make nets, canoes, tools and weapons. His adopted son Tundun was the ancestor of the tribe.

MURAIAN: Australian Aborigine, Van Arnhem Land. Culture hero of the

Kakadu tribe. Known as 'the Turtle Man'.

MURUGAN: Hindu. Chief god of the ancient Tamils. Attended by mountain fairies.

MUSEOS: ('Muse-Man') Greek. Son of Hecate.

MWARI – see MUARI.

MYESTAS, MYESYATS: Slavonic Moon god – but sometimes appears as the Sun's beautiful young bride whom he marries each Spring and abandons each Winter. As Moon god, his wife in some versions is Dennitsa (Svezda Dennitsa), the Morning Star (Venus) goddess.

MYRDDIN – see MERLIN.

MYRMIDONS – see AEACUS.

NABU, NEBO: Assyro-Babylonian and Chaldaean. God of wisdom, patron of scribes. In charge of the Tablets of Fate. Son of MARDUK, and husband of Tashmit (Urmit, Varamit), who helped him invent writing, or in other versions of the grain goddess Nisaba or of Ishtar.

NAGAS, NAGIS: Hindu serpent gods, living with their wives, the Naginis, in a magnificent underground kingdom. They can be tricky or helpful. Their father is Kashyapa, their mother Kadru and their ruler VASUKI. They always walk or run; their flying equivalents are the Sarpis. Apparently based on a pre-Hindu serpent-totem people whom the invading Hindus conquered. Statues of Nagas and Naginis are widely worshipped in South India, always under a tree.

NAGENTZANI and THOBADESTCHIN: Amerindian, Navajo. Twin culture heroes, revered warriors, sons of the Earth mother Estanatlehi.

NAGO: Haitian voodoo, of African (Yoruba) origin. A god of power; also associated with family lineage. He has a traditional drum-beat rhythm.

NAH-HUNTE: Assyro-Babylonian. Sun god of the Elamites. God of light, law and order.

NAI-NO-KAMI: Japanese earthquake god.

NAKA-YAMA-TSU-MI: Japanese god of mountain slopes.

NAKKI: Finnish. Water god, who lives in a splendid palace reached through bottomless lakes. He surfaces to visit Earth at sunrise and sunset and can assume many shapes. Swimmers must placate him.

NALA: Hindu. Son of the smith god VISVAKARMA and 'as skilful as his father'. With the aid of monkeys, he built a bridge across Ocean for RAMA and his brother Lakshmana to use.

NAMTAR, NAMTARU: Assyro-Babylonian. Plague-bringer, living in Arallu, the Underworld.

NANAN-BOUCLOU: Benin (Ewe peoples) and Haitian voodoo. In Africa, a bisexual deity who produced the twins Mawu-Lisa, from whom all the gods and goddesses sprang. In Haiti, a god of herbs and medicines.

NANCOMALA: Costa Rican, Guaymi Indians. Father by the water goddess Rutbe of the Sun and Moon, who were the ancestors of mankind.

NANDEREVUSU: Brazilian civilizing hero, and father by Nandecy of the storm god TUPAN.

NANNA: Chaldaean and Sumerian Moon god. Son of ENLIL and the grain goddess Ninlil. (Do not confuse with Scandinavian Nanna, wife of BALDUR.)

NANNAR, ENZU: Chaldaean. Moon god of the city of Ur (which means 'Light'). Equated with SIN.

NARA: Hindu. He and his wife Nari (a form of the mother goddess) sometimes appear as the primordial man and woman.

NARASINHA: Hindu. The fourth avatar of VISHNU, as a lion-headed man.

NARAYANA, HIRANYAGARBHA: Hindu. Born from the primordial egg (or a name for the egg itself), he willed the universe into being. Sometimes regarded as an aspect of BRAHMA and sometimes of VISHNU.

NARBROOI: New Guinean. Woodland spirit who stole the souls of the sick and only returned from them when propitiated with gifts.

NA REAU, NARUAU: Polynesian, Gilbert Islands. He and his daughter Kobine together created Heaven and Earth. When he created the first man and woman, he ordered them not to have children. They disobeyed him and had three – the Sun, Moon and Sea. He was furious, but forgave them.

NASATYAS, ASVINS, THE: Hindu. Dasra and Nasatya, twin sons of the goddess Saranyu, doctors to the gods and friends of the sick and unfortunate. They share one wife, the Sun goddess Surya. They make a path through the clouds for the dawn goddess Ushas, and perform a similar function at sunset. Said to be the inventors of mead.

NASR: Arabic, pre-Islamic vulture god. Condemned in the Koran as one of the five idols erected by the sons of Cain.

NATA: The Aztec Noah. His wife was Nena. They were commanded by TEZCATLIPOCA to build a ship to save themselves from the Deluge.

NATARA – see NETER.

NATARAJA: Hindu. A name for SHIVA as the master of dance and rhythm.

NATIGAI: Mongolian, Siberian, northern Chinese. Earth god, originating among the Tartars. Mentioned several times by Marco Polo: 'These two gods, Natigai and his wife, are the gods of Earth and watch over their flocks and crops and all their earthly goods.'

NORIANAHARY: Madagascan. Supreme god. Father of Ataokoloinona, whom he sent to Earth to consider the advisability of creating mankind but who never returned. He sent (and continues to send) messengers to Earth to look for him, and these became the human race.

NEBO – see NABU.

NEFERTUM: Egyptian, god of the setting Sun (later replaced by IMHOTEP) and of the lotus blossom. At Memphis, called the son of PTAH and Sekhmet; but at Buto in the Delta, his mother was said to be the cobra goddess Wadjet. Other versions make his mother the cat goddess Bast or make him a personification of Ptah.

NEHE, HEH: ('Eternity') Egyptian. One of two deities holding up the pillars of the sky, the other being (his wife?) Djet. Personification of eternity and of a long happy life.

NEKHEBKAU, NEHEBU-KAU: Egyptian. An Underworld serpent god with human limbs. His mother was the fertility and scorpion goddess Selkhet; other versions give his parents as the Earth god GEB and the harvest goddess Rennutet. Together he and Selkhet sometimes bound the dead with chains but sometimes looked after and helped them. Protective of royalty.

NEMED: Irish. Leader of one of the early peoples to occupy Ireland in the mythological cycle. Husband of Macha, the (probably pre-Celtic) Ulster goddess.

NEMQUETCHA: Colombian, Chibcha Indian, culture hero. His wife, Hunthaca, in a temper, flooded the Cundinamarea Table Land, so was banished to the sky and became the Moon.

NEMU: New Guinean, Kai tribe. Demigods who inhabited the Earth before mankind, whom they created. They were finally destroyed by a great flood.

NENAUNIR: African, Masai. Storm god and spirit of evil.

NEPER: Egyptian grain god, particularly of barley and emmer wheat.

NEPTUNE: Roman sea god. His feast was the Neptunalia, 23 July, when huts of branches were built as protection against the sun – i.e., against drought, Neptune being originally a freshwater god, acquiring his maritime status (and most of his characteristics) when he became equated with the Greek POSEIDON. His wife was Salacia, goddess of salt water. 777: Tarot: Hanged Man, (Cups) Queens, Moon; gems: beryl, aquamarine, pearl; plants: lotus, all water plants, unicellular organisms, opium poppy; animals: eagle-snake-scorpion (Cherub of Water), fish, dolphins; minerals: sulphates; perfumes: onycha, myrrh, ambergris; magical weapons: Cup and Cross of Suffering, Wine, Twilight of the Place and Magic Mirror.

NEREUS: Greek. A sea god, son of PONTUS and Gaia, living in a cave in the Aegean Sea. Known as 'the Truthful' and as 'Old Man of the Sea'. Father by Doris of the fifty Nereids, sea nymphs helpful to sailors. By one of these, Thetis, he was the grandfather of Achilles. In some versions, also father of the sea goddess Amphitrite.

NERGAL, MESHLAMTHEA: Assyro-Babylonian war and Underworld god, husband of Queen of the Underworld Ereshkigal, whom he first demoted and then married. In earlier legends, his wife was Laz, a prehistoric goddess of Cuthac.

NETER, NATARA: Egyptian. A name for the ultimate God, the active power of which all other god-forms were aspects. Feminine equivalent Neteret (Natarat).

NGAHUE: New Zealand, Maori. Afterworld god.

NGAI: African, Masai. Supreme deity, creator of the universe.

NGENDEI, NGENDEL: Melanesian, Fiji Islands. Supreme god who upholds the Earth, causes earthquakes and rules the dead. Comets are his children. In some versions, he created the world and mankind. Envisaged as half snake, half man. His mother was a stone.

NGURVILU: Chilean, Araucanian Indian. God of water, rivers and lakes, who assumes the form of a wild cat, his tail ending in a claw. Blamed for any boating or swimming accident.

NGWOREKARA: Congo, Pahouin tribe. An ugly and wicked god who can condemn souls to a second death.

NICHANT: Amerindian, Algonquin, Gros-Ventre tribe. The god who destroyed the world by fire and water.

NICK: The 'Old Nick' of British folklore seems to have been a late masculine variant of the Teutonic Nixe, priestesses (or spirits) of lakes, rivers and wells.

NIDIM: Babylonian. An early name for EA.

NIJUHACHI BUSHU, THE: Japanese. The twenty-eight deities symbolizing the constellations.

NIKKAL SEN: India. 'A sect in the Punjab worshipped a deity whom they called Nikkal Sen. This Nikkal Sen was no other than the redoubtable General Nicholson, and nothing that the general could do or say damped the ardour of his adorers' (Frazer, *The Golden Bough*, p. 132). Frazer remarks that 'to this day in India all living persons remarkable for great strength or valour or for supposed miraculous powers run the risk of being worshipped as gods.'

NINGIRSU, NINURTA: Assyro-Babylonian irrigation and fertility god. Also a war and hunting god – the concept being that he fought the chaotic aspects of Nature to ensure fertility. Personification of the South Wind. His wife was Bau (Bohu, Bahu, Gur), primeval goddess of the Dark Waters of the deep. Their marriage was celebrated at the Babylonian New Year, which followed the harvest. Other versions make his wife Gula or Nin-karrak, both health goddesses.

NINIGI: Japanese. Young god, grandson of Sun goddess Amaterasu, and husband of rice goddess Kono-Hana-Sakuya-Hime or of Shitateru-Hime.

NINIGIKU: ('King of the Sacred Eye') Assyro-Babylonian. A name for EA in his wisdom aspect.

NINURTA – see NINGIRSU.

NIORD, NJORD, NJOERD: Scandinavian giant, patriarchal masculinization of the early fertility goddess Narthus. Husband of Skadi, and father of FREY and Freya. He lived by the sea-shore, but Skadi preferred her native mountains; eventually she returned to them.

NIPARAYA: Amerindian, Pericu, creator god. He had no body, yet his wife Amayicoyondi bore him three sons, one of whom was Man.

NIRRITA: Hindu. With his wife, Nirriti, Vedic deities of death.

NJORD, NJOERD: – see NIORD.

NOBU, NOHU: Melanesian, New Hebrides. Creator of the world.

NODENS: British. A Severn estuary river god who had a temple at Lydney Park in Gloucestershire. Some confusion with LUDD: they may originally have been the same.

NOESARNAK: Eskimo. Lives on land, dressed in deerskin with a deerskin mask. Looks like a tiny woman. To be treated cautiously.

NOH: African. The Hottentot Adam. His Eve was Hingnoh.

NOHOCHACYUM. ('Grandfather') Mayan, Yucatan. Beneficient creator god. Perpetually at war with the evil HAPIKERN.

NOHU – see NOBU.

NONCOMALA: Costa Rican. Creator of the Earth and mankind, and father of the Sun and the Moon. When mankind became wicked, he sent a deluge to destroy them.

NOOTAIKOK: Eskimo. Helpful iceberg spirit who procures seals.

NOTUS: Greek god of the South Wind. Son, with the other three Winds (see BOREAS, EURUS, ZEPHYRUS), of the Titan ASTRAEUS and the dawn goddess Eos. Roman equivalent AUSTER.

NU – see NUN.

NUAD, NUADA: Irish. A king of the Tuatha Dé Danann, who lost his hand in the First Battle of Mag Tuireadh (Moytura) and so had to abdicate, as Celtic kings had to be physically perfect; but MIACH and his sister Airmid made him a silver one, and he regained his throne, thereafter being known as Argetlamh ('Silver Hand'). See also LUDD.

NUDA, NUDD – see LUDD.

NUDIMMUD: Babylonian. An early name for EA.

NUN, NU, NUNU: Egyptian. God of the primordial waters; 'father of the gods'. With his wife Naunet (Nunut), the first couple of the Ogdoad of Hermopolis. The Ogdoad were the first eight living beings, the males being frogs and the females serpents. 777: Tarot: Fool; gems: topaz, chalcedony; plant: aspen; animal: eagle or man (Cherub of Air); perfume: galbanum; magical weapon: Dagger or Fan.

NURELLI: Australian Aborigine, Wiimbaio tribe. Created the land and brought law and order to the tribe. He had two wives, each carrying two spears. Eventually ascended to the sky as a constellation.

NURRUNDERE – see BUNJIL.

NUSKU: Assyro-Babylonian. A fire god, associated with burnt offerings. Son of SIN or of ANU. In early versions, a minister of ENLIL, and a god of justice. His symbol was a lamp.

NWYVRE: ('Sky, Space, Firmament') Welsh. Husband of the goddess Arianrhod. He has survived in name only.

NYAME: African, Ashanti. Supreme god, and god of the sky, storms and lightning. He was driven from Earth to the sky by the noise of the pounding of grain. Gave mankind the Sun, Moon, rain and other gifts, after the spider ANANSE had reported their needs to him.

NYAMIA: Guinean, Agni tribe. Supreme god, which he became under Moslem influence; before that, he was a sky and storm god equal to the Earth goddess Asia, to the bush god Asia-Bussu and to the cultivation god Pan.

NYYRIKKI – see TAPIO.

NZAMBE, NZAME: African, Bantu. Supreme god. The first man he created became evil, so he buried him and created another, shaping a wife for him from wood; these became the ancestors of mankind.

OAK KING: Celtic god of the Waxing Year. See Chapter IX.

OANNES: Babylonian god of wisdom. Half man, half fish. Brought culture to mankind; perhaps a memory of an early conquest of Babylon by a sea-going people. Said to have been the father, by the fish goddess Ataryatis Derketo of Askalon, of Semiramis, a historical queen of Babylon (believed to be mythical until 1909, when an inscription about her was found). Egyptian early Christians identified John the Baptist with him.

OBATALA: Nigerian, Yoruba tribe, and Brazilian voodoo. Sky god. He and

Earth goddess Odudua were created by the supreme god OLORUN as an Adam and Eve, with their Eden on the island of Ife. He was very pure, but she was interested in procreation and had many lovers.

OBERON. Shakespeare's King of the Fairies also appears in the medieval epic *Huon de Bordeaux*. In that, he is also a fairy king with magical powers, ruling a kingdom called Mommur. He is a dwarf, though with an angelic face, and son of Julius Caesar and the Lady of the Hidden Isle. She was apparently ageless; according to the epic, seven centuries earlier (in fact, it would have been three), she had been mother to Alexander the Great. At the end of the tale, Oberon is taken up to Heaven by angels, leaving Huon to rule Mommur as 'King of all Faerie'. Titania, Oberon's queen in Shakespeare's *A Midsummer Night's Dream*, was in fact the Roman goddess Diana, whom Ovid calls by that name in *Metamorphoses* 3:173.

OCEANUS: Greek. Son of URANUS and Gaia – the only one not to rebel against his father. God (and personification) of the great river which girdled the universe, embracing the sea but not mingling with it, and giving birth to all the waters on Earth. By his sister Tethys, father of the 3,000 Oceanids, sea and river nymphs, and of Metis ('Wisdom, Counsel'), who became ZEUS's first wife. According to one version, he and Tethys cared for the infant Hera (who became Zeus's second wife) in their palace at the western edge of the world. As the Olympians established themselves, his rule over the waters of Earth was transferred to POSEIDON, and he retired to the encircling river.

ODIN: Scandinavian. Chief god, and god of war, magic, poetry, cunning and the dead. King of the AESIR. Son of BOR or THOR and the giantess Bestla. Probably originally a historical person, chief of a powerful raven clan, early becoming a god of nocturnal storms. Gradually replaced Thor as head of the AESIR (Thor being the peasants' god, Odin the warriors'). Known as the All-Father. At the creation of the world, he set the Sun and Moon in motion. With HOENIR and LODUR, he made ASK and Embla, the first human couple. He lived in Valhalla, attended by the Valkyries, and with two ravens, Hugin and Munin, who kept him informed on events on Earth. He had an eight-legged horse, Sleipnir, a spear, Gungnir, and a magic ring, Draupnir. His wife was Frigg, who bore him BALDUR, Bali, BRAGI, HODER, THOR, TYR and VIDAR. At Ragnarok, the Twilight of the Gods, he was consumed by the FENRIS WOLF. Identified with the German WOTAN and the Anglo-Saxon WODEN. 777: Tarot: Twos, Kings or Knights, Eights; gems: star ruby, turquoise, opal, especially fire opal; plants: amaranth, moly, anhalonium lewinii; animals: man, hermaphrodite, jackal; minerals: phosphorus, mercury; perfumes: musk, storax; magical weapons: Lingam, Inner robe of Glory, Names and Versicles and Apron. (Note: 777 gives different correspondences for Odin and Wotan.)

ODOMANKOMA: African, Ashanti. Creator of Earth and all things thereon, including mankind – and death, which ultimately overcame him too.

ODYSSEUS, ULYSSES, ULIXES: Greek. Hero of Homer's *Odyssey* which is the story of his wanderings after the siege of Troy. Archetype of human ingenuity and endurance. King of Ithica, son of Laertes and Anticela, husband of Penelope, and father of Telemachus. Ulysses or Ulixes was his Roman name.

OG – see GOG.

OGHMA: Irish god of wisdom and writing. See p.20.

OGUN: Nigerian, Yoruba tribe, and Brazilian voodoo. War and fire god. Son of AGANJU and Yemaja. One of the many lovers of the love goddess Erzulie.

OHDOWAS, THE: Amerindian, Iroquois. Dwarfs who live underground, in charge of all kinds of monsters.

OISÍN, OSSIAN: ('Fawn') Irish. Son of FIONN MAC CUMHAL and the deer goddess Sadhbh. She was lured away from Fionn's house by magic before Oisín was born, and turned into a deer; Fionn never found her, but the boy Oisíon came to him and grew up to be an inspired poet. The only man on record to stand up to St Patrick in argument. He went with Niamh of the Golden Hair to Tír na nÓg (the Celtic Land of Youth), where she bore him two sons (Fionn, after Oisín's father, and Osgar, 'He Who Loves the Deer'), and a daughter (Plur na mBan, 'Flower of Women').

OIWA DAIMYOJIN: Japanese, Shinto. A god of rock.

OKITSU-HIKO: Japanese kitchen god, with female counterpart Okitsu-Hime.

O-KUNI-NUSHI: Japanese. Earth god and god of medicine. Son of the sea and fertility god SUSANOWO when he went to live in Izumo province. His sister and wife was Suseri-Hime. When his jealous brothers killed him, the seed goddess Kami-Musumi ('Divine Generative Force') brought him back to life. He became ruler of Izumo.

OLLE: Amerindian, Tuleyone. When the evil spirit Sahte tried to destroy the Earth with a fire, Olle put it out with a great flood, submerging everything except one mountaintop on which the survivors gathered. Sometimes called COYOTE. See also WEKWEK.

OLOFAET: Melanesian, Caroline Islands. Fire god. He gave fire to a bird, who flew from tree to tree on Earth implanting its forces in them, so that men could draw it out by friction.

OLOKUN: Nigerian, Yoruba tribe. God of the primeval ocean or of the great ocean of the sky. Son of AGANJU and Yemaja, and father of OLORUN.

OLORUN: Nigerian, Yoruba tribe. Supreme god over a large pantheon, but in a passive role, not the central subject of myth or worship. Son of OLOKUN. See OBATALA.

OLUKSAK: Eskimo. God of lakes, living on their banks.

OLYMPIANS, THE: Greek. The pantheon of the Classical period, said to dwell on Mount Olympus, on the borders of Macedonia and Thessaly. The 'Twelve Olympians' were the gods ZEUS, POSEIDON, HEPHAESTUS, HERMES, ARES and APOLLO and the goddesses, Hera, Athene, Artemis, Hestia, Aphrodite and Demeter. Other minor deities beside the Twelve also lived on Olympus.

OMACATL: ('Two Reeds') Aztec. God of happiness and festivity. At his feasts, maize paste images of his bones were made and eaten.

OMETECUCHTLI, OMETEOTL, TLOQUE NAHUAQUE: Aztec creator god. His wife, creator goddess Omeciuatl, may be a deity earlier than he. Sometimes they are regarded as male and female aspects of the same deity.

OMONGA: Indonesian, Celebes, Tomori tribe. A rice spirit who dwells in the Moon. If he is not treated with respect, he will come and eat twice as much rice in the barn as its owners take out of it.

ONAMUJI: Japanese. Earth god, son of SUSANOWO. Forced to abdicate in favour of NINIGI.

ONI, THE: Japanese Buddhist. Spirits who bring diseases. They are dressed in red. Not unduly dangerous and may even be converted to Buddhism.

ONNIONI: Amerindian, Huron. A horned snake god, whose horn could pierce mountains and rocks. Warriors carried pieces of 'Onnioni's horn' into battle to give them courage.

ONO: Polynesian, Marquesas Islands. Local name for RONGO.

ONURIS, ANHUR, ANHURT: ('The One Who Leads Back the Distant One') Egyptian. Warrior and hunter god originating at This near Abydos. His name (Anhur in Egyptian) refers to the legend of his journey south to capture the lion goddess Mekhit who became his consort.

OONAWIEH UNGGI: ('The Oldest Wind') Amerindian, Cherokee. Wind god.

OOYARRAUYAMITOK: Eskimo. Lives sometimes on Earth, sometimes in Heaven. Helps hunters to find meat.

OPHION: Greek. The Cosmic Snake. The Pelasgians claimed to descend from his mating with the Oceanid Euronyme.

OPOCHTLI: Aztec. God of fishermen and bird-snarers.

ORCUS: Roman. God of death, who took the living by force and carried them off to the Underworld. Identified with DIS, PLUTO and the Greek HADES. Also a name for the Underworld itself.

ORION: Greek. A hunter who fell in love with seven daughters of ATLAS and the oceanid Pleione. ZEUS placed them in the heavens to help them escape him, where they became the Pleiades. The dawn goddess Eos fell in love with him and carried him away, but he was accidentally killed by Artemis. He too became a constellation in the sky, where he still pursues the Pleiades. (The Australian Aborigines have an almost identical story about these two constellations.) The Egyptians associated the Orion constellation with OSIRIS.

ORISHAKO: Nigerian, Yoruba tribe. Agricultural god. Sometimes named as the husband of Earth goddess Odudua (see OBATALA).

ORKO: Basque thunder god. *Orkeguna* is the Basque name for Thursday.

ORMAZD – see AHURA MAZDA.

ORO: Polynesian war god. Son of creator god TAAROA by Hina-of-the-Land, wife of Sea-for-Swimming-in, who adopted him as his son. In Tahiti the king was regarded as his human manifestation.

ORONGO – see RONGO.

ORUNJAN. Nigerian, Yoruba tribe, and Brazilian voodoo. Midday Sun god, son of AGANJU and Yemaja. Orunjan raped his mother, and she gave birth to eleven gods and goddesses, plus the Sun and Moon, and two streams of water came from her breasts to form a great lake.

ORVANDIL, EGIL:

OSGAR – see OISIN.

OSHALLA: Nigerian, Yoruba tribe. A secondary god, son of the Sun god and husband of the Earth goddess.

OSIRIS: Egyptian. God of vegetation, fertility and the afterlife. See Chapter XVIII. 777: Tarot: Tens, Empresses or Princesses, Hierophant; gems: rock crystal, topaz; plants: willow, lily, ivy, mallow; animals: sphinx, bull (Cherub of Earth); mineral: magnesium sulphate; perfumes: dittany of Crete, storax; magical weapons: Magical Circle and Triangle, Labour of Preparation.

OTOS: ('Reason') Phoenician. In the Damascius creation legend, son of Air and Aura.

OULOMUS: Phoenician. In the Mochus creation legend, son of Ether and Air. From him sprang the primeval egg from which came URANUS and Gaia.

OURANOS – see URANUS.

OUSOOS: Phoenician. In the Philo Byblos creation legend, giant son of Fire. He was the first to make garments from skins, in conflict with his brother Hyposouranios, first builder of cities. Probably a memory of country/town friction.

OVINNIK: Slavonic. God of barns.

O-WATA-TSU-MI: Japanese. Chief sea god. Also known as Shio-Zuchi ('Old Man of the Tide').

O-YAMA-TSU-MI: Japanese. Chief god of mountains.

PA-CHA: Chinese. A 'Great General', invoked against locusts. Envisaged as a man with bird's beak and feet, his hands tipped with claws, and wearing a petticoat.

PACHACAMAC: Inca; pre-Inca in origin. Outside the main Inca pantheon, worshipped as supreme god by the coastal Peruvians. A universal creator god, born of the Earth Mother goddess Mama Pacha (Pachamama). Fire god (particularly of underground fire), so the Incas made him son of the Sun. He created men and women (or improved those created by VIRACOCHA, whom he rivalled) and gave them the necessities and also the fine things of life. He required human sacrifice. He was invisible, and it was forbidden to portray him. His cult centre, a great temple near today's Lima, was looted by the Spaniards.

PAEON: Greek. An early healer god, supplanted by APOLLO.

PAHA – see HIISI.

PA-HSIEN: Chinese, Taoist. The Eight Immortals, humans who achieved immortality through practising Taoist doctrines. They have the right to attend the banquets of the Lady Wang, wife of the AUGUST PERSONAGE OF JADE (see under JADE).

PAIKEA. Polynesian, Mangaia Island. God of the sea monsters. Son of RANGI and the mother goddess Papa-Tu-Anuku. Also the name of a whale, and of a hero of a swimming story.

PÄIVÄ: Finno-Ugric Sun god.

PALAEMON: Greek. Born human as Melicertes, he became a sea god. His mother, Ino, jumped into the sea with him in her arms, to escape her husband, Athamas, King of Boeotia, who had gone mad and killed her other son. Nereids befriended her, and she became a goddess protecting mariners, under the name Leucothea. Dolphins bore the body of Melicertes, who had drowned, to Corinth, where he became venerated as a god. Often portrayed as a child carried by dolphins.

PALES: Roman. Originally a god of pastures and cattle, and protector of shepherds, who later became a goddess with the same name and functions. His/her festivals, the Palilia, were on 21 April, traditional date of the founding of Rome. As a god, sometimes identified with FAUNUS, and as a goddess, with Vesta. Gave his/her name to the Palatine Hill.

PAMOLA: Amerindian, Algonquin. An evil spirit of the night who was defeated by the culture hero GLOOSKAP.

PAN (1) Greek. God of all Nature, the countryside and the woods. See Chapter XVII. Identified by the Romans with FAUNUS. 777: Tarot: Devil; gem: black diamond; plants: Indian hemp, orchis root, thistle; animals: goat, ass; mineral: carbon; perfumes: musk, civet (also Saturnian perfumes); magical weapons: Secret Force, Lamp.

PAN (2) – see NYAMIA.

PANCHAMUKHI-MARUTI: Hindu. Western Indian name for SHIVA. Invoked when weights had to be lifted.

PANEBTAWY: Egyptian. A young god, 'Lord of the Two Lands'. Son of HAROERIS and Tasenetofret ('The Good or Beautiful Sister'), he represents the legitimacy of the Pharaoh.

P'AN-KU: Chinese. A cosmic being born from the primordial egg, thousands of years before it divided into YANG and Yin. He (or, more strictly, It) grew with the universe and was co-extensive with it. Other versions make him a giant who evolved from the Yang and Yin.

PAPSUKAL: Babylonian. A messenger of the gods, who brought to SHAMASH the news of Ishtar's imprisonment in the Underworld (see p.87).

PARASHURAMA: Hindu. The sixth avatar of VISHNU, as RAMA with the axe, in which he defeated the Kshatriyas, followers of INDRA, in twenty-one battles (a story to explain the displacement of Indra by Vishnu). He married Dharani, an incarnation of Lakshmi particularly connected with the Earth.

PARIS: Greek. The prince of Troy whose abduction of Helen, wife of Menelaus of Sparta, caused the Trojan War. This arose from the 'Judgement of Paris', when he had been asked which was the fairest of the goddesses Hera, Athene and Aphrodite; Hera offered him wealth and power, Athene wisdom and Aphrodite the most beautiful woman in the world. To the other two's fury, Aphrodite won, and his fateful reward was Helen, who was the daughter of ZEUS and Leda; so the Olympians were involved, and intervened, on both sides of the resulting war. In that war, he killed ACHILLES and finally died himself.

PARJANYA: Hindu. A form of the Sun god, when he hides in clouds and sends down rain to fertilize the Earth.

PARTHOLON: Irish. Leader of the second people (twenty-five men and twenty-four women) to occupy Ireland in the mythological cycle. They brought agriculture and craftsmanship to the island.

PATECATL: Aztec. God of drink and drunkenness.

PATOL: Mayan, chief god of the Tzental tribe. His wife was Alaghom Naum (Istat Ix), 'the Mother of Mind', creatress of mind and thought.

PAYNAL: Aztec. Messenger god, assistant of HUITZILOPOCHTLI.

PEIROUN: Chinese, Taiwan (Formosa). Hero of a Deluge legend, in which he escaped by boat.

PELEUS: Greek. His marriage to the Nereid Thetis, and their failure to invite the goddess of discord, Eris, to it, led to the Judgement of PARIS and thus to the Trojan War. Their son was ACHILLES.

PELLERVOINEN: Finno-Ugric. God of fields, protector of trees and plants.

PENATES: Roman household gods – indoor, of hearth and pantry, compared with LARES, who were outdoor. Always two in number. They had a shrine just inside the front door to which visitors paid their respects.

PENEUS: Greek. A river god, of one of the two rivers (the other being the ALPHAEUS) which HERAKLES diverted to clean out the Augean Stables.

PERKUNAS: Lithuanian thunder god. An alternative form of PERUN.

PEROUN – see PERUN.

PERSES: Greek. He and his wife, Asteria, both Titans, were symbols of shining light and were the parents of Hecate in the earliest tradition.

PERSEUS: Greek. A hero, son of ZEUS and Danaë. He killed the Gorgon Medusa with Athene's help and created the Atlas Mountains by showing ATLAS the head of Medusa and turning him to stone. He rescued Andromeda from the sea monster and married her; their grandson Perses was the legendary ancestor of the Persians.

PERUDA: Brazilian. Tupi-Guarani tribes. One of three creator gods, the others being GUARACY and JACY. Concerned with human reproduction.

PERUN, PEROUN, PYERUN: Slavonic. Sun, lightning and war god, and lord of the thunderbolt, whose worship persisted well into the Christian era, especially around Kiev. Gave his name to Thursday (*Perendan*). His weapon was the bow. Also a harvest god. May be a form of THOR brought by Scandinavian traders to Novgorod and Kiev. Later, in Christian times, merged with the prophet Elijah. See also TROJANU.

PETESUCHOS – see SEBEK.

PIGUERAO: ('White Bird') Inca. Twin brother of APOCATEQUIL. Because of them, twins were regarded as sacred.

PHAETON (1): Greek. Son of HELIOS and Clymene, who tried to drive his father's Sun-chariot but failed to control it, and set fire to the Earth. ZEUS killed him to prevent the fire destroying everything. His mourning sisters became poplars, weeping amber tears into the River Po (southern end of the overland amber-trade route from the Baltic).

PHAETON (2): Greek. Son of Cephalus and the dawn goddess Eos. Carried off as a child by Aphrodite to be 'the nocturnal guardian of her sacred temples'.

PHANES: ('Light', 'He Who Appears') Greek. In the Orphic tradition, first being to be born from the Cosmic Egg. By union with Night, he created Heaven and Earth and engendered ZEUS. Described as having golden wings and the heads of ram, bull, snake and lion.

PHEBELE: Congo, Mundang tribe. Male member of the triad MASSIM-BIAMBE (omnipotent, immaterial creator), Phebele (god) and Mebeli (goddess). Phebele and Mebeli gave birth to Man, and Massim-Biamba gave him a soul and the breath of life.

PHOBOS: ('Fright') Greek. One of the sons of ARES who accompanied him to battle, the other being Deimos ('Fear').

PHOEBUS: ('Shining') Another name for APOLLO.

PHORCYS: Greek. An early sea god, son of PONTUS and Gaia. Father by his sister Ceto of the Gorgons, the Graeae, the dragon Ladon and perhaps the Hesperides; and by Hecate of Scylla, who was turned by Circe into one of the two deadly monsters guarding the Straits of Messina. (Scylla lived by a rock, as the other monster, Charybdis, did in a whirlpool, both of which were a danger to boats.) These awesome offspring suggest that Phorcys represented the sea in its threatening aspect.

PHOSPHORUS: Greek. Son of ASTREUS and the dawn goddess Eos. Personification of the planet Venus as Morning Star. Envisaged as a winged spirit with a torch in his hand, flying in the sky before his mother's chariot. His Evening Star brother was HESPERUS.

PICUNNUS: Roman. With his twin brother, Pilumnus, protective gods of the newborn. A bed was made for them in the conjugal chamber.

PICUS: ('Woodpecker') Roman. Son of SATURN and father by Canente of FAUNUS.

PIHUECHENYI: Chilean, Araucanian Indian. A vampire sucking the blood of those who sleep in the forest overnight. Portrayed as a winged snake.

PILAN, PILLAN: ('Supreme Essence') Chilean, Aurucanian Indian. Supreme god and thunder god. Lightning and earthquakes were caused by him. Tribal chiefs and warriors went to him after death and became respectively volcanoes and clouds. He commanded spirits called Huecuvus, who could bring disaster and disease, and others called Cherruve, who caused comets and shooting stars, omens of calamity. He gradually became abstract and invoked only in extreme emergencies.

PILTZINECUHTLI – see TONATIUH.

PILUMNUS – see PICUNNUS.

PINGA: Eskimo. Watches over hunting and game animals, the caribou especially. One of the deities supervising the souls of the dead.

PINON: Brazilian, Tupi-Guarani tribes, Uapes branch. Born girdled with a star serpent, he became the constellation Orion, and his sister, born with seven stars, became the Pleiades.

PLOUGHING, GOD OF: Chinese. An impersonal god, without myths, but invoked at the appropriate time. At his festival, the emperor himself put his hand to a plough.

PLUTO: Roman equivalent of the Greek HADES. The Romans had no great Underworld divinities of their own, so his mythology was essentially that of Hades. 777: Wheel of Fortune, Judgement, (Wands) Kings or Knights;

gems: amethyst, lapis lazuli, fire opal; plants: hyssop, oak, poplar, fig, red poppy, hibiscus, nettle; animals: eagle, lion (Cherub of Fire); mineral: nitrates; perfumes: saffron, all generous odours, olibanum, all fiery odours; magical weapons: Sceptre, Wand or Lamp, Pyramid of Fire.

PLUTUS: Greek. Son of IASION and Demeter. God of wealth. ZEUS was said to have blinded him so that his gifts would go to the deserving and the undeserving alike.

PO: Polynesian. The original Void, without light, heat, sound, form or movement; all these materialized gradually from it, and finally Father Sky and Mother Earth, parents of the gods and of mankind and Nature.

POLEVIK: Slavonic. A field spirit; every field had its own. Couid be mischievous or helpful. Placated with offerings, in a ditch, of two eggs and an old cockerel who could no longer crow. In northern Russia, sometimes replaced by the Poludnitsa, a beautiful girl spirit.

POLLUX, POLYDEUCES – see CASTOR AND POLLUX.

PONTUS: ('Sea') Greek, originally Phoenician. An early sea god. He and his brother URANUS ('Heaven') were the parthenogenic sons of Earth Mother goddess Gaia; in another version, Pontus was the son of Gaia by Uranus.

POOKA, THE: Irish. A pre-Celtic god who degenerated into a mere malicious spirit, taking many forms – especially that of a black horse. Origin of the English Puck.

PORENTIUS, POREVIT: Slavonic. Five-headed god of the island of Rügen. He had one head at each of the cardinal points and one on his chest. Similar to RUGIEVIT, SLANTOVIT and TRIGLAV.

POSEIDON: Greek. The most important god of the sea, and one of the twelve OLYMPIANS. Son of CRONUS and Rhea. He lived at the bottom of the sea with his wife, Amphitrite. Father by her of TRITON, and by other mothers of THESEUS, Polymephus, ORION and ANTAEUS: and by the Gorgon Medusa of the winged horse Pegasus. A rival of ZEUS on many occasions. Favoured the Greeks in the Trojan War. Believed to cause earthquakes, and thus called 'the Earth-Shaker'. Rode the sea in a horse-drawn chariot; the horse and the dolphin were sacred to him. He (offering the horse) and Athene (offering the olive tree) competed for the patronage of Athens; Athene won, but the Athenians placated Poseidon by building him a temple on nearby Cape Sounion, the remains of which still stand. Roman equivalent NEPTUNE: 777: Tarot: Fours, Hanged Man, (Cups) Queens, Moon; gems: amethyst, sapphire, beryl or aquamarine, pearl; animals: unicorn, eagle-snake-scorpion (Cherub of Water), fish, dolphin; mineral: sulphates; perfumes: cedar, onycha, myrrh, ambergris; magical weapons: Wand, Sceptre or Crook, Cup and Cross of Suffering, Wine, Twilight of the Place and Magic Mirror.

POSHAIYANKAYA: Amerindian, Pueblo, Zuñi. Hero of the Deluge legend, who led the survivors out of the caves in which they had taken refuge.

POTOS: ('Desire') In one of the four main Phoenician creation legends, the goddess Omicle was mother of all things by Potos. May just be a way of saying that she created all things out of her own desire.

PRAJAPATI: Hindu. The master of created beings, and protector of those who beget offspring, including the gods. At one extreme, identified with SAVITAR or SOMA: at the other, so abstract as to be the absolute, BRAHMA, or the indefinable absolute known as '*Ka?*' ('Who?').

PRAMZIMAS: Lithuanian. At the Deluge, he threw a nutshell into the water, in which two survivors escaped.

PRIAPARCHIS – see KREMARA.

PRIAPUS: Greek. Originally a fertility god of the coasts of Asia Minor, the Greeks made him the son of Aphrodite by DIONYSUS. Fig-wood carvings of him, small but with a huge erect phallus, were set up in orchards and gardens to ensure fertility, and at fishing harbours for good catches. Also a protector of shepherds. *777*: Tarot: Devil; gem: black diamond; plants: Indian hemp, orchis root, thistle; animals: goat, ass; perfumes: musk, civet (also Saturnian perfumes); magical weapons: Secret Force, Lamp.

PROMETHEUS: ('He Who Foresees') Greek. Son of the Titan IAPETUS and the oceanid Clymene or the Titaness Themis. Personification of wise advice, much venerated by the Athenians. Neutral during the war of the Olympians against the TITANS, and so admitted to Olympus. He and his brother Epimetheus ('He Who Looks Back on Events') were entrusted by ZEUS with the creation of men and women, and fashioned them out of clay and water in the likeness of the gods; Athene then breathed life into them. Epimetheus had given animals all the gifts which mankind had, so Prometheus gave them fire to make them superior and became their champion against the Olympians. Zeus therefore took fire away from them, but Prometheus stole it from Heaven in a reed and gave it back to them again. Zeus punished mankind by sending Pandora, with her box of disasters, and punished Prometheus by chaining him to a mountain, with an eagle to consume his liver daily. Finally HERAKLES, with Zeus's permission, rescued him from this plight, and he was readmitted to Olympus. Prometheus warned his son DEUCALION of the coming Deluge and told him to build an ark to escape it.

PROTEUS (1): Greek. An early sea god, son of OCEANUS and Tethys. Guardian of POSEIDON's herd of seals. He had the gift of prophecy, but one had to catch him and make him speak, undeterred by his other gift, that of shape-changing. Said to live on the Egyptian coastal island of Pharos (probably by confusion with (2) below).

PROTEUS (2): Greek. A legendary king of Egypt, said to have welcomed PARIS and Helen when they fled from Sparta. POSEIDON hollowed out a tunnel for him from the Egyptian coast to Pharos.

PROTOGONOS: ('Firstborn') In the Philo Byblos Phoenician creation legend, son of primordial goddess Baau and the wind god KOLPA.

PRYDERI: Welsh. Son of PWYLL and the fertility and Otherworld goddess Rhiannon. She was punished for having allegedly killed the boy, but he was afterwards found to have been kidnapped. Accompanied BRAN on his expedition against Matholwch, of which he was one of the seven survivors. He married Kicva.

PTAH: Egyptian. Creator and craftsman god. See p.31. *777*: Tarot: Aces;

gem: diamond; plant: almond in flower; animal: god; mineral: aur. pot.; perfume: ambergris; magical weapons: Swastika or Fylfat Cross, Crown.

PUANG MATOWA: Melanesian, Celebes, Toradja tribe. Sky god, ancestor of the ruling family.

PUCHAN – see PUSHAN.

PUCK – see POOKA, THE.

PUHSIEN – see PUSHAN.

PULUG: Indian Ocean, Andaman Islands. Thunder god.

PUNCHAU: Inca. Sun god, depicted as a warrior armed with darts.

PUN-GEL – see BUNJIL.

PURA: Melanesian, New Britain and Rooke Island. White-skinned gods with whom Europeans were at first identified when they arrived.

PURUSHA, SKAMBHA: Hindu. In Vedic myth, the male aspect of BRAHMA, in contrast to Satarupa, the female aspect. Also envisaged as a primeval giant from whose dead body the world was created.

PURUTABBUI: Amerindian, Pericu. Creator of the stars, which were pieces of burning metal.

PUSHAN, PUCHAN, PUHSIEN: Hindu. A form of the Sun god. He brings all things, animate and inanimate, into relationship with each other, and thus presides over marriage. Guardian of roads and cattle, and guide of the dead into the Underworld. One of the ADITYAS.

PWYLL: Welsh. King of Annwn, the happy Otherworld, and first husband of Rhiannon (see PRYDERI).

PYERUN – see PERUN.

QAT: Banks Island, off Queensland, Australia. He made the first men and women out of wood and brought them to life by dancing and beating a drum. In one account, he created pigs too, with no difference from humans till he gave the pigs four legs. At first the sunlight was endless, and his brothers complained; so he went to see Night, who lived in another country, and Night taught him how to bring night and day to Earth. Identifiable with QUAT.

QEBEHSENUF – see HORUS, FOUR SONS OF.

QUAAYAYP: ('Man') Amerindian, Pericu. One of the three sons of NIPARAYA and Amayicoyondi. He came down to Earth with many servants, to teach the Indians of the South, who finally murdered him. He is still dead, but incorruptible, and his blood still flows. He does not speak, but an owl speaks to him.

QUAHOOTZE: Amerindian, Nootka. War god.

QUAMTA: African, Kaffir. Supreme god. Mounds of stones characterize his worship; each passer-by adds a stone.

QUAT: Melanesian, New Hebrides. Principal god, alongside TAAROA. Identifiable with QAT.

QUETZALCOATL: ('Plumed Serpent') Aztec. An early Toltec god who became one of the major Aztec deities. God of wind, life, fertility, wisdom and practical knowledge. Said to have invented agriculture and the calendar. Identified with Venus as the Morning Star, his twin XOLOTL being the Evening Star. Portrayed sometimes as a feathered serpent, sometimes as a bearded man. Identified in legend with a semi-historical priest-king, who sailed away promising to return; when Cortes landed, many Mexicans welcomed him and his army, thinking Quetzalcoatl had come home at last.

QUIATEOT: Nicaraguan, Niquiran. Rain god.

QUIRINUS: Early Italian war god. When ROMULUS was deified, he was worshipped under the name of Quirinus, as the son of MARS.

RA (1), RE: Egyptian. Sun god, and chief god of the Heliopolis pantheon. See Chapter XXVII. 777: Tarot: Sixes, Emperors or Princes, Sun; gems: topaz, yellow diamond, crysoleth; plants: acacia, bay, laurel, vine, sunflower, heliotrope; animals: phoenix, lion, child, sparrowhawk; perfumes: olibanum, cinnamon, all glorious odours; magical weapons: Lamen or Rosy Cross or Bow and Arrow.

RA (2): Polynesian, Raiatea. Sun god. He married Tu-Papa (Tu-Neta), youngest daughter of Earth Mother Papa, and lived with her in the Underworld.

RABEFIHAZA: Madagascan. Taught men to hunt and fish and invented snares.

RA-HARAKHTE: ('Ra of the Horizon') Egyptian. A title of RA as the rising Sun.

RAIDEN: Japanese. A thunder god, portrayed as a demon, often with claws and carrying a drum.

RAINBOW SNAKE, THE: Australian Aborigine. In some areas male, in others female. Represents rain and water and their life-giving qualities. The Rainbow Snake features in many seasonal rituals and is a frequent subject of Aborigine art.

RAINI: Brazilian, Tupi-Guarani, Mundruku tribe. Created the world by placing a flat stone on the head of another god.

RAKSHASAS, THE: Hindu. Semi-divine beings, not evil in themselves but destined by fate (*dharma*) to bring disaster to men and women – often as a natural result of the human's *karma*. They live in a beautiful city and treat each other affectionately and honestly.

RAKTAVIJA: Hindu. Chief of the demon army. Representations of Kali show her carrying his severed head.

RAMA: Hindu. Any one of three avatars of VISHNU –see RAMA-CHANDRA, PARASHURAMA and BALARAMA.

RAMACHANDRA: Hindu. The seventh avatar of VISHNU, often known simply as Rama. His wife in that incarnation was Sri, herself an incarnation of Lakshmi.

RAMMAN, RAMMON, RIMMON: Babylonian. Storm god equatable with HADAD. Associated with the Deluge, when, 'The whirlwind of Ramman mounted up in the heavens and light was turned into darkness.' The pomegranate was sacred to him. The Rimmon of the Old Testament. His wife was Shala the Compassionate.

RANGI (1): Maori. Sky god, who fell in love with Papa, the Earth Mother, during the primeval darkness. Their embrace crushed the gods to whom they gave birth, and all other creatures, and nothing could grow or bear fruit. So the gods decided to separate them (in one version, at Rangi's request). Thereafter light spread over the world, and creation could continue. Rangi's tears at the separation are the dew, and his sighs are the winter ice.

RANGI (2): (Distantly the same as (1).) Polynesian, Mangaia Island. Underworld and war god. First ruler of Mangaia after a deluge which had overwhelmed it. Grandson of Earth Mother Papa. His wife was Tepotatango ('Bottom of Hades').

RASHNU: Persian, Zoroastrian. Co-judge with MITHRA of the souls of the dead.

RATI-MBATI-NDUA: ('Lord with One Tooth') Melanesian, Fiji Islands. Underworld god.

RAVANA: Hindu. Originally a heavenly being, he offended VISHNU and was given the choice of three Earthly incarnations as Vishnu's enemy or seven as his friend; he chose the former, as it would be over sooner. In his first incarnation, as Hiranyakasipu, a demon king, he dethroned INDRA and took over Heaven, but Vishnu defeated him. In his second, as Ravana, he abducted Sita, wife of RAMA, who eventually killed him and rescued her. In his third, as Sisupala, he was born son of a king but with three eyes and four arms; his extra eye and arms withered away when KRISHNA, visiting his parents, took him on his knee. As a young man, he insulted and threatened an old man, and Krishna caused his death. Ravana's punishment was thus complete, and he was forgiven.

RAVEN: Amerindian, Pacific North-West. Creator and trickster, equivalent to the COYOTE of other tribes. He made the dry land by dropping stones to give himself perching-places. He created all living creatures – including men and women out of wood and clay.

RE – see RA.

REMUS – see ROMULUS AND REMUS.

RERIR: Scandinavian. Son of ODIN's son SIGI, and founder and king of the VOLSUNGS.

RESHEF: Assyro-Babylonian slayer god, associated with Ishtar in her battle aspect. A variant of Reshep (see RESHPU (1)).

RESHPU (1), RESHEP, RESHEP-SHULMAN: Originally Syrian, brought to Egypt in the Eighteenth Dynasty (c.1567-1320 BC). War god who could be appealed to for military success and also for healing. Portrayed as bearded, wearing the crown of Upper Egypt with a gazelle's head in front.

RESHPU (2): Phoenician. 'The Luminous.' Often associated with the Syrian/Egyptian goddess Qedeshet.

RHADAMANTHUS: Greek. Son of ZEUS and Europa and brother of MINOS. Renowned for his wisdom and justice, he was tutor to HERAKLES. After his death, he became one of the judges of the Underworld. 777: Tarot: Justice; gem: emerald; plant: aloe; animal: elephant; perfume: galbanum; magical weapon: Cross of Equilibrium.

RIMMON – see RAMMAN.

RISHIS, THE: Hindu. Sons of the gods, appearing in various roles. They included seven sages who preserved and handed down the wisdom of the Vedas; these were the stars of Ursa Major.

ROBIGUS: Roman. God who protected crops from blight (robigo). Sometimes seen as a goddess, Robigo.

ROHE: Maori. Ruler of three of the ten levels of the Underworld. The upper four levels were ruled by Hine-nui-te-po, the bottom three by the goddess Miru.

ROMULUS AND REMUS: Roman. Twin sons of MARS and Rhea Silvia, and legendary founders of Rome. Put adrift as babies by their uncle Amulius, they were rescued and reared by a she-wolf. They built Rome (traditionally in April 753 BC) and Romulus killed Remus in an argument. Romulus became first king of Rome and after his death was deified and worshipped as the war god QUIRINUS.

RONGO, ORONGO: Polynesian, Indonesian. Son of Earth Mother Papa. Variously a fertility, agriculture, war and Underworld god, and patron of music. Widely worshipped at harvest. Known as Ono in the Marquesas, and equatable with the Tahitan ONO. His consort was Itum, a healer goddess.

ROT: Finno-Ugric, Lapland. Underworld god.

RU: Polynesian, Tahiti. God of the East Wind.

RUAHATU: Polynesian. A war and sea god, honoured particularly in Tahiti.

RUDA: North Arabian. The Evening Star (Venus).

RUDRA: Hindu. An early Earth and mountain god, from whom SHIVA evolved. Sometimes also seen as a storm god. Prince of demons. Also god of the dead. A skilled archer, his arrows brought disease. Addressed as 'ruddy divine boar'. His wife was the Earth and cow goddess Prisni. They were the parents of the eleven MARUTS who became the companions of INDRA. The early Vedic storm and lightning goddess Rodasi is also named as his wife.

RUDRAS, THE – see MARUTS, THE.

RUGIEVIT: Slavonic. A seven-faced god of the island of Rügen in the Baltic. Similar to PORENTIUS, SVANTOVIT and TRIGLAV.

RUTI: ('He Who Resembles a Lion'). Phoenician. God of Byblos, portrayed in human form with a lion's head.

SAA: Egyptian. Son of RA who sits in his father's boat and also attends the judgement of the dead. May be the same as HU.

SABAZIUS: Greek, Thracian Hellespont and Phrygia. Sun god. His wife was the Moon goddess Bendis. As Dionysus Sabazius, a barley god, and according to Plutarch and Tacitus, the original of the Jewish god.

SAE-NO-KAMI: Japanese. Collective term for various gods who ward off misfortune.

SAGBATA: Benin. Smallpox god.

SAHAR, SHAHAR: Phoenician. The Morning Star, Venus; he and his twin brother SALEM, Venus as the Evening Star, were sons of EL and Ashera or Rahmaya. When they were born, they stretched their lips to Heaven and Earth, feeding on birds and fish, which established them as gods. Sahar was also a Moon god of the northern and southern Semites.

SAHSNOT, SAXNEAT: ('Sword-Bearer') An old Saxon name for TIWAZ.

SAHTE – see OLLE.

SAKA-NO-MI-WO-NO-KAMI: Japanese god of mountain slopes.

SAKARABRU: Guinean, Agni tribe. He is both just and terrible; demon of darkness but also a healer and dispenser of justice. Represented by a ball of maize.

SAKRA: ('Powerful') A title of INDRA (1).

SAKYAMUNI: Chinese name for the BUDDHA.

SALEM, SHALEM, SHELIM: Phoenician. The Evening Star, Venus; see SAHAR. The name seems to be preserved in that of Jerusalem.

SAMAEL: Hebrew, a name for Satan.

SAMAS: Sun god of the northern Semites. The southern Semites had a corresponding Sun goddess, Sams. Doubtless related to SHAMASH.

SAOSHYANT: Persian, Zoroastrian. A *psychopompos* conducting dead souls for judgement by MITHRA and RASHNU.

SARAPIS, SERAPIS: Egyptian. Greek name for the APIS Bull of Memphis, regarded as an incarnation of OSIRIS (or sometimes of PTAH). In Ptolemaic times, he became the chief deity of Alexandria. As such, he was virtually a new god invented by Ptolemy I's advisers Manetho and Timotheus, whom he had commissioned to harmonize the Egyptian and Greek pantheons. Most Egyptian deities could be reasonably equated with Greek ones, but Osiris presented difficulties. They required a consort for the increasingly international Isis, so Sarapis absorbed Osiris in their scheme, yet was equatable with ZEUS and POSEIDON. He became accepted as Isis's partner outside Egypt but always remained secondary to her.

SARUTO-HIKO: Japanese: Commander of the armed forces of NINIGI.

SASABONSUM: African, Kaffir. A forest demon who devoured travellers. His wife, the silk cotton tree dryad Srahman, however, taught him the secrets of the forest and of herbs.

SATAN: ('Adversary') The Devil in Christian terminology. See Chapter XIII.

SATURN: Roman. An early god of planting and harvest, said to have been a king during the Golden Age; driven from the sky by JUPITER, he hid (*latuit*) in the land which became called Latium – more precisely, beneath the Capitol at Rome. His wife was the fertility goddess Ops ('Plenty'). He became identified with the Greek CRONUS, and she with Rhea or Cybele. His festival, the Saturnalia, was from 17-23 December, involving feasting, merriment, the giving of presents and role-reversal (e.g. masters waiting on slaves). Saturday is named after him. Astrologically, regarded as restrictive, limit-setting; Cabalistically, the planet of Binah, restrictive in the form-giving sense. 777: Tarot: Threes, Queens, World; gems: star sapphire, pearl, onyx: plants: cypress, opium poppy, ash, hellebore, yew, nightshade; animals; woman, crocodile; mineral: lead; perfumes: myrrh, civet, asafoetida, scammony, indigo, sulphur, all evil odours; magical weapons: Yoni, Outer Robe of Concealment, Sickle.

SATYRS: Greek. Forest and mountain spirits, originally crudely animal in form, with hairy bodies, goats' hooves, horns and pointed ears; sensual, fond of chasing nymphs. Later became more graceful, given to music and dance, but still horned and orgiastic.

SAVITAR, SAVITRI: Hindu. The god of movement, causing the Sun to rise and set, the winds to blow and the waves to circulate, and making the gods immortal. Invoked for the remission of sins and as a *psychopompos*. Portrayed with golden tongue, eyes and arms. Son of Aditi, Mother of the Gods.

SAXNEAT – see SAHSNOT.

SCAMANDER, XANTHUS: Greek. A Phrygian river god. HERAKLES, when thirsty, scooped out the earth and made the river gush forth. Scamander took part in the Trojan War, catching Achilles in his nets; HEPHAESTUS intervened to save him.

SEB: Egyptian. An alternative name for GEB.

SEBEK: Egyptian. Associated with the Pharaohs of the Thirteenth Dynasty (c.1786-1633 BC). Depicted as a crocodile, or crocodile-headed. Originally a crocodile totem god of the Fayoum, apparently predating RA – with whom he became identified as Sebek-Ra – and SET, with whom he was also often identified.

SEBIUMEKER: Sudanese, Meroitic culture (c.300 BC – AD 500). God of procreation. Main centre of worship the temple complex at Musawwarat el-Sufra near the Sixth Cataract of the Nile. (See also APEDEMAK.)

SEF: ('Yesterday') Egyptian. Lion god, personification of 'yesterday', together with his brother DUA ('Today').

SEGOMO: Continental Celtic. A war god, also known as Cocidius.

SEKER: ('Close of the Day') Egyptian. An early vegetation god, later a god of the Memphis necropolis and the Underworld. His realm, dark and populated by evil spirits and reptiles, was lit up only when RA's boat passed through it each night. Depicted hawk-headed or as a mummified hawk carried in Ra's boat. Closely identified with OSIRIS, who was known at Memphis as Seker-Osiris. Called Soucharis by the Greeks.

SEMO SANCTUS: Roman, Latin origin. God of oaths.

SEPA: Egyptian. Centipede god from Heliopolis, who could ward off snake-bites. Sometimes shown with the head of a donkey or mummified with two short horns.

SEPTU – see SOPEDU.

SERAPHIM: Hebrew. Fiery celestial beings, originally serpent-like but probably later human-bodied; described in Isaiah's vision (vi:2,6) as having six wings – one pair covering the face, one pair the feet, and one pair for flying. Serpents were regarded as temple guardians.

SERAPIS – see SARAPIS.

SESHA – see SHESHA.

SET, SETH: Egyptian. A god with a complex history. For his final form, see Chapter XVIII. Set was originally a pre-dynastic tribal Sun and sky god with a totem animal similar to a pig; associated with him was a ritually sacrificed Divine King. A god of royalty as late as the Twentieth Dynasty (c.1200-1085 BC). As he became absorbed into the RA pantheon, these aspects were forgotten, and Set degenerated into the chief of the powers of evil. In this role, he personified the ever-threatening and destructive aridity of the desert. 777: Tarot: Devil; gem: black diamond; plants: Indian hemp, orchis root, thistle; animals: goat, ass; perfumes: musk, civet, also Saturnian perfumes; magical weapons: Secret Force, Lamp.

SETHLANS: Etruscan artificer god.

SEYON: Indian, Tamil. One of their principal gods.

SHAHAR – see SAHAR.

SHAI: Egyptian god of destiny. His wife was Meshkent, goddess of childbirth. He shadowed the soul during life and appeared at its judgement after death. Sometimes appears in feminine form as Shait. Coalesced in Graeco-Roman period with AGATHODAIMON.

SHAITAN: Islamic name for Devil, from a Semitic word meaning 'adversary', and origin of the modern name SATAN.

SHAKURU: Amerindian, Pawnee. On the orders of TIRAWA, he mated with the Moon goddess, Pah, to produce the first man, while the Morning and Evening stars produced the first woman. Shakuru's festival, the Dance of the Sun, is the most important of the year among the Plains Indians and lasts a week.

SHALEM – see SALEM.

SHAMASH: Assyro-Babylonian Sun god, and deity of righteousness and law. Also of divination, through his soothsayer-priest the baru. Son of the Moon god SIN and the Earth goddess Ningal, and brother to supreme goddess Inanna/Ishtar and to Underworld goddess Ereshkigal. His wife was the dawn goddess Aya, who bore him MISHARU and Kittu. In his earlier Chaldaean form, he was known as Shamash-Bubbar, and his wife was the Moon goddess Sirdu or Sirrida. He is the Chemosh of the Old Testament. Called Heres by the Canaanites. Originally Semitic, brought to Mesopotamia by the Akkadians. Sumerian equivalent UTU.

SHANGO: Nigerian, Yoruba tribe. Son of AGANJU and Yemaja, or in some versions of their son ORUNJAN. Thunder god. Legendary first king of the tribe, with a splendid metal palace (the 'City of Brass' of the *Thousand and One Nights*) and hundreds of horses. His wife was the fertility and water goddess Oya, priestess of the River Niger. At the end of a long and warlike life, he disappeared into the Earth and was worshipped thereafter with an established priesthood and human sacrifice.

SHANG-TI: Chinese. God of the Shang Bronze Age culture of north China, c.2000 BC. Perhaps originally a vegetation or rice god, he became lord of Tien, or Heaven. Human sacrifices were offered to him.

SHANKPANNA: Nigerian, Yoruba tribe. God of smallpox.

SHEDU, THE – see UTUKKU, THE.

SHEN-NUNG: Chinese. An emperor of c.2700 BC who taught the people agriculture and was deified after death. His wife, Shen-Tsan, became the goddess of silk-culture.

SHESHA, SESHA: Hindu. A thousand-headed serpent born from the mouth of BALARAMA, an avatar of VISHNU, as he was dying. Cradled Vishnu between incarnations. A king of the NAGAS.

SHEZMU, SHESMU: Egyptian. God of wine and unguent oil-presses. Could be cruel or beneficial; in his earlier form, the god who dismembered sinners in the Underworld; later the emphasis was on his role as master of perfumes. Both stemmed from his original role as attendant on the Pharaoh. Portrayed in human form, but later in lion form.

SHICHI FUKUJIN, THE: Japanese. The seven deities of luck – six gods (BISHAMON, DAIKOKU, EBISU, FUKUROKUJU, HOTEI and

JOROJIN) and the sea goddess Benten. This category seems to have originated in the seventeenth century to accommodate popular deities who did not fit in the official Buddhist pantheon.

SHIGI-YAMA-TSU-MI: Japanese god of the mountain foot.

SHIHOTSUCHI: Japanese. A sea god.

SHINA-TSU-HIKO: Japanese. God of wind. Associated with him was the goddess Shina-to-Be, who blew away mists from the Earth. Both born of IZANAGI's breath.

SHI TENNO, THE: Japanese. Guardians of the four cardinal points; BISHAMON (TAMON) (North), JIKOKU (East), KOMOKU (South) and ZOCHO (West). All under the command of Taishaku-ten.

SHIVA, SIVA: Hindu. See Chapter XXVII. 777: Tarot: Twos, Kings or Knights, Hierophant; gems: ruby, star ruby, turquoise; plants: amaranth, tiger lily, geranium; animals: man, ram, owl; mineral: phosphorus; perfumes: musk, dragon's blood; magical weapons: Lingam, Inner Robe of Glory, Horns, Energy, Burin. (As Sacred Bull) Tarot: Hierophant; gem: topaz; plant: mallow; animal: bull (Cherub of Earth); perfume: storax; magical weapon: Labour of Preparation.

SHODEN: The Japanese name for the Hindu GANESHA.

SHONEY: Scottish and Irish Celtic. A sea god to whom libations of ale were offered till late into the nineteenth century by fishermen in Ireland and the Isle of Lewis.

SHOU-HSING: Chinese. God of long life. He knows the date of everyone's death but by honour and sacrifice can sometimes be persuaded to put it back. Portrayed as an old, bald, white-bearded man carrying a staff and the peach of immortality.

SHU: Egyptian air god. See p.81. 777: Tarot: Nines; gem: quartz; plants: banyan, mandrake, damiana; animal: elephant; mineral: lead; perfume: jasmine, ginseng, all odiferous roots; magical weapons: Perfumes and Sandals.

SHUI-KUAN: ('Agent of Water') A god who averts evil. One of a triad with T'IEN KUAN and TI-KUAN.

SIA: Egyptian. An intellectual god, representing the perceptive mind. Born of the blood dripping from the phallus of RA.

SIAPPADIKARAM, SILAPPADIKARAM: Hindu. Brother of SHIVA. His wife was the Tamil victory goddess Korraval.

SIDA: Melanesian, Torres Islands. Culture hero and fertility god, originating in New Guinea. Taught the islanders language, stocked the reefs with coral and introduced useful plants. His ritual includes a dance explaining life after death.

SIDDHARTHA: Buddhist. The son born to Maya, who became the BUDDHA.

SIEGFRIED – see SIGMUND.

SIGI: Scandinavian. A son of ODIN. King of the Huns and father of RERIR.

SIGMUND: Scandinavian hero, who both benefited and suffered from ODIN's treatment. Odin, in disguise, thrust a sword into a tree, saying it would belong to the man who could pull it out. Sigmund was the only one who could, and from then on won many victories with it. But in the end Odin, in the same disguise, confronted him and broke the sword with a wooden lance, mortally wounding him. His wife Hjordis tried to treat his wounds, but he refused; if Odin (whom he now recognized) wished him to die, he must submit. He asked only that his sword be restored; it was inherited by his son Sigurd (the Siegfried of German legend and Wagner's operas).

SIGU: Guyanese, Arawak tribe. Lord of the beasts of the forest created by his father, Makonaima. In the forest was a tree of knowledge which Sigu cut down to plant its seeds around the Earth; but water gushed from the stump and flooded the Earth. He led those animals which could not fly or climb into a mountain cave, where they survived the deluge.

SIGURD – see SIGMUND.

SILAPPADIKARAM: Hindu. The Tamil name for BALARAMA. His wife was the victory goddess Korraval.

SILENUS: Greek. An attendant of DIONYSUS, fat, bald, cheerful and always drunk, yet full of wisdom and knowledge; he was Dionysus's tutor. He could tell the future of anyone who could tie him up during his drunken sleep. Son of HERMES and Gaia, or born of the blood of URANUS after CRONUS had castrated him. According to Pindar, his wife was Nais. He usually rode an ass. In fact, Silenus was a generic term for a class of river and spring spirits, originally Phrygian, and often confused with the SATYRS.

SILTIM: Persian, Zoroastrian. A malignant forest demon.

SILVANUS, SYLVANUS: Roman: God of fields, woods and flocks and of clearing trees to make fields. Guardian of boundary lines. Often confused with FAUNUS and with PAN, whom he resembled in appearance.

SIMBI: Haitian voodoo. Patron of springs and rain and of magicians. Symbol a snake. Occupies a central position in the pantheon, overlapping several other deities.

SIN: Chaldean, Sumerian, Assyro-Babylonian. Moon god, wisdom god and time-measurer; the Babylonian calendar was lunar. Known as 'He whose deep heart no god can penetrate'. At the end of every month, the gods came to consult him, and he made decisions for them. Enemy of evildoers (because the Moon illuminates the night when they operate). Son of ENLIL and Ninlil. Portrayed as an old man with a beard the colour of lapis lazuli. Father of the Sun god SHAMASH and the fire god NUSKU, and one of the named fathers of Ishtar (the others being ANU and ENKI). His wife was the Moon goddess Ningal, 'the Great Lady'. He was known as NANNAR at Ur. Mount Sinai was named after him; the Levites were originally lunar priests. (Do not confuse with Teutonic truth goddess Sin.)

SITRAGUPTA: Indian. Son of INDRA and Indrani.

SIVA – see SHIVA.

SKAMBHA – see PERUSHA.

SKANDA – see KARTIKEYA.

SO – see KHEBIESO.

SOBO: Haitian voodoo, Benin origin. Sky and thunder god. Associated with DAMBALLAH. Son of the twins MAWU-LISA and brother of BADÉ.

SOL: Roman Sun god. Often referred to as Sol Invictus ('Unconquered'). Identified with the Greek HELIOS.

SOMA: Hindu. Both a plant and a god. The plant was part of sacrificial offerings, and its nectar was the drink of the gods, giving immortality to all who imbibe it. God of inspiration, link between Heaven and Earth. Also (and particularly later) a Moon god; the twenty-seven lunar stations, daughters of DAKSHA, were his wives.

SOMANATHA: ('Lord of the Moon') Hindu, Gujarat. A title of SHIVA.

SOMASUNDARA: Hindu, Tamil. Perhaps an avatar of SHIVA. His wife was Tadategei, unbeatable in knowledge of war.

SOPEDU, SOPD, SOPDU, SEPTU: Egyptian. Defender of the Eastern frontier; known as 'Lord of the East' and 'Scourge of Asiatics'. Also protector of the Sinai peninsula turquoise mines. But earlier a stellar god, equated with the teeth of the Pharaoh when the latter himself became a star god. In this role, known as Horus-Sopedu, born of the mystical union of the Pharaoh with the goddess Isis as Sothis, the Dog Star Sirius, which heralded the Nile inundation. Portrayed either as a crouching falcon or as a Bedouin warrior with a crown of tall plumes.

SOUCHARIS – see SEKER.

SOUCHOS – see SEBEK.

SOWA: Arabic. A pre-Islamic god condemned in the Koran as an idol worshipped by the Sons of Cain.

SPHINX: Egyptian. Usually a combined image of a Pharaoh and the Sun god RA (or one of his many-named aspects), with a man's or animal's head and a lion's body. Avenues of Sphinxes were often set up as guardians to the entrances to tombs or temples. The most famous Sphinx is the Fourth Dynasty (c.2613-2494 BC) one beside the Great Pyramid of Gizeh, which has a small temple between its forepaws; it probably commemorates the Pharaoh Chephren (Khafre). (Not to be confused with the Greek Sphinx, which was part woman, part bird and part lioness.)

SRAOSHA: Persian, Zoroastrian. The Angel of Obedience and Sacrifice, who took the souls of the good to Paradise.

STRIBOG: Slavonic. God of cold and frost. His statue stood in Kiev with those of DA-BOG, KHORS and PERUN.

SUCELLOS: Gaulish. His consort was Nantosuelta ('of the Winding Stream').

SUCHOS – see SOBEK.

SUGAAR: Basque. Son/husband of the supreme goddess Mari. He rides the night sky as a burning crescent but is not lunar – the Basques' Moon is always female.

SUITENGU: Japanese. Very popular protector of sailors. Said to be a child himself, and therefore a protector and comforter of sick children.

SUMMANUS: Roman. An early god of thunder, especially nocturnal thunder.

SUN HOU-TZU: Chinese. A monkey god, ruler of the monkeys. He became immortal when he was taken to the Underworld and found and tore up the page with his name on it. He carries a magic wand. Hero of many stories, in which he represents human nature.

SUN PIN: Japanese. A fourth century BC general who had his toes cut off and hid his deformity in leather sheathes; he became the god of shoemakers.

SUPAI, SUPAY: Inca. God of the dead, ruling those spirits who did not go to the land of the Sun but were confined under the Earth. He demanded human sacrifice, including one hundred children a year.

SURMA: Finno-Ugric. A monster personifying fatal destiny and violent death, who protected the entrance to the realm of the goddess Kalma, ruler of graves.

SURT: Scandinavian. King of Muspelheim, the land of fire. At Ragnarok, the Twilight of the Gods, he led the capture of Asgard, defeated FREY and destroyed the world by fire.

SURYA: Hindu. Sun god. One of the ADITYAS. His wife Sanjna or Saranyu left him because she could not stand his brightness; to win her back, he gave up one-eighth of his rays. In earlier versions, Sanjna/Saranyu had been wife of VIVASVAT. In some myths, Surya is feminine.

SUSANOWO, SUSA-NO-O: Japanese. God of the sea, fertility, thunder and rain. Son of IZANAGI and Izanami, or born from Izanagi's nose when he was bathing in the sea. Also a Moon god. Conflict with his sister the Sun goddess Amaterasu resulted in his being banished from Heaven to Earth, to Izumo province.

SUS'SISTINNAKO: Amerindian, Sia. Creator god. He created mankind by singing, accompanying himself by using a spider's web as a harp.

SUT, SUTEKH (1): A Hyksos warrior god worshipped in Egypt in the Fifteenth and Sixteenth Dynasties (c.1674-1567) and identified with SET.

SUT, SUTEKH (2): Islamic, a son of IBLIS who inspires lies. Probably a relic of (1).

SVANTOVIT, SWIETOWIT: Slavonic. A warrior god and god of plenty, with prophetic powers. His cult centre was at Arcona on Rügen Island in the Baltic. Envisaged with four heads, a bow in his left hand and a drinking horn in his right. Overlaps SVAROG.

SVAROG: Slavonic. Sky god, ruler of the universe, progenitor of the Slavonic deities. His son DA-BOG represented the Sun.

SVAROZHICH, SVAROGICH: ('Son of SVAROG') Slavonic. Fire god. Brother of DA-BOG, though sometimes regarded as the same.

SWIETOWIT – see SVANTOVIT.

SYEN: Southern Slavonic. Guardian spirits of the home who can enter the bodies of men, dogs, snakes or hens.

SYLVANUS – see SILVANUS.

TAAROA, TANGAROA, TANGALOA: Polynesian creator god. Son of VATEA and the Earth Mother Papa, and twin brother of RONGO. He hatched the world from a primordial egg, dividing it into Earth and sky. Father by Hina-of-the-Land of the war god ORO.

TAAUT, TAAUTOS: Phoenician equivalent of THOTH. Inventor of writing.

TAGES: Etruscan. An Underworld god who taught divination by examining entrails and observing lightning.

TAGTUG: Sumerian prediluvian culture hero who became deified. May be equated with Ziudsuddu. Linked with the Sun god UTU and the Babylonian MARDUK.

TAISHAKU: Japanese name for INDRA.

TAISHAKU-TEN – see SHI TENNO, THE.

T'AI SHAN, T'AI-YUEH-TA-TI, TUNG-YUEH-TA-TI: Chinese. 'The Great Emperor of the Eastern Peak' – a mountain in northern China. Delegated by the AUGUST PERSONAGE OF JADE to oversee the deeds of all Earthly creatures including mankind. A magnificient temple was built for him in Peking.

TAKA-KI-NO-KAMI, TAKA-MI-MUSUBI-NO-KAMI: Japanese. Collaborator with the Sun goddess Amaterasu; she is the supreme deity but is directly responsible only for the Heavenly plane, being kept informed about Earth by other deities. His wife is Kami-mi-musubi-no-Mikoto.

TAKA-OKAME: Japanese. A mountain-dwelling rain god.

TAKE-MIKAZUCHI: Japanese, perhaps of Chinese origin. A thunder god, sent by the gods to force the abdication of ONAMUJI in favour of NINIGI.

TAKI-TSU-HIKO: ('Prince-Cataract') Japanese. A rock god who can be prayed to for rain. Son of AJI-SUKI-TAKAHIKONE.

TAKSHAKA: Hindu. A serpent god, one of the named kings of the NAGAS.

TALIESIN: ('Radiant Brow') Welsh. Son of Cerridwen, who gave birth to him after swallowing GWION. A barley god who overlaps a sixth-century bard of the same name, which may have become the title of several chief bards; the Cerridwen story may enshrine a bardic initiation ritual.

TAMAA: Polynesian, Marquesas Islands. God who guards the coconut tree in the Underworld, where many kinds of tree are believed to originate.

TAMAGOSTAD: Nicaraguan, Niquiran tribe. With his consort Zipaltonal he created the Earth and everything in it. They live in the East.

TAMAKAIA: Melanesian, New Hebrides. Created the world, with the help of MAUI (2).

TAMISU: Hittite. When KUMARBIS fought with ANU and bit off his genitals, he spat out part of them, which became the god Tamisu and the River Tigris.

TAMMUZ: Assyro-Babylonian. See Chapter XIX.

TAMON – see BISHAMON.

TAMU – see KAMU.

TANE: Polynesian and Maori creator god. Son of RANGI and the Earth Mother Papa. He separated Earth and sky (his parents), thus bringing light to the Earth, and placed the stars. He created Hine-Ahu-One, the Polynesian Eve, out of his red clay with other gods' help. He had a daughter, Hina-Titama, by her, and then several children by Hina-Titama before she discovered he was her father. When she did, she fled in shame to the Underworld and became its ruler as Hine-Nui-Te-Po. Known in Hawaii as Kane.

TANGALOA, TANGAROA – see TAAROA.

TANNUS, TINNUS: ('Oak') Gaulish and British. A thunder god. Adopted into the Etruscan pantheon as TINA. His name survives in the word 'tinder', and in the Gaelic *'teine'* (fire) and also in place-names, such as Tan Hill in Wensleydale and St Anne's (originally Tan) Hill in Wiltshire. Elsewhere confused with St Anthony, whose feast corresponds with the midwinter fire festival.

TANTALUS: Greek. A divine king figure, son of ZEUS, who offered his son Pelops as a meal for the gods. Zeus had Pelops restored to life and banished Tantalus to Hades within sight of water and delicious food which he could never reach; hence the word 'tantalize'. His wife was Moon goddess Euryanassa (a form of Eurynome).

TAPIO: Finno-Ugric. Forest god, with his wife Mielikki, his son Nyyrikki and his daughter Tuulikki. They had power over all who walked or hunted in the woods and were invoked by the Finns for abundance of game. Tapio was envisaged as dark-bearded, with a fir hat and a moss cloak, and his wife as stately and beautiful. His forest realm was called Tapiola.

TARANIS: ('The Thunderer') Gaulish, also found in Britain. His symbol was the wheel, and sometimes a spiral representing lightning. Human sacrifices were offered to him.

TARVOS: An early British bull god.

TATENEN: ('Exalted Earth') Egyptian. Symbolized the fertile silt emerging as the annual Nile inundation withdrew.

TATSUTA-HIKO: Japanese wind god. With his female counterpart, Tatsuta-Hime, he is prayed to for good harvests and venerated by sailors and fishermen.

TAUKIYOMI: Japanese Moon god, brother of the Sun goddess Amaterasu.

TAUS: ('Peacock Angel') A pre-Islamic name for IBLIS.

TAWENDUARE: Brazilian, Tupi-Guarani tribe. God of daylight, constantly vanquishing his brother ARIKUTE, god of night. In another version, the brothers are heroes of the Deluge story.

TAWHAKI: Maori. God of thunder and clouds, sometimes seen as ruling the kingdom of the dead. In Polynesia generally, hero of many legends, dating at the latest from AD 700.

TAWHIRI: Polynesian storm god, son of sky god RANGI and Earth Mother Papa. Father of thirteen children – two strong winds and eleven clouds of various kinds.

TAWISKARA – see IOSKEHA.

TEGID VOEL: Welsh. A nobleman of Penllyn, husband of Moon and grain goddess Cerridwen, who bore him Avagdu (the ugliest boy in the world) and Creirwy (the most beautiful girl).

TEHUTI – see THOTH.

TEI SEIKO – see COXINGA.

TEKKEITSERKTOK: Eskimo. Earth god, most powerful in the pantheon. All deer belong to him. Sacrifices are made to him before the hunting season.

TELEPINU: Hittite fertility god. When he left Earth, it suffered drought and famine; the mother goddess Hannahannas sent a bee to find him, and it brought him back when all other methods had failed.

TELLUNO: Roman. A very early fertility god, together with his female counterpart, Tellus Mater; she was later associated with JUPITER.

TEM – see ATUM.

TEMMANGU, TENJIN: Japanese. God of learning and calligraphy.

TENAGIS: Greek. One of the seven heliads, sons of HELIOS and Rhodos. All seven were highly intelligent, but he excelled the other six, so they murdered him through jealousy.

TENGU, THE: Japanese. Playful and sometimes malicious spirits who live in treetops, especially on mountains. Envisaged as small birdlike men, hatched from eggs.

TENJIN – see TEMMANGU.

TEOYAOMIQUI, HUAHUANTLI: Aztec god of dead warriors; a variant of MICTLA. Ruled the sixth hour of the day.

TEPEYOLLOTL: ('Heart of the Mountains') Aztec. A puma god, lord of the eighth hour of the night.

TEPICTOTON, THE: Aztec. Dwarf protectors of mountains, to whom children were sacrificed.

TERAH: An ancient Semitic name for the Moon – see EL. Also equated with Terah, father of Abraham.

TERMINUS: Roman. God of property and fixer of boundaries, which were marked by stones (once plain, later human-headed) called *termini*, sacred to JUPITER. 'Terminus' was originally a title of Jupiter but became an independent god.

TESHUB, TESHUP: Hittite storm god and king of the gods, whose worship spread to surrounding lands. His wife was the presiding goddess Hepatu (Hebat).

TETHRA: Irish. A chief of the Fomors who was also king of Lochlann, their mythical undersea home.

TEUTATES: Gaulish. A war god, worshipped with human sacrifice. The name is cognate with *Tuatha*, Gaelic for 'People'.

TEYRNON: Welsh. An early god who became a mortal. He brought up PRYDERI, the kidnapped son of PWYLL and Rhiannon, till he was restored to them.

TEZCATLIPOCA: ('Smoking Mirror') Aztec Sun god, particularly of the summer Sun which can bring fertility or drought. Also god of music and dancing. Each year the handsomest of prisoners was identified with him, royally treated and given four girls (personifying four goddessess) as wives, and sacrificed at the end of a long festival. Tezcatlipoca fell in love with Xochiquetzal, Moon and love goddess, wife of rain god TLALOC, and took her away from him. Lord of the tenth hour of the day. He commanded NATA, the Aztec Noah, to build a ship to escape the Deluge.

THANATOS: ('Death') Greek. A minor Underworld god, little more than a personification. See also HYPNOS and MORPHEUS.

THAUMAS: Greek. Son of PONTUS and Gaia. His wife was the marine goddess Electra, one of the Pleiades, who bore him Iris, rainbow messenger of the gods, and the Harpies, frightening creatures with women's heads and birds' bodies.

THESEUS: Greek. Athenian hero who slew the MINOTAUR with the help of Ariadne, whom he later abandoned on the island of Naxos. He succeeded his father, Pittheus, to the throne of Athens. He seized Hippolyte, Queen of the Amazons, as his wife and defeated the Amazons when they attacked Athens in revenge.

THIEN-LUNG: Chinese. His wife was Earth Mother Ti-Ya (Ti-Mu), Ancestress of the World. Both may be Indian in origin.

THINGS – see TYR.

THOBADESTCHIN – see NAGENATZANI.

THOR: Scandinavian. Sky and thunder god. Son of ODIN and his wife Fjorgyn, Jord (originally an Earth goddess) or Hlodyn – all three named mothers being giantesses. (These complications may be due to Thor having been a pre-AESIR culture hero who had to be fitted into the pantheon.) Second only to his father. Popular with sailors, farmers, emigrants to Iceland and the lower classes generally, in contrast to Odin, who was the god of kings and fighting aristocrats. Well disposed to mankind. With his magic hammer, Mjolnir, he broke up the ice of winter each spring. His chariot was drawn by goats. His mansion was named Bilskinir. Envisaged as red-bearded and very strong. Thursday was named after him and was regarded as a propitious day for marriages; these occasions, as well as funerals and civil contracts, were hallowed by his blacksmith's hammer (cf. Gretna Green). His Teutonic equivalent was DONAR. 777: Tarot: Fives; gem: ruby; plants: oak, nux vomica, nettle; animal: basilisk; minerals: iron, sulphur; perfume: tobacco; magical weapons: Sword, Spear, Scourge, or Chain.

THOTH: Egyptian. God of wisdom and writing. See Chapter XX. 777: Tarot: Eights; gem: opal, especially fire opal; plants: moly, anhalonium lewinii; animals: hermaphrodite, jackal; mineral: mercury; perfume: storax; magical weapons: Names and Versicles and Apron.

THOUME KENE KIMTE CACOUNCHE: Amerindian, Natchez. Creator god. He first made men, but they were bored, so he created tobacco. They were still unsatisfied, so he created women.

THUNAR: Anglo-Saxon thunder god, equivalent of the Teutonic DONAR and the Scandinavian THOR. Like Thor, a god of the people rather than of the military aristocracy.

THUNDERBIRD, THE: Amerindian. In the mythology of some Western tribes, a great bird like an eagle who produced thunder, lightning and rain for the crops.

TIBERINUS: Roman. The god of the River Tiber, particularly venerated in Rome. Each year, on 15 May, to prevent him overflowing, Vestal Virgins threw twenty-four wicker mannikins from the Sublicius bridge – doubtless in memory of a human sacrifice. His Ludi Piscatori, festival of fishermen and divers, was on 17 June, and his main festival, the Tiberinalia, on 17 August.

TIEN: Chinese. God of the vault of Heaven, who later became that vault itself, ruled over by SHANG-TI.

TIEN-KUAN: ('Agent of Heaven') Chinese. A god who bestows happiness and well-being, for example on family occasions or theatrical performances. Portrayed dressed as a mandarin and carrying a scroll of blessings. See also

TI-KUAN snd SHUI-KUAN.

TI'I: Polynesian first man. His wife was Hina-Mitigator-of-Many-Things, who was both a woman and a goddess. The royal families of Tahiti claimed descent from them. See also TIKI.

TI-JEAN PETRO: Haitian voodoo. A one-footed or footless (snake?) god. His wife is the corn goddess Marinette. The Petro rites are of Amerindian rather than African origin.

TIKI: Polynesian. A god who created the world – in some versions by bringing it up from the depths of the sea. Or was created by TANE, and then himself created the Moon goddess Hina and married her. Overlaps TI'I, and in Hawaii known as Ki'i.

TI-KUAN: ('Agent of Earth') Chinese. Remitter of sins.

TILO: Mozambican. Sky god and god of rain and thunder.

TINA, TINIA: Etruscan. Thunder and fire god, chief god of the pantheon. Wherever his thunderbolts struck became a sacred place.

TINIRAU: Polynesian and Maori. Both human and divine. As a man, hero of many legends. As a god, a sea deity, sometimes incarnate in a whale. Guardian deity of New Zealand.

TINNUS – see TANNUS.

TIPHARETH: ('Beauty') The sixth Sephira of the Cabalistic Tree of Life. The solar sphere; in Christian Cabalism, the Christ sphere ('Tiphareth the Son showeth us Kether the Father' – though strictly speaking Kether is sexless). The Sacrificed God sphere. The Sephira which links the whole Tree together and balances it. Cabalistic symbols: the Lamen, the Rosy Cross, the Calvary Cross, the Truncated Pyramid, the Cube. Tarot: Sixes. Magical image: a majestic king, a child, a sacrificed god.

TIRAWA, ATIUS-TIRAWA: Amerindian, Pawnee. Great Spirit and creator god, sometimes a Sun or thunder god. At one stage he tried to destroy the world by fire, but it was put out by a deluge. His wife is Atira.

TISHTRIYA: Persian. The Dog Star, Sirius.

TITANS, THE: Greek. The twelve children of URANUS and Gaia. Personification of violence in Nature, before the rule of the OLYMPIANS. Under their king and queen, CRONUS and Rhea, they overthrew their father and then (all except OCEANUS) made war on the Olympians. Defeated, they were confined by ZEUS to Tartarus, the lowest region of Hades.

TITHONOS: Greek. Human husband of the dawn goddess Eos. She asked ZEUS to grant him immortality but forgot to ask for eternal youth, so he gradually became decrepit. In pity, the gods turned him into a cicada.

TITI: Bolivian and north-west Brazilian, Anti Indian. When mankind had been destroyed by fire, he opened a tree, from which he brought forth the tribal ancestor Ule ('tree'), his wife and others, to repopulate the world.

TIUZ, TIW, TIWAZ – see TYR.

TLAHUIZCALPANTECUHTLI: ('Lord of the House of Dawn') Aztec. God of the Morning Star, Venus. Lord of the twelfth hour of the day.

TLALCHITONATIUH: Aztec. God of the late afternoon Sun.

TLALOC: ('Pulp of the Earth') Aztec. Pre-Aztec in origin but became one of their most important gods. Mountain, rain and thunder god. His mountain dwelling, Tlalocan, was abundant with food. Portrayed as black, with a garland of white feathers and a green plume. His rituals were the cruellest of all, with the sacrifice of many children and babies at the breast. His wife, the water goddess Chalchiuhtlicue ('Emerald Lady'), however, was protectress of newborn children, marriages and chaste lovers. Another named wife was Xochiquetzal, the Aztec Eve and Moon goddess of flowers, love, marriage, art, singing, dance, spinning and weaving. She bore him the Toltec culture hero QUETZALCOATL, who became an Aztec god. She was finally stolen from Tlaloc (see TEZCATLIPOCA).

TLALOQUES, THE: Aztec. Cloud spirits, servants of TLALOC as rain god.

TLALTECUHTLI: ('Lord of the Earth') Aztec. Earth monster god. Lord of the second hour of the day.

TLOQUE NAHUAQUE – see OMETECUHTLI.

TOHIL: Guatemalan, Quiche Indian. Fire god.

TONACATECUHTLI: ('Lord of our Subsistence') Aztec creator god. His wife was Tonacacihuatl, said to have given birth to an obsidian knife from which sprang 1,600 demigods who peopled the Earth.

TONATIUH, PILTZINTECUTLI: Aztec. Sun god. Fed and cooled by human sacrifice. His home, House of the Sun, was the abode of warriors. Warriors raised him to the zenith each day, and women who had died in childbirth lowered him into the Underworld each night. Lord of the East and of the fourth hour of the day.

TORNAQS, TORNATS, TORNGAKS, THE: Eskimo. Spirits of localities, who can also protect individuals.

TORNARSUK, TORNGARSAK: Eskimo. Chief god, and ruler of the TORNAQS. Called 'The Great Spirit'.

TORUGUENKET: Brazilian, northern Tupi-Guarani tribes. Moon god, principle of evil; the Moon is believed to be the cause of floods and thunderstorms and periodically to fall to Earth and destroy it. Seems to be a local form of JACY. Cf. TORUSHOMPEK.

TORUSHOMPEK. Brazilian, northern Tupi-Guarani tribes. Sun god, principle of good; CF. TORUGUENKET.

TRIGLAV: Slavonic. A god of Stettin (Szczein) where he had four temples. He had three heads, representing Heaven, Earth and the Underworld; the faces were veiled so that he might not see the sins of the world. He had a black horse which gave omens.

TRIPTOLEMUS: Greek. Son of King Celeus of Eleusis. The corn goddess Demeter taught him the art of ploughing and harvesting, and he toured Greece spreading the knowledge. His name may be cognate with *tripolos*, the 'thrice-ploughed furrow' in which grain was sown and in which Demeter lay with her lover IASION.

TRISTAN, TRISTRAM: Celtic. Lover of Iseult, who represents the Triple Goddess; Tristan is the Young God who must come to terms with her; see *The Witches' Goddess*, p. 34.

TRITA: Hindu. In Vedic myth, conqueror of the serpent god AHI (1). Later superseded by INDRA as conqueror of Ahi or Vritra.

TRITON: Greek. Son of POSEIDON and Amphitrite. Part man and part sea-serpent, he blew his conch shell to stir up or calm the waves. Amphitrite's chariot was escorted by similar beings, called Tritons.

TROJANU: Slavonic. The Roman Emperor Trajan, deified in some parts of Russia under this name. Attributes similar to PERUN.

TS'AI-LUN: Chinese. God of stationers, inventor of paper.

TS'AI-SHEN: Chinese. God of Wealth. His birthday, the fifth day of the first month of the Chinese year, is celebrated with special rituals.

TS'ANG-CHIEH: Chinese. God of public story-tellers, inventor of writing.

TSAO-WANG: Chinese hearth god, helped by his wife Tsao-Wang Nai-Nai, who also keeps a record of the women's sayings and doings. He reports annually to the AUGUST PERSONAGE OF JADE, and his departure and return are marked with firecrackers.

TSUI GOAB: African, Hottentot. A culture hero, probably originally historical. Central figure of a cult honouring a mound of stones believed to be his grave.

TSUKIYOMI: ('Counter of Months') Japanese Moon god, son of IZANAGI and Izanami, or born from Izanagi's right eye when he washed it. Brother of the Sun goddess Amaterasu.

TSUL 'KALU: ('Slanting Eyes') Amerindian, Cherokee. Hunting god of the Blue Ridge Mountains of Virginia.

TU: Polynesian. War god, but his role as such was largely taken over by ORO. In the Society Islands, a creator god. Called Ku in Hawaii.

TUAMUTEF: Alternative spelling of Duamutef; see HORUS, FOUR SONS OF.

TUISTO: Teutonic. According to Tacitus, a god or giant of the west German tribes (ancestors of today's Germans), born of the Earth and father of the first man, Mannus. The name Tuisto seems to mean 'two-sexed being', and Mannus a human endowed with thought and will.

TUNDUN – see MUNGAN-NGANA.

TUNG WANG KUNG – see JADE, AUGUST PERSONAGE OF.

TUNG-YUEH-TA-TI – see T'AI-SHEN.

TUONI: Finno-Ugric god of Tuonela or Manala, the Underworld. His wife was Tuonetar. Their daughters were goddesses of death (Kalma), disease (Loviatar and Kipu-Tytto/Kivutar) and suffering (Vammatar).

TUPAN, TUPI: Brazilian, Tupi-Guarani tribe. Storm god, son of NANDEREVUSU and Nandecy. Tupan lives in the west, and there are storms every time he travels to visit his mother Nandecy in the east.

TUPURAN – see WAC.

TURSAS: Finno-Ugric. A monster who rises from the bottom of the sea and sets fire to grass.

T'U-TI: Chinese. Gods of place. Every town, village, street and dwelling has one.

TVASHTAR, TVASHTRI: Hindu. A solar-type craftsman god and 'universal exciter'. He forged the thunderbolt of INDRA and the Moon-cup for ambrosia. Father of cloud goddess Saranyu, wife of Sun god SURYA.

TWANYRIKA: Australian Aborigine. The great spirit whose voice is heard in the bull-roarer.

TYPHOEUS: Greek. Spirit of the hurricane. See p.121.

TYPHON: Greek storm god. A snake-headed giant, born parthenogenetically to Hera during her rage at ZEUS's giving birth to Athene from his head. Hera used him to try to prevent Leto giving birth to APOLLO, but POSEIDON frustrated his attempt. Typhon lived in a cave on Mount Parnassus. Often confused with TYPHOEUS; some authorities treat them as the same. In Egypt (where he was taken by the Hyksos invaders) Typhon became another name for SET in the Nineteenth Dynasty (c.1320-1200 BC). 777 Tarot: Death; gem: snakestone; plant: cactus; animals: scorpion, beetle, lobster or crayfish, wolf; perfumes: Siamese benzoin, opoponax; magical weapon: Pain of the Obligation.

TYR: Scandinavian and Teutonic. In various versions, son of FRIGG, ODIN or HYMIR. Originally a law-giving god, later a war god, and patron of athletes. As with THOR, a peasant god, gradually superseded by ODIN. Called Ziu by the south Germans, Tiuz by the north Germans, and Tiw by the Anglo-Saxons (hence Tuesday) and identified with MARS by the Romans (hence the French *mardi*, Tuesday). All these names are cognate with the Sanskrit *dyaus*, the Latin *deus* and the Greek *ZEUS* – all simply meaning 'divinity'. Another Germanic name for him was *Things* (from *thing*, council) from his original function (hence the German *Dienstag*, Tuesday).

TZITZIMIME: ('Monsters Descending from Above') Aztec. A minor stellar god, probably connected with meteors – hence the name.

UAYAYAB: Mayan. God of the five intercalary days.

UEUETEOTL: Aztec. God of fire, both creative and destructive. He lived in the Pole Star.

UITZILOPOCHTLI – see HUITZILOPOCHTLI.

UKKO: Finno-Ugric. The supreme sky and air god in later mythology, taking the place of JUMALA. Also thunder god, causing the rain to fall, and he supported the world. His wife was Akka (Rauni, or in Estonia Maa-Emoinen), the Earth Mother goddess.

UKWA: Sudanese, Shilluk tribe. Grandson of Kola. He married two Nile priestesses and became the ancestor of the tribe.

ULLER, ULLUR, ULLR: Scandinavian, Icelandic and Teutonic. A god of the sky, hunting, archery and winter. One of the AESIR. Son of Earth Mother Sif and stepson of THOR, who seems to have replaced him.

ULYSSES, ULIXES – see ODYSSEUS.

UMINA: Ecuadorean. God of medicine of the pre-Colombian Caranques. Represented by a large emerald.

UNKULUNKULU: African, Bantu. The progenitor and teacher of mankind, himself born of the reeds. He sent a chameleon to tell humans they were immortal, but the chameleon lingered, so he sent a lizard with the opposite message. The lizard got there first, so mankind became mortal.

UNNEFER: ('The Good Being') Egyptian. A name for OSIRIS as ruler of Amenti, land of the dead.

UNTUNKTAHE: Amerindian, Dakota. Water god and master of magic, often invoked against the thunder bird WAUKHEON.

UPELLURI, UPELLURIS: Hurrian. A giant who held up the Earth and the sky.

U-PIDI-NI-NO-KAMI: ('Mud-Earth Lord'). Japanese. He and his sister-wife Suhiji-ni-no-kami ('Mud-Earth Lady') were deities of the fertility of vegetation.

UPUAUT – see WEPWAWET.

UPULERO: Indonesian, Babar. Sun god. A woman wanting a child will ask a man who has fathered many children to invoke Upulero for her, in a ritual involving the suckling of a doll and the sacrifice of a chicken.

URAEUS: Egyptian. A flame-breathing asp who destroyed RA's enemies. A symbol of power, worn on the front of royal crowns.

URANUS: Greek. Personification of the sky. Youngest son of Earth Mother Gaia, and father by her of the CYCLOPES, Hecatonchires and TITANS. See p.120. 777: Tarot: Twos, Kings or Knights; gems: star ruby, turquoise; plant: amaranth; animal: man; mineral: phosphorus; perfume: musk; magical weapons: Lingam, Inner Robe of Glory.

URCAGUAY: Inca. God of underground treasures. Portrayed as a large snake with a deer's head, his tail decorated with little gold chains.

URSHANABI: Sumerian equivalent of the Greek CHARON.

URUTAETAE: Polynesian, Tahiti. Ruler of the level of the Afterworld reserved for the elect, the Areoi.

USUKUN: Mayan. A god ill-disposed to mankind, whose assistant was the earthquake god Kisin.

UTA-NAPISHTIM, UTNAPISHTIM: Assyro-Babylonian equivalent of Noah. His Flood story, involving EA and Ishtar, appears in the GILGAMESH epic and closely parallels the biblical one. Also a god of the Underworld.

UTHER PENDRAGON: British. King of southern Britain during the Saxon invasions. He fell in love with Igraine, wife of the Duke of Cornwall, and MERLIN magically gave him the Duke's appearance for one night, as a result of which she conceived ARTHUR.

UTTU: Sumerian. Sun god, equivalent of the Babylonian SHAMASH. Son of NANNA or SIN and Ningal, and brother of Ereshkigal, Queen of the Underworld, and Inanna, Queen of Heaven. Reputation as a fair judge and legislator. (Do not confuse with Uttu, Chaldaean and Sumerian goddess of vegetation, weaving and clothes.)

UTUKKU, THE: Assyro-Babylonian. Good and evil genii. The good ones, the Shedu or Lamassu, were guardian spirits of individual humans. The evil ones included the Edimmu, souls of the unburied dead or those whose funeral rites had been inadequate, who revenged themselves by tormenting the living; these could be appeased.

UYITZIN: Mayan. A god benevolent to mankind.

VAHARA – see VARAHA.

VAINAMOINEN: Finno-Ugric. Hero of the national epic Kalevala. The first man, a bard, born parthenogenetically (or, according to the epic, through impregnation by the East Wind) to creator goddess Luonnotar (Ilmatar), daughter of the air god ILMA.

VAINEMUINE: Estonian. God of music, who left mankind because they did not appreciate his songs. Local version of VANAMOINEN.

VAIROCANA – see DHYANI-BUDDHAS, THE.

VAISRAVANA – see MO-LI, THE.

VAIVASVATA – see MANU.

VA-KUL': Finno-Ugric, Zyrian. A malevolent water spirit who could appear as either a man or a woman, with long hair.

VALI: Scandinavian. Son of ODIN and Rinda, or of LOKI and Siguna. One of the AESIR. He slew HODER to avenge the death of BALDUR. His twin brother was VIDAR.

VAMANA: Hindu. The fifth avatar of VISHNU, as a dwarf who defeated the demon Bali who was menacing Heaven and Earth.

VANIR, THE: Scandinavian. A beneficent race of deities, including FREY and Freya, who were gods and goddesses of fertility and protectors of all living creatures. They first fought with the AESIR and then joined them in Valhalla; probably a memory of actual conflict and compromise between two invading races.

VANTH: Etruscan. Leader of benevolent spirits who gave help at the moment of death. His malevolent counterpart was Charun.

VARAHA, VAHARA: Hindu. The third avatar of VISHNU, as a boar who rescued Earth from the Deluge by killing the demon HIRANYAKSHA who was holding it underwater. His wife in that incarnation was Sukara-preyasi, 'Beloved of the Boar'.

VARUNA: Hindu. An early Vedic sky and water god, maintaining justice and order in the universe. Witness of oaths and guarantor of mercy. Later became a Moon god and lord of the dead. Son of the sky or Sun god DYAUS and the Earth goddess Privthi – or of Aditi, the Cosmic Matrix mother goddess, and brother of Sun god MITHRA sand the ADITYAS, twelve month gods. Husband of Varuni, goddess of spiritous liquor – or of Varunari, Varuni being his daughter. Portrayed as a white man riding a sea monster and carrying a lasso (from his function as a judge).

VASEDUVA: Hindu. An early Sun god, at one stage partially supplanting KRISHNA, the dark Sun. Later regarded as Krishna's father by Devaki.

VASUKI: Hindu. A huge snake, one of the rulers of the NAGAS. The gods used him as a rope to churn the sea. Similar to SHESHA.

VASUS, THE: Hindu. A group of eight deities attendant upon INDRA. They are the mother goddess Aditi, Antariksha ('Sky'), AGNI, CHANDRA, Dyu ('Heaven'), the Nakshrates ('Stars'), Earth and fertility goddess Privthi and VAYU.

VATA, VAYU: Hindu. God of wind, and father of HANUMAN; later considered father of the MARUTS. One of the VASUS. His importance declined as INDRA's increased.

VATEA: Polynesian. Father of TAAROA and RONGO by Earth Mother Papa. The Sun and Moon were regarded as his eyes.

VATES: Polynesian, Indonesian. Underworld god, son of Vari-Ma-Te-Takere, great Mother of gods and men who live in Aviki, land of the dead.

VAYA – see VATA.

VE – see BOR.

VELCHANOS – see VULCAN.

VELES – see VOLOS.

VERETHAGHNA: Persian, Zoroastrian. God of victory in war.

VERTUMNUS: Roman. God of gardens and orchards, sharing this duty with his consort Pomona and with Flora. A shape-changer (*vertere*, to change).

VETISL: Etruscan. God of night.

VIDAR: Scandinavian. A son of ODIN and Siguna, or of LOKI and Rinda. A strong and silent god, one of the AESIR, who killed the FENRIS-WOLF and survived Ragnarok as a god of the awaited Golden Age. His twin brother was VALI.

VIDYADHARAS, THE: Hindu air spirits. Their female equivalents are the Vidyadharis.

VILI – see BOR.

VIRACOCHA, CHUN: Inca, adopted from pre-Inca. Creator god of the Sun, Moon and stars, of water, thunder, rain and growing things. He lived in the depths of lake Titicaca. He had neither flesh nor bones, yet could run very fast. Children and animals were sacrificed to him. His sister and wife was the rain and sea goddess Mama Cocha, mother of all mankind.

VIRAJ – see MANU.

VIRBIUS: Roman. A consort of Diana of whom little is known but who seems to have filled a Sacrificed King role.

VIRUDHAKA and VIRUPKSA – see MO-LI, THE.

VISHNU: Hindu. A Vedic Sun god, who became the second of the supreme triad, the first and third being BRAHMA and SHIVA. Believed to have had nine avatars (incarnations) so far: (1) MATSYA, as a fish; (2) KURMA, tortoise; (3) VARAHA, boar; (4) NARASINHA, lion-headed man; (5) VAMANA, dwarf; (6) PARASHURAMA, RAMA with the axe; (7) RAMA-CHANDRA; (8) KRISHNA; (9) BUDDHA. Still to come is (10) KALKI, a giant with a horse's head, who will manifest in a new and better world. The first three are aspects of the Deluge story. Vishnu being a much-loved god of the people, some of the remainder (e.g. Buddha) represent a compromise between traditions; others enshrine changes following invasions. The development from fish through reptile and mammal to semi-human and human, and finally to fully enlightened human, even suggests an evolutionary theme. Vishnu is often portrayed blue-skinned, yellow-clothed, with a mace, shell, disc and lotus in his four hands. His consort is Lakshmi, goddess of good fortune and beauty, said to have been his wife, in various forms, in each of his avatars; she was probably an early Earth mother, perhaps originally Vishnu's mother. 777 gives different correspondences for eight of the avatars: (Matsya) Tarot: Moon; gem: pearl; plants: unicellular organisms, opium poppy; animals: fish, dolphin; perfume: ambergris; magical weapons: Twilight of the Place and Magic Mirror. (Kurma) Tarot: Nines; gem: quartz; plants: banyan, mandrake, damiana; animal: elephant; mineral: lead; perfumes: jasmine, ginseng, all odiferous roots; magical weapons: Perfume and Sandals. (Varruna (Varaha?)) Tarot: Fives, gem: ruby; plants: oak, nux vomica, nettle; animal: basilisk; minerals: iron, sulphur; perfume: tobacco; magical weapons: Sword, Spear, Scourge or Chain. (Nara-Singh

(Narisinha)) Tarot: Strength; gem: cat's eye; plant: sunflower; animal: lion (Cherub of Fire) perfume: olibanum; magical weapon: Discipline (Preliminary). (Parasu-Rama) Tarot: Magician; gems: opal, agate; plants: vervain, herb mercury, marjolane, palm; animals: swallow, ibis, ape; mineral: mercury; perfumes; mastic, white sandal, mace, storax, all fugitive odours; magical weapons: Wand or Caduceus. (Krishna) Tarot: Sixes, Emperors or Princes; gems: topaz, yellow diamond; plants: acacia, bay, laurel, vine; animals: phoenix, lion, child; perfume: olibanum; magical weapons: Lamen or Rosy Cross. (Buddha) Tarot: Twos, Kings or Knights; gems: star ruby, turquoise; plant: amaranth; animal man; mineral: phosphorus; perfume: musk magical weapons: Lingam, Inner Robe of Glory. (Horse (Kalki)) Tarot: Temperance; gem: jacinth; plant: rush; animals: man or eagle (Cherub of Air), peacock; perfume: lign-aloes; magical weapon: Arrow.

VISVAKARMA: Hindu. The universal agent, complementing PRA-JAPATI, master of created beings. Architect and craftsman for the gods, who built the cities of Lanka (in Sri Lanka) and Amaravati (in Swarga, the Heaven of Indra). He forged the disc of VISHNU, the trident of SHIVA, the lance of KARTTIKEYA and the weapons of KUBERA from the one-eighth of SURYA's light which he gave up to regain Saranyu, who was Visvakarma's daughter. Once an epithet of INDRA and the Sun. Later identified with TVASHTAR.

VIVASVAT – see SURYA.

VIZETOT: Nicaraguan, Niquiran tribe. God of famine.

VIZI-EMBER – see VU-MURT.

VLKODLAKS, VOOKODLAKS: Slavonic name for the werewolf. Believed to cause eclipses of the Sun and Moon.

VODYANOI, THE: Slavonic. Dangerous water spirits, inhabiting lakes, pools and rivers, particularly near mill-dams. Could assume many shapes, including those of a fish, a giant man or a naked woman combing water from her hair. They drew humans into drowning, their victims becoming slaves in their underwater palaces.

VOHU-MANO: Persian, Zoroastrian. Spirit of wisdom.

VOLKH: Slavonic. A shape-changing being who could appear as a bird, animal or insect. Protector of the city of Kiev.

VOLOS, VOLUSU: Slavonic. An early god of animals, also sometimes of war. Became a peasants' god, protector of shepherds and cattle. Among the Czechs, named Veles and regarded as a demon.

VOLSUNG: Scandinavian. Son of RERIR, and grandson of ODIN's son SIGI. Father by Liod of SIGMUND. Also, as the Volsungs, a name for the whole family.

VÖLUND: Scandinavian name of Wayland the Smith; see Chapter XXVIII.

VOOKODLAKS – see VLKODLAKS.

VOTAN: Guatemalan, Quiche Indian. A god corresponding to the Aztec TEPEYOLLOTL.

VU-KUTIS: Finno-Ugric, Votyak. A water spirit who cured diseases.

VULCAN: Roman. God of fire and metal-working, corresponding to the Greek HEPHAESTUS, from whom he acquired most of his legend – as did his wife Venus from Hephaestus's wife Aphrodite. According to Graves (*The White Goddess*, p. 331) his original was Velchanos, 'a Cretan Cock-demon who became Vulcan when his worship was introduced into Italy'. *777*: Tarot: Justice, Judgement, (Wands) Kings or Knights; gems: emerald, fire opal; plants: aloe, red poppy, hibiscus, nettle; animals: elephant, lion (Cherub of Fire); minerals: nitrates; perfumes: galbanum, olibanum, all fiery odours; magical weapons: Cross of Equilibrium, Wand or Lamp, Pyramid of Fire.

VU-MURT: Finno-Ugric, Votyak. A water spirit. Magyar equivalent Vizi-ember.

VU-NUNA: ('Water-Uncle') Finno-Ugric, Votyak. A water spirit who protected against the malevolent Yanki-murt.

VU-VOZO: Finno-Ugric, Votyak. A malevolent water spirit.

WAC, TUPURAN: Amerindian, Pericu. A god who rebelled against Niparaya but was defeated and expelled from Heaven with his followers and confined to an underground cave, where he had to look after whales and see they did not escape.

WADD: Arabic, pre-Islamic. One of the gods worshipped by the descendants of Cain, and condemned in the Koran.

WADJ WER: ('Great Green') Egyptian. Fertility god personifying either the Mediterranean off the Egyptian coast or the major lagoons of the Nile Delta itself. Represented androgynously, with a prominent breast and a pregnant-looking belly.

WAKA-MI-KE-NU-NO-MIKITO: Japanese. Son of sea goddess Tamayori-Bime-No-Mikoto. Later, called Jimmy Tenno, said to have been the first emperor of Japan.

WAKONDA: Amerindian, Sioux. The Great Spirit, Father of the Sky and supreme being, source of all life and power, as Mother Earth is its start and finish. The TIRAWA of the Pawnees.

WALGINO: Slavonic, Polish. Protector of Cattle.

WARMARA: Ugandan. Father of four gods – the Sun and Moon god, the god of cattle, the water god and a fourth who was the hero of many adventures.

WAUKHEON: Amerindian, Dakota. The Thunder Bird, in constant conflict with the water god UNTUNKTAHE.

WAYLAND THE SMITH – see Chapter XXVIII.

WEI-T'O – see IDA-TEN.

WEKWEK: Amerindian, Tuleyone. A falcon who stole fire from Heaven and set the Earth ablaze; the fire was put out by OLLE's sending rain. The same story is told with Sahte as the arsonist.

WENCESLAS: In Slavonic myth, King Wenceslas of Bohemia sleeps under a mountain with his knights, awaiting the call of their country's needs.

WEN CH'ANG. Chinese. An ancient god of literature. Possibly a great philosopher deified after death. Portrayed as a seated mandarin carrying a sceptre. His assistant is K'UEI-HSING.

WENEG: Egyptian. Son and scribe of RA in Old Kingdom texts, representing cosmic order – similar in this to his much more important sister Ma'at.

WEPWWET, UPUAUT: ('Opener of the Ways') Egyptian, jackal- or dog-headed god of Upper Egypt, champion of the Pharaoh, both in war and in the Underworld. Apparently of Predynastic origin. At Abydos in the Middle Kingdom (where he was also known as KHENTI-AMENTIU) a 'procession of Wepwawet' opened the mysteries of OSIRIS, who was referred to as his father. Occasionally, in his role as 'opener', he appeared as a god of the rising Sun, guiding the ship of RA.

WEYLAND – see Chapter XXVIII.

WHERO-AO: Polynesian. A primal god, ancestor of TAWHAKI.

WIELAND – see WAYLAND THE SMITH.

WINABOJO – see MANABOZHO.

WISAKA: Amerindian, Sac and Fox. Ancestor of the tribe and hero of a Deluge story.

WODAN, WODEN: The Anglo-Saxon form of ODIN.

WOTAN: The Teutonic form of ODIN. Owing to Christian suppression of the Germanic myths, little is known of him apart from what can be learned from the Odin myths. But 777 gives different correspondences for Wotan: Tarot: Aces, Fours; gems: diamond, amethyst, sapphire; plants: almond in flower, olive, shamrock; animals: god, unicorn; mineral: aur. pot.; perfumes: ambergris, cedar; magical weapons: Swastika or Fylfat Cross, Crown, Wand, Sceptre or Crook.

WU-CH'ANG: ('Without Duration') Chinese. Two gods, one white and one black, who bring souls to the Underworld.

XAMANIQUINQU: Mayan, Yucatan. Spirit of the North.

XANTHUS – see SCAMANDER.

XELHUA: Aztec. A giant who escaped the Deluge by going to the top of TLALOC's mountain. Credited with building the Cholula step pyramid.

XIPE, XIPE TOTEC: Aztec. God of Spring growth, vegetation and flowers. Known as 'Our Lord the Flayed God'.

XISUTHROS: Babylonian. The tenth pre-diluvian king, and hero of a Deluge legend. May be the same as UTA-NAPISHTIM.

XIUHTECUTLI: Aztec. Fire god and ruler of the Sun. Lord of the year, the first hour of the day, and the first hour of the night. Human sacrifices to him were thrown into flames. Also called Huehueteotl (the Old God).

XOCHIPILLI ('Flower Prince'), MACUILXOCHITL: Aztec corn god, central character of the Spring Equinox fertility ritual. God of love, dancing, music and youth. Lord of the seventh hour of the day. Son of and lover of the Moon, love and marriage, flower, art, singing, dance, spinning and weaving goddess Xochiquetzal. These were deities of the two sexes.

XOLOTL: Aztec. Patron and guardian of twins, and himself the twin brother of QUETZALCOATL. Also god of ball-play. A shape-changer, and thus god of magicians. Represented the planet Venus as Evening Star, his brother being the Morning Star.

XPIYACOC: Guatemalan, Quiche Indian. In their creation legend, which reflects Mayan beliefs and perhaps some Aztec, he and his consort, Xmucane, first made animals and then human beings. Cf. OMETECUCHTLI.

YABUNE: Japanese. An early house god.

YACATECUHTLI: ('The Lord Who Guides') Aztec. God of merchants and travellers. Slaves were sacrificed to him.

YACHIMATA-HIKO: Japanese god 'of innumerable roads', with his female counterpart Yachimato-Hime.

YAGHUTH: ('He Who Helps') Arabic, pre-Islamic. One of the gods worshipped by the descendants of Cain and condemned in the Koran. Worshipped north of the Yemen, in the form of a lion. Cognate with the Uz and Jeush of Genesis.

YAH, YAHWEH: The Hebrew god. See Chapter XII.

YAKUSHI NYORAI: Japanese Buddhist. Divine healer who stops epidemics. Portrayed as a Buddha holding a flask of medicine and often flanked by symbols of the Sun and Moon. Very popular from the eighth century onwards.

YAMA: The Hindu Adam. In early Vedic myth, he and his twin sister, Yami, were born of Saranyu, wife of the Sun, and were the ancestors of the human race. Yami was the first of all beings to die, and they became king and queen of a secret sanctuary in Heaven where dead friends and families reunite and live happily. Under later Brahmanic theology, Yama became a grimmer figure. 777: Tarot: Justice, Judgement, (Wands) Kings or Knights; gems: emerald, fire opal; plants: aloe, red poppy, hibiscus, nettle; animals: elephant, lion (Cherub of Fire); minerals: nitrates; perfumes: galibanum, olibanum, all fiery odours; magical weapons: Cross of Equilibrium, Wand or Lamp, Pyramid of Fire.

YAMA-KINGS, THE: Chinese. The ten rulers and judges of the ten courts of Hell, with precisely defined functions. The end of their process for the individual soul is either immortality, or almost immediate reincarnation (either as a human or as an animal), or a period of suitable punishment before reincarnation. Chief of the Yama-Kings is YEN-WANG.

YAMANTAKA: Buddhistic Hindu. A terrifying figure with several faces and many arms, and a necklace of skulls.

YAMM (1): Babylonian. A sea god killed by BAAL.

YAMM (2): Egyptian. Tyrannical sea god, known only from a fragmentary papyrus, and doubtless the same as (1).

YANG: Chinese. The masculine, Heaven, active principle, in harmonious balance with Yin, the feminine, Earth, receptive principle. (Yang is the white segment of the Yang-Yin symbol.)

YANGWU: Chinese. A sun crow, equatable with the Japanese Yatagrasu.

YARIKH, YARIH, YERAH: Canaanite Moon god. He married Nikkal, goddess of the fruits of the Earth, paying her father, HIRIBI, 'the Summer's King', 10,000 gold shekels for her hand.

YARILO: Slavonic. God of passion and sexual love and of fertility. Young girls held a flower festival for him in the spring, and at the end of summer his funeral rites were marked by dancing and feasting.

YASO-MAGA-TSU-BI: Japanese. God of multiple calamities, born of the mud which IZANAGI washed off after visiting Hell.

YATUS, THE: Hindu and Persian, Zoroastrian. In Vedic myth, a group of holy men who were killed by INDRA (probably an early Brahmanic anti-Indra invention). The name of a present Jain sect. In Zoroastrian myth, evil spirits with powers of sorcery.

YA'UK: ('He Who Prevents, or Keeps') Arabic, pre-Islamic. One of the gods worshipped by the descendants of Cain and condemned in the Koran.

YAZATAS, THE: Persian, Zoroastrian. Benevolent spirits representing the astral counterparts of physical objects, and the types of moral force, in the universe. Many similarities to the AMESHAS SPENTAS.

YEN-WANG: Chinese. God of the world of the dead, and chief of the YAMA-KINGS. He decides the time and manner of death, the human or animal form of reincarnation, and the reward of immortality for good or the nature of punishment for evil.

YERAH – see YARIKH.

YESOD: ('Foundation') The ninth Sephirah of the Cabalistic Tree of Life, the lunar sphere – in some aspects masculine, in some feminine. Its traditional definition is 'the foundation of the universe, established in strength'. Sphere of the astral plane, linking the rest of the Tree to physical manifestation (the tenth Sephira, Malkuth); it 'purifies the emanations' of the first eight Sephiroth and offers 'a vision of the machinery of the universe'. Cabalistic symbols: the Perfume and Sandals. Tarot: Nines. Magical image: a beautiful naked man, very strong.

YETL: Amerindian, Athapascan. A great thunder-raven who dragged the flooded Earth above the water.

YIMA: Persian, Zoroastrian. The Noah of the Deluge myth very similar to the biblical one, except that he was instructed (by AHURA MAZDA) to build a cave instead of an ark. Modern tradition says his treasure is still hidden in the cave.

YMIR: Scandinavian. Father of all the giants and, through his daughter Bestla, grandfather of ODIN (though another version makes Bestla the daughter of BOLTHORN). He was killed by Odin and the other gods, and the sea, Earth and Heaven were created from his body, and the world-tree Yggdrasil grew from it.

YNG, YNGVI, YNGIFREY: Swedish names for FREY.

YOHUAL-TECUHTIN, THE: Aztec. Ten lords of the night who decide men's destinies.

YSBADADDEN: Welsh. A king of the Giants, father of Olwyn; he knew he must die if his daughter (a May Queen type) married, but failed to prevent it.

YU-CH'IH CHING-TE and CH'IN SHU-PAO: Chinese – see GENERAL, THE SNIFFING and GENERAL, THE PUFFING.

YUH-HUANG-SHANG-TI – see JADE, AUGUST PERSONAGE OF.

YUM CAAX, YUM KAAX, GHANAN: Mayan. Corn and agriculture god, honoured at the planting and harvesting of maize.

YUNCEMIL: Mayan, Yucatan. Lord of death.

YU-TI – see JADE, AUGUST PERSONAGE OF.

YU-TZU: Chinese. Master of rain, sprinkling it with his sword from a pot he carries.

YUN-T'UNG: Chinese. Little Boy of the Clouds, who piles them up in the sky during storms.

YURUPARI: Brazilian, Tupian Indian (Amazon). A forest god, or ogre, according to the tribe.

ZAGREUS: Cretan. Probably originally a ZEUS-type god; identified by the Greeks, under the influence of Orphism, with DIONYSUS as Dionysus-Zagreus.

ZAMBA: Cameroons. Supreme god of the Yaunde tribe. He created the Earth and then came down to it and had four sons; N'kokon the wise, Otukut the idiot, Ngi the gorilla and Wo the chimpanzee. He taught the Yaunde and alloted their duties.

ZAMBI: Angolan. Supreme god, who lives in the sky and judges the dead.

ZAMNA – see ITZAMNA.

ZAQAR: Assyro-Babylonian. Messenger of the Moon god SIN, bringing dreams to mankind.

ZEPHYRUS: Greek god of the West Wind. Son, with the other three Winds (see BOREAS, EURUS, NOTUS), of the Titan ASTRAEUS and the dawn goddess Eos. His wife was Iris, rainbow messenger of the gods.

ZERVAN AKARANA: Persian, Zoroastrian. God of time and destiny, and father of AHURA MAZDA and AHRIMAN.

ZEUS: Greek. Supreme god. See Chapter XXV. 777: Tarot: Aces, Nines, Fool, (Swords) Emperors or Princes, Wheel of Fortune; gems: diamond, quartz, topaz, chalcedony, amethyst, lapis lazuli; plants: almond in flower, banyan, mandrake, damiana, aspen, hyssop, oak, poplar, fig; animals: god, elephant, eagle or man (Cherub of Air); minerals: aur. pot., lead; perfumes: ambergris, jasmine, ginseng, all odiferous roots, galbanum, saffron, all generous odours; magical weapons: Swastika or Fylfat Cross, Crown, Perfume and Sandals, Dagger or Fan, Sceptre.

ZIO, ZIU, ZIUMEN, ZIU-WARI – see TYR.

ZOCHO: Japanese. Guardian deity of the West.

ZOTZILAHA CHIMALMAN: Mayan. Bat god. Same as the Quiche CAMAZOTZ.

ZU: Assyro-Babylonian. Storm and chaos god, in the form of a bird. Son of the bird-goddess Siris. He stole the Tablets of Creation from ENLIL and hid them in a mountain top. SHAMASH eventually netted him and recovered the Tablets.

Appendix I
Casting and Banishing the Circle

As in *The Witches' Goddess*, we felt that the rituals we have given in this book would be incomplete without instructions for Casting and Banishing the Circle which must precede and follow them. (The exceptions are of course the Egyptian rituals, about which see Appendix II.) We therefore give these instructions below, to make this book self-contained. Explanations and footnotes have not been included: these will be found in our *Eight Sabbats for Witches*, Sections I and III.

Casting the Circle

The tools are on the altar in the North, with the sword laid on the ground before it. At least one candle (preferably three) is on the altar, and one each in the East, South and West points of the perimeter. Incense is burning in the censer on the altar. A bowl of water and one of salt are also on the altar.

The High Priestess and High Priest kneel before the altar. The rest of the coven stand outside the North-East of the Circle.

The High Priestess puts the bowl of water on the pentacle, and the tip of her athame in it, and says: '*I exorcize thee, O Creature of Water, that thou cast out from thee all the impurities and uncleanness of the spirits of the world of phantasm, in the names of Cernunnos and Aradia.*' (Or whatever god- and goddess-names are being used.)

She holds up the bowl of water before her. The High Priest puts the bowl of salt on the pentacle, and the tip of his athame in it, and says: '*Blessings be upon this Creature of Salt; let all malignity and hindrance be cast forth thencefrom, and let all good enter therein. Wherefore I bless thee and invoke thee, that thou mayest aid me, in the name of Cernunnos and Aradia.*'

He pours the salt into the High Priestess's bowl of water, and they replace both bowls on the altar. The High Priest leaves the Circle to join the coven in the North-East.

The High Priestess casts the Circle with the sword, proceeding deosil from North to North. As she passes the North-East, she raises the sword higher than the heads of the coven to leave a gateway. As she casts the Circle, she says:

'*I conjure thee, O Circle of Power, that thou beest a meeting-place of love and joy and truth; a shield against all wickedness and evil; a boundary between the world of men and the realms of the Mighty Ones; a rampart and protection that shall preserve and contain the power that we shall raise within thee. Wherefore, I bless thee and consecrate thee, in the names of Cernunnos and Aradia.*'

She lays down the sword and admits the High Priest to the Circle with a kiss, spinning with him deosil. The High Priest admits a woman in the same way; the woman admits a man; and so on till all are inside. The High Priestess picks up the sword and closes the gateway with a deosil sweep of it.

The High Priestess names three witches. The first carries the bowl of water deosil round the Circle from North to North, sprinkling the perimeter. He then sprinkles each person in turn. If he is a man, he ends by sprinkling the high Priestess, who sprinkles him; if she is a woman, she ends by sprinkling the High Priest, who sprinkles her. The bowl is returned to the altar.

The second named witch carries the smoking censer deosil round the Circle from North to North and replaces it on the altar. The third carries an altar candle round in the same way and replaces it.

All take their athames and face East, with the High Priestess in front. She draws the Invoking Pentagram of Earth (apex, bottom left, far right, far left, bottom right and apex again) in the air before her, saying: '*Ye Lords of the Watchtowers of the East, ye Lords of Air; I do summon, stir*

and call you up, to witness our rites and to guard the Circle.'
The rest of the coven copy her gestures with their athames.
The same to the South, saying: *'Ye Lords of the Watchtowers of the South, ye Lords of Fire; I do summon ...'* etc.
The same to the West, saying: *'Ye Lords of the Watchtowers of the West ye Lords of Water; Lords of Death and of Initiation; I do summon ...'* etc.
The same to the North, saying: *'Ye Lords of the Watchtowers of the North, ye Lords of Earth; Boreas, thou guardian of the Northern portals; thou powerful God, thou gentle Goddess; I do summon ...'* etc.

All replace their athames on the altar, and the coven kneel in the South of the Circle facing North. The High Priestess stands with her back to the altar, with the wand in her right hand and a scourge in her left, crossed over her breasts. The High Priest kneels before her and gives her the Fivefold Kiss, saying:

'Blessed be thy feet, that have brought thee in these ways' (kissing her right foot then her left).

'Blessed be thy knees, that shall kneel at the sacred altar' (kissing her right knee then her left).

'Blessed be thy womb, without which we would not be' (kissing her just above the pubic hair).

'Blessed be thy breasts, formed in beauty' (kissing her right breast then her left; she spreads her arms for this).

'Blessed be thy lips, that shall utter the sacred Names' (kissing her on the lips).

He then 'Draws Down the Moon' on her by kneeling again and touching her with his right forefinger on her right breast, left breast and womb; the same three points again; and finally the right breast. As he does so, he says:

'I invoke thee and call upon thee, Mighty Mother of us all, bringer of all fruitfulness; by seed and root, by stem and bud, by leaf and flower and fruit, by life and love do I invoke thee to descend upon the body of this thy servant and priestess.'
Still kneeling, he says:

'Hail, Aradia! From the Amalthean horn
Pour fourth thy store of love; I lowly bend
Before thee, I adore thee to the end
With loving sacrifice thy shrine adorn.
Thy foot is to my lip (kissing it), *my prayer upborns*
Upon the rising incense-smoke; then spend
Thine ancient love, O Mighty One, descend
To aid me, who without thee am forlorn.'

He stands up and takes a pace backwards. The High Priestess draws the Invoking Pentagram of Earth in front of him with the wand, saying:

'Of the Mother darksome and divine
Mine the scourge, and mine the kiss;
The five-point star of love and bliss –
Here I charge you, with this sign.'

The High Priest and High Priestess now both stand with their backs to the altar and deliver the Charge, as follows:

High Priest: *'Listen to the words of the Great Mother; she who of old was also called among men Artemis, Astarte, Athene, Dione, Melusine, Aphrodite, Cerridwen, Dana, Arianrhod, Isis, Brid, and by many other names.'*

High Priestess: *'Whenever ye have need of any thing, once in the month, and better it be when the Moon is full, then shall ye assemble in some secret place and adore the spirit of me, who am Queen of all witches. There shall ye assemble, ye who are fain to learn all sorcery, yet have not won its deepest secrets; to these will I teach things that are yet unknown. And ye shall be free from slavery; and as a sign that ye be really free, ye shall be naked in your rites; and ye shall dance, sing, feast, make music and love, all in my praise. For mine is the ecstasy of the spirit, and mine also is joy on earth; for my law is love unto all beings. Keep pure your highest ideal; strive ever towards it; let naught stop you or turn you aside. For mine is the secret door which opens upon the Land of Youth, and mine is the cup of the wine of life, and the Cauldron of Cerridwen, which is the Holy Grail of immortality. I am the gracious Goddess, who gives the gift of joy unto the heart of man. Upon Earth, I give the knowledge of the spirit eternal; and beyond death, I give peace, and freedom, and reunion with those who have gone before. Nor do I demand sacrifice; for behold, I am the Mother of all living, and my love is poured out upon the Earth.'*

High Priest: *'Hear ye the words of the Star Goddess; she in the dust of whose feet are the hosts of heaven, and whose body encirlces the universe.'*

High Priestess: *'I who am the beauty of the green Earth, and the white Moon among the stars, and the mystery of the waters, and the desire of the heart of man, call unto thy soul. Arise, and come unto me. For I am the soul of Nature, who gives life to the universe. From me all things proceed, and unto me all things must return; and before my face, beloved of Gods and of men, let thine innermost divine self be enfolded in the rapture of the infinite. Let my worship be within the heart that rejoiceth; for behold, all acts of love and pleasure are my rituals. And therefore let there be beauty and strength, power and compassion, honour and humility, mirth and reverence within you. And thou who thinkest to seek for me, know thy seeking and yearning shall avail thee not, unless thou knowest the mystery; that if that which thou seekest thou findest not within thee, then thou shalt never find it without thee. For behold, I have been with thee from the beginning; and I am that which is attained at the end of desire.'*

All stand. The High Priest raises his arms wide and says:

'Bagahi laca bachahe
Lamac cahi achabahe
Karrelyos
Lamac lamec bachalyos
Cabahagi sabalyos
Baryolas
Lagozatha cabyolas
Samahac et famyolas
Harrahya!'

The High Priestess and coven repeat: *'Harrahya!'*

The High Priestess and High Priest face the altar with their arms raised in the Horned God salute (fists clenched, palms forward, first and little fingers pointing upwards). The High Priest says:

'Great God Cernunnos, return to Earth again!
Come at my call and show thyself to men.
Shepherd of Goats, upon the wild hill's way,
Lead thy lost flock from darkness unto day.
Forgotten are the ways of sleep and night –
Men seek for them, whose eyes have lost the light.
Open the door, the door that hath no key,
The door of dreams, whereby men come to thee.
Shepherd of Goats, O answer unto me!'

The High Priestess and High Priest together say: *'Akhera goiti'*, lower their hands and say *'Akhera beiti!'*

The High Priestess, High Priest and coven now form a ring facing inwards, men and women alternately as far as possible, and link hands. They circle deosil, chanting the Witches' Rune:

'Eko, Eko, Azarak,)
Eko, Eko, Zomelak,) [repeated
Eko, Eko, Cernunnos,) three times]
Eko, Eko, Aradia!)
Darksome night and shining Moon,
East, then South, then West, then North,
Hearken to the Witches' Rune –
Here we come to call thee forth!
Earth and water, air and fire,
Wand and pentacle and sword,
Work ye unto our desire,
Hearken ye unto our word!

Cords and censer, scourge and knife.
Powers of the witch's blade –
Waken all ye unto life,
Come ye as the charm is made!
Queen of heaven, Queen of hell,
Horned hunter of the night –
Lend your power unto the spell,
And work our will by magic rite!
In the earth and air and sea,
By the light of Moon or Sun,
As we do will, so mote it be.
Chant the spell and be it done!
Eko, Eko, Azarak,   )
Eko, Eko, Zomelak,   ) [repeated
Eko, Eko, Cernunnos,   ) till ready]
Eko, Eko, Aradia!   )

When the High Priestess decides it is time, she orders *'Down!'* and all sit, still in a ring facing inwards.

Banishing the Circle

All take their athames and face East, with the High Priestess in front. The High Priestess draws the Banishing Pentagram of Earth (bottom left, apex, bottom right, far left, far right, bottom left again) in the air before her, saying:

'*Ye Lords of the Watchtowers of the East, ye Lords of Air; we do thank you for attending our rites; and ere ye depart to your pleasant and lovely realms, we bid you hail and farewell ... Hail and farewell.*'

The coven copy her gestures and say the second '*Hail and farewell*' with her.

The same to the South, saying: '*Ye Lords of the Watchtowers of the South, ye Lords of Fire; we do thank you ...*' etc.

The same to the West, saying '*Ye Lords of the Watchtowers of the West, ye Lords of Water; ye Lords of Death and of initiation; we do thank you ...*' etc.

The same to the North, saying: '*Ye Lords of the Watchtowers of the North, ye Lords of Earth, Boreas, thou guardian of the Northern portals; thou powerful God, thou gentle Goddess; we do thank you ...*' etc.

This completes the banishing of the Circle.

Appendix II
The Egyptian Ritual

The Egyptian temple, opening ritual and ritual robes are described in greater detail on pp. 177-82 of *The Witches' Goddess*, but the outline below should be enough for the rituals suggested in the present book for Osiris, Thoth and Ra.

Egyptian temples were rectangular, with the altar in the East. No objects of iron were found in them.

The relation of the elements to the cardinal points was different from Craft or Western occult practice but in accordance with the Egyptian environment: Fire in the East (the rising Sun), Air in the West (sky of the desert), Water in the South (whence the Nile flows), and Earth in the North (to which the Nile brings fertility). The guardian deities were Neith and Duamutef (East), Selkhet and Qebehsenuf (West), Isis and Imset (South), and Nephthys and Hapy (North).

Priests wore knee-length kilts. Priestesses wore ankle-length skirts, bare-breasted, held up by shoulder straps parallel at the back and meeting in the cleavage in front. Both were barefoot and often wore circular decorative pectorals round their necks, bracelets round their wrists and sometimes at their armpits, and sometimes anklets as well.

The Opening Ritual

This requires the Priest, Priestess and four other people, though Priest and Priestess can work it alone. (Unlike in Wiccan ritual, there is no reason why Priest and Priestess may not exchange the roles given below if they wish.)

The altar carries an ankh symbol (see Figure 4 on p.136), three lit candles and a bowl with an uncracked egg in it for the sacrifice. Other candles may be at the other three cardinal points or wherever convenient for illumination.

One person stands in the North for Earth, bearing a bowl of salt; another in the South for Water, with a bowl of water; another in the West for Air, carrying a sistrum or bell; and another beside the altar in the East for Fire, carrying a lit candle. If Priest and Priestess are working alone, these objects are placed at the four quarters.

The Priest and Priestess face the altar. He says '*Sayga oo-dan!*' ('Silence for the Offering.') She says '*Natara di zeem a Koeten!*' ('May the god bless our rite.') ('*Koetan*' is pronounced like 'curtain' without the r-sound. If the rite were for a goddess, '*Natara*' would be '*Natarat*'.)

The Priest holds up the egg bowl, and the Priestess breaks the egg into it. They hold it up together in salute, then replace it on the altar.

The Priest remains at the altar, while the Priestess goes to the North. She takes (or picks up) the bowl of salt and walks deosil round the perimeter, sprinkling a little as she goes.

Meanwhile the Priest says: '*Nephthys, Lady of the North; Lord Hapy, Royal Son of Horus, Earth God and Lord of the North, keeper and guardian of the lungs; with the casting of this sacred salt, fertilize and sanctify this holy ground with your being, so that we may be strong in all things.*'

When she has completed her circuit from North to North, the Priestess goes and places the salt bowl on the altar. She then goes to the South and takes (or picks up) the bowl of water. She walks round the perimeter deosil, sprinkling a little water as she goes.

Meanwhile the Priest says: '*Isis, Lady of the South; Lord Imset, Water God and Lord of the South, keeper and guardian of the liver; with the sprinkling of this sacred water, sanctify and cleanse this holy sanctum of all its impurities and the vanities of men.*'

When she has completed her circuit from South to South, the Priestess goes and places the water bowl on the altar. She then goes to the West and takes (or picks up) the sistrum or bell. She walks round the perimeter, deosil, shaking it as she goes.

Meanwhile the Priest says: '*Selkhet, Lady of the West; Lord Qebehsenuf, Air God and Lord of the West, keeper and guardian of the intestines; with the disturbance of air with this music, descend from your cardinal point, purify and sanctify the area of this holy sanctum.*'

When she has completed her circuit from West to West, the Priestess goes and puts the sistrum or bell on the altar. She then takes (or picks up) the lit candle and carries it deosil round the perimeter.

Meanwhile the Priest says: '*Neith, Lady of the East; Lord Duamutef, Fire God and Lord of the East, keeper and guardian of the stomach; with the burning of this ritual fire, the all-consuming element, sanctify and purify this temple from all violations.*'

When she has completed her circuit from East to East, the Priestess replaces the lit candle on the altar and stands beside the Priest. The main ritual may now begin.

Closing the Temple
Unlike the Wiccan Circle, the Egyptian temple is not 'banished' at the end of a ritual but is left to disperse of its own accord.

Bibliography

Beltz, Walter – *God and the Gods*, trans. by Peter Heinegg (Penguin, Harmondsworth, Middlesex, 1983)

Bord, Janet and Colin – *Earth Rites* (Granada Publishing, St Albans, Herts, 1982)

Bradford, Ernle – *Ulysses Found* (Hodder & Stoughton, London, 1963; paperback Sphere Books, London, 1967)

Branston, Brian – *The Lost Gods of England* (Thames & Hudson, London, 1957)

British Museum – *A General Introductory Guide to the Egyptian Collections* (Trustees of the British Museum, London, 1969). The Dynastic dates given in our text are as defined in this guide.

Budge, Sir E.A. Wallis – *The Book of the Dead*, trans. with comments (second edition, Routledge & Kegan Paul, London, 1969). *Egyptian Magic* (Routledge & Kegan Paul, reprint 1972). *Egyptian Religion* (Routledge & Kegan Paul, reprint 1972). *Osiris and the Egyptian Resurrection* (two volumes, Dover Publications, New York, reprint 1973)

Campbell, Joseph – *The Masks of God: Primitive Mythology* (Viking Press, New York, 1959; Souvenir Press, London, 1971)

Coghlan, Ronan – *Dictionary of Irish Myth and Legend* (Donard Publishing Co, Bangor, Co. Down, 1979)

Crossley-Holland, Kevin (trans.) – *Beowulf* (Folio Society, London, 1973)

Crowley, Aleister – *777 Revised* (Neptune Press, London 1952)

Deren, Maya – *Divine Horsemen* (Thames & Hudson, London, 1953; paperback under title *The Voodoo Gods*, Granada, St Albans, 1975)

Dillon, Myles, and Chadwick, Nora – *The Celtic Realms* (Weidenfeld & Nicolson, London, 1967; paperback Cardinal, London 1973)

Durdin-Robertson, Lawrence – *The Goddesses of Chaldaea, Syria and Egypt* (Cesara Publications, Clonegal, Ireland, 1975). *The Goddesses of India, Tibet, China and Japan* (Cesara, 1976)

Evans-Wentz, W.Y. – *The Fairy-Faith in Celtic Countries* (Oxford University Press, 1911; Colin Smythe Ltd, Gerrards Cross, Bucks., 1977)

Farmer, David Hugh – *The Oxford Dictionary of Saints* (Clarendon Press, Oxford, 1978)

Farrar, Frank A. – *Old Greek Nature Stories* (Harrap, London, 1910)

Farrar, Janet and Stewart – *Eight Sabbats for Witches* (Robert Hale, London, 1981). *The Witches' Way* (Hale, 1984). American edition of these two under titles *A Witches' Bible*, two volumes (Magickal Childe, New York, 1984). *The Witches' Goddess: The Feminine Principle of Divinity* (Hale, London, 1987). *Life and Times of a Modern Witch* (Piatkus Books, London, 1987); paperback Headline, London, 1988). All these titles also Phoenix Publishing, Custer, Wa, USA, 1988.

Farrar, Stewart – *What Witches Do* (originally published 1971; second edition, Phoenix Publishing, Custer, Wa., USA, 1983)

Folklore, Myths and Legends of Britain (Reader's Digest Association, London, 1973)

Fortune, Dion – *The Mystical Qabalah* (Eernest Benn, London, 1935). *The Sea Priestess* (Aquarian Press, London, 1957; paperback Wyndham Publications, London 1976)

Frazer, Sir J.G. – *The Golden Bough* (abridged edition) (Macmillan, London, paperback, 1974). Our page references are to this edition.

Freud, Sigmund, (trans. and ed. James Strachey), *The Standard Edition of the Complete Psychological Works* (24 Volumes, Hogarth Press, London, for the Institute of Psycho-Analysis, 1953 onwards)

Gantz, Jeffrey, trans. – *The Mabinogion* (Penguin, Harmondsworth, Middlesex, 1976)

Grahame, Kenneth – *The Wind in the Willows* (Methuen, London, 1908)

Graves, Robert – *The White Goddess* (third edition, Faber & Faber, London, 1952). *The Greek Myths, Volumes I and II* (Penguin, London, 1960 edition)

Gray, John – *Near Eastern Mythology* (Hamlyn, London, 1969)

Green, Roger Lancelyn – *Myths of the Norsemen* (Puffin Books, Harmondsworth, Middlesex, 1970 reissue; original 1960 title *The Saga of Asgard*)

Hart, George – *A Dictionary of Egyptian Gods and Goddesses* (Routledge & Kegan Paul, London, 1986)

Hawkes, Jacquetta – *Dawn of the Gods* (Chatto & Windus, London, 1968; paperback Sphere Books, London, 1972)

Herm, Gerhard – *The Celts* (Weidenfeld & Nicolson, London, 1975)

Hooke, S.H. – *Middle Eastern Mythology* (Pelican Books, Harmondsworth, Middlesex, 1963)

Ions, Veronica – *Egyptian Mythology* (Hamlyn, Feltham, Middlesex, 1968)

Jansen, Sally E. – *A Guide to the Practical Use of Incense* (second edition, Triad Library & Publishing Co, St Ives, NSW, 1972)

Joyce, Donovan – *The Jesus Scroll* (Angus & Robertson, London, 1973; paperback Sphere Books, London, 1975)

Jung, Carl Gustav – *Collected Works Vol. 7: Two Essays on Analytical Psychology* (second edition, Routledge & Kegan Paul, London, 1966)

Kaufmann, Friedrich (trans. M. Steel Smith) – *Northern Mythology* (J.M. Dent, London, 1903)

Kinsella, Thomas (trans.) – *The Táin* (Oxford University Press, London, 1970)

Larousse Encyclopaedia of Mythology (Hamlyn, London, 1959)

Leland, Charles G. – *Aradia; the Gospel of the Witches* (C.W. Daniel Co, London, 1974)

Lethbridge, T.C. – *Witches: Investigating an Ancient Religion* (Routledge & Kegan Paul, London, 1962)

MacAlister, Stewart (ed. and trans.) – *Lebor Gabála Érenn, the Book of the Taking of Ireland*, Parts I-V (Irish Texts Society, Dublin, 1938-56). Commonly known as *The Book of Invasions*, this is a collection of medieval texts in which monks recorded very much older, originally oral material.

Mac Cana, Proinsias – *Celtic Mythology* (Hamlyn, London, 1970)

MacNeill, Maire – *The Festival of Lughnasadh* (Oxford University Press, 1962; paperback, two volumes, Comhairle Bheadolais Éireann, University College, Dublin, 1982)

MacQuitty, William – *Buddha* (Thomas Nelson, London, 1969)

Maple, Eric – *The Magic of Perfume* (Aquarian Press, Wellingborough, Northants, 1973)

Markale, Jean (trans. A. Mygind, C. Hauch and P. Henry) – *Women of the Celts* (Cremonesi, London, 1975; paperback Inner Traditions International, Rochester, Vermont, 1987)

Mascaro, Juan (trans,) – *The Bhagavad Gita* (Penguin, Harmondsworth, Middlesex, 1962)

Mathers, S. Lidell MacGregor (trans. and ed.) – *The Key of Solomon the King (Clavicula Solomonis)* (Originally published 1888; Routledge & Kegan Paul, London, 1972)

Montet, Pierre (trans. Doreen Weightman) – *Eternal Egypt* (Weidenfeld & Nicolson, London, 1965)

Morganweg, Iolo (compiler) – *The Triads of Britain* (Wildwood House, London, 1977)

Patai, Dr Raphael – *Man and Temple in Ancient Jewish Myth and Ritual* (Nelson, London, 1947). *The Hebrew Goddess* (Ktav Publishing House, New York, 1968)

Patrick, Richard – *All Colour Book of Greek Mythology* (Octopus Books, London, 1972). *All Colour Book of Egyptian Mythology*, Octopus, London, 1972)

Peake, Arthur S. – *Commentary on the Bible* (Nelson, London, 1919)

Perowne, Stewart – *Roman Mythology* (Hamlyn, London, 1969)

Phipps, W.E. – *Was Jesus Married?* (Harper & Row, New York, 1970)

Pinsent, John – *Greek Mythology* (Hamlyn, London, 1969)

Poignant, Roslyn – *Myths and Legends of the South Seas* (Hamlyn, London, 1970)

Reed, A.W. – *Aboriginal Myths: Tales of the Dreamtime* (Reed Books, French's Forest, NSW, 1978). *Aboriginal Legends: Animal Tales* (Reed Books, 1978)

Rees, Alwyn, and Rees, Brinley – *Celtic Heritage* (Thames & Hudson, London, 1961)

Richmond, I.A. – *The Pelican History of England: 1. Roman Britain* (second edition, Penguin, Harmondsworth, Middlesex, 1963)

Ross, Anne – *Pagan Celtic Britain* (Routledge & Kegan Paul, London, 1967; paperback Sphere Books, London, 1974)

Rowan, John – *The Horned God: Feminism and Men as Wounding and Healing* (Routledge & Kegan Paul, London and New York, 1987)

Schonfield, Hugo J. – *The Passover Plot* (Hutchinson, London, 1965; paperback Corgi, London, 1967)

St. Clair, David – *Drum and Candle* (Macdonald, London, 1971)

Sety, Omm, and Elzeini, Hanny – *Abydos: Holy City of Ancient Egypt* (LL Company, Los Angeles, 1981)

Shapiro, Max S., and Hendricks, Rhoda A. – *Mythologies of the World: A Concise Encyclopaedia* (Doubleday, New York, 1979); UK edition under title *A Dictionary of Mythologies* (Paladin, London, 1981)

Shorter, Alan W. – *The Egyptian Gods: A Handbook* (Routledge & Kegan Paul, London, 1937, reprint 1983)

Soustelle, Jacques – *The Daily Life of the Aztecs* (French original Librairie Hachette, Paris, 1955; English translation Weidenfeld & Nicolson, London, 1961; paperback Pelican Books, Harmondsworth, Middlesex, 1964)

Stone, Merlin – *The Paradise Papers* (Virago, London, hardback 1976, paperback 1977)

Sykes, Egerton – *Everyman's Dictionary of Non-Classical Mythology* (J.M. Dent, London, 1968)

Valiente, Doreen – *An ABC of Witchcraft Past and Present* (Robert Hale, London, 1973). *Natural Magic* (Hale, 1975). *Witchcraft for Tomorrow* (Hale, 1978)

Valliant, George C. – *The Aztecs of Mexico* (Doubleday, Doran Inc., New York, 1944; Pelican Books, Harmondsworth, Middlesex, 1950)

Vinci, Leo – *Incense: its Ritual, Significance, Use and Preparation* (Aquarian Press, Wellingborough, Northants, 1980)

Wilhelm, Richard (trans. Cary F. Baynes) – *The I Ching or Book of Changes* (third edition, Routledge & Kegan Paul, London, 1968)

Witt, R.E. – *Isis in the Graeco-Roman World* (Thames & Hudson, London, 1971)

Wood, Frederick H. – *This Egyptian Miracle* (John M. Watkins, London, 1955)

Index

To keep this index within bounds, god-names which appear only as alphabetical headings to entries in Part III, Gods of the World, have not been included. So both lists should be consulted. Internal references in the Part III entries, however, have been included, with the exception of the 777 items.